Edward Frederick Knight

The Falcon on the Baltic

A Coasting Voyage from Hammersmith to Copehagen in a three-ton Yacht

Edward Frederick Knight

The Falcon on the Baltic
A Coasting Voyage from Hammersmith to Copehagen in a three-ton Yacht

ISBN/EAN: 9783337297107

Printed in Europe, USA, Canada, Australia, Japan

Cover: Foto ©Andreas Hilbeck / pixelio.de

More available books at **www.hansebooks.com**

THE "FALCON" ON THE BALTIC.

A COASTING VOYAGE FROM HAMMERSMITH TO COPENHAGEN IN A THREE-TON YACHT.

BY

E. F. KNIGHT,

AUTHOR OF "THE CRUISE OF THE FALCON," ETC.

WITH MAP AND ILLUSTRATIONS BY
ARTHUR SHEPHARD.

LONDON:
W. H. ALLEN & CO., 13 WATERLOO PLACE,
PALL MALL. S.W.
1889.

CONTENTS.

CHAPTER	PAGE
I.—I GET A NEW BOAT	1
II.—THE NEW BOAT LEAKS	14
III.—ACROSS THE NORTH SEA	33
IV.—FROM ROTTERDAM TO AMSTERDAM	57
V.—ON THE ZUIDER ZEE	81
VI.—TO THE DOLLART	108
VII.—THE FRISIAN ISLANDS	128
VIII.—FROM THE JADE TO THE EIDER	155
IX.—KIEL BAY	172
X.—THE FIORDS OF SCHLESWIG	191
XI.—THE LITTLE BELT AND VEILE FIORD	215
XII.—ACROSS THE GREAT BELT	236
XIII.—THE KATTEGAT AND ISE FIORD	259
XIV.—GILLELIE AND THE SOUND	282
XV.—COPENHAGEN AND HOME	302

LIST OF ILLUSTRATIONS.

Water Tower at Hoorn	*Frontispiece*
Approach to the Island of Urk	*to face page* 101
North shore of Eckernforde Fiord	,, 19
Village of Slieby	,, 201
Village of Horup Hav	,, 210
Veile	,, 243
Village below Tirsback and entrance to Fiord of Veile	,, 246
Seiero Island and Lighthouse	,, 257
Lighthouse on Nakke Head	,, 294
Kronberg Castle, Elsinore	,, 303

THE "FALCON" ON THE BALTIC.

CHAPTER I.

I GET A NEW BOAT.

In the summer of '86 I was without my favourite toy, a yacht, and had no intention of purchasing a vessel. I had just returned from a winter cruise about the Spanish Main and through the West Indies, and any voyage more extensive than a boating expedition on the upper Thames was quite out of my mind, when I by chance came across a boat lying at Hammersmith— of all unlikely places—which appeared to me to be singularly adapted for the realisation of one of my earliest yachting dreams.

For many years I had talked of visiting the Baltic in a small yacht, and I had often taken up the charts and pilot-books of that tideless sea and planned pleasant cruises among the deep winding fiords and narrow sounds of the Danish islands; and now I saw before me the very boat for the purpose.

"The smaller the yacht the better the sport," is a maxim which, in my opinion, holds good in most waters, but especially so when a cruise on the Baltic is in question. For on all the shores of that sea, even where the map indicates long straight stretches of iron-bound coast, there are innumerable small artificial havens which have been constructed by the herring fishermen for the accommodation of their shallow craft; and again, on many of the islands, the only harbours are those affording shelter to the ferry-boats which ply to the mainland—harbours, as a rule, having no more than three feet of water.

Therefore small yachts only can visit these out-of-the-way spots. A cruise among the islands affords some of the fascination of a voyage of discovery; at many of them sea-going vessels never call; and as all the English yachts that enter the Baltic are of considerable tonnage, the English yachtsman knows but little of the charms of the best cruising-ground in Europe.

The Baltic is a treacherous sea; settled weather can never be depended on, gales spring up very unexpectedly, and a nasty sea rises quickly on its shallow waters. But a little yacht following the coast has nearly always some snug harbour to run for should bad weather come on; whereas a larger craft with deeper draught must needs stand out to sea and make the best of it she can.

The small yacht is certainly the one for the Baltic, but to get her there is a somewhat difficult task. To arrive at the mouth of the river Eider, whence the Baltic can be reached by canal, involves a voyage across the North Sea and a lengthy cruise along the coast of Holland and Germany. Unless the yachtsman has exceptional luck with his weather this journey is likely to cause him a considerable amount of anxiety; for the east coast of the North Sea, with its dangerous shoals, tumbling seas, and lack of harbours to run for, is certainly the last the skipper of a small yacht would select for a pleasure cruise. But once let him reach the mouth of the Eider and he will be more than compensated for his preliminary difficulties and hardships.

The yacht at Hammersmith possessed two qualities not usually found together. She was of very light draught and yet she was an excellent sea-boat. She drew something under three feet, and so could enter the shallowest Danish boat-harbour. With her if I saw a port before me I could run in boldly, not needing a pilot, and without troubling my head about the depth of water; for, where any other boat had gone before, mine was able to follow. She also looked like a craft that would put up with a good deal of heavy weather, and could be trusted to carry one safely across the North Sea. I saw that she was, in short, the very vessel I required; so I came to terms with her owner, and soon found that I had no reason to be disappointed with my bargain.

The *Falcon*—for so I named her after my former

vessel—was an old P. and O. lifeboat, and had doubtlessly made many a voyage to India and back on a steamer's deck. As is the way with lifeboats, her bow and stern were alike, and she had far more sheer than is ever given to a yacht. She had been built in the strongest manner by the well-known lifeboat builder, White, of Cowes. She was double-skinned, both skins being of the best teak, the outer of horizontal, the inner of diagonal, planking.

The gentleman from whom I bought her had converted her into a yawl, or, to be more correct, a ketch, for her mizen-mast was well in-board, so that her mainsail was smaller and her mizen larger than is the case with yawls (an advantage as far as handiness is concerned). The water-tight compartments had been taken out of her, a false keel had been fastened on, and she had been decked all over with the exception of a small well. There was no appliance for covering over this well in bad weather, but I have never seen a pint of water tumble into it, so buoyant and admirable a sea-boat did the little vessel prove to be.

The *Falcon* is jury-rigged; too much so indeed, her spars and sails being rather too small. Her mainmast lowers on a tabernacle, a system which I do not like for sea-work, but which proved useful on the Norfolk broads. She is twenty-nine feet long and of three tons register.

When I bought her, the season was so far advanced that I had to postpone my Baltic expedition until the following summer; but I made a pleasant trial cruise in her down our east coast and on the broads and rivers of Norfolk.

I succeeded in exploring all the portions of those inland waters which are practicable to a yacht of three-feet draught; but, as might be expected from so long and shallow a boat, she was slow in stays and ill-adapted for the narrow streams beloved of the East Anglian yachtsman.

This cruise over, the *Falcon* was brought back to Hammersmith, and during the winter all was got ready for her Baltic voyage. So strong are lifeboats when built on this diagonal system that it is considered unnecessary to timber them; but when one of them is converted into a yacht and it is intended to subject her to the great strain of rigging, it becomes advisable to place some timbers into her, especially under the channel plates. So I had seven stout timbers put in on either side, and, among other improvements, a strong oak rubbing-piece was carried round her, a new and larger rudder fitted on, and a stout rail placed on her bulwarks. After all this, built as she was of imperishable wood and copper-fastened, she seemed as safe a little vessel as a sailor's heart could desire.

Her cabin was a spacious one for a boat of her tonnage. There was not much head room in it, but I do not hold, as some do, that to be able to stand up in one's cabin is an essential on a small yacht. If one wishes to assume an erect position one can always go on deck.

The shingle ballast which she contained when I purchased her was taken out and somewhat more than a ton of iron substituted. Many told me that this was far from sufficient. But a shallow boat should always be kept light. With more ballast she will certainly turn to windward better in smooth water, but it is of far greater importance to keep her lively and safe in a heavy sea.

It is rare indeed that a yacht is fitted out at Hammersmith for a foreign cruise, and it is certainly not one of the best places in England for this purpose. But somehow or other—not without much wrath on the part of all concerned, and not without much of the work having to be pulled to pieces as utterly bad and done over again — everything was satisfactorily completed at last; and as the *Falcon* lay off the "Doves Inn" she looked far more smart and ready for business than she had ever done in her previous existence. When I bought her, her sides were tarred, an act of atrocious vandalism, for her skin was of the cleanest and most beautifully-grained teak; so now all the tar was burnt off, she was scraped and her natural loveliness revealed. When she had been sand-papered and varnished she looked a very different sort of craft from of old. No picture-dealer who discovers some rare old master under a smoky daub ever effected so marvellous a transformation as did we with this once black, heavy-looking old tub.

In the second week in May the finishing touches were given to the yacht and the stores were brought on board. A goodly supply of tinned meats and pickles was stowed in the lockers. For the benefit of inexperienced yachtsmen, I may state that the above, together with tea, sugar, and coffee, are the only provisions of which it is advisable to carry a large quantity from England. Everything else is much cheaper abroad.

We did all our cooking with a large spirit-stove, which answered admirably. Mr. George Wilson, of Glasshouse Street, supplies similar stoves in several sizes. I have used petroleum on small yachts, but I shall never do so again, the spirit-stove is far cleaner and better in every respect. We did a good deal of cooking each day with this kitchener, and yet we consumed only a shilling's worth of spirit per week. I took a large supply of methylated spirit with me from England. As an old traveller I should have known better, for burning spirit is nearly twice as dear in England as in the countries I visited, and it is easy to procure it even in small foreign towns.

I did not forget to lay up a stock of old rum. True it is that spirits for internal application are also cheaper abroad; but then one does not at once acquire the taste for Scandinavian *aqua vitæ* and the fire-water of Holland and Germany.

Of tobacco I took but sufficient to last me across the German Ocean, not being one of those who cannot smoke Dutch tobacco because it costs little more a pound than the English does an ounce.

A considerable number of charts were necessary for

my projected cruise; these I procured in London—a great mistake on my part. Danish and Swedish charts for the Baltic are better than those of our English Admiralty, which last do not indicate the snug little fishing-harbours I have mentioned above. One of the best-known map and chart sellers in London sold me, for twenty-five shillings, what he called the only reliable maps of the Dutch canals. They proved to be quite useless; but while walking through the Hague later on I saw some really admirable maps of the Low Countries in a shop window, which I purchased for three shillings.

The vessel was of course provided with riding-lights, side-lights, an aneroid, and all the manifold articles necessary for a small yacht bound "foreign." I brought with me my quant, a relic of the Norfolk Broads, and very useful too it often proved to be. A rifle and shot-gun were not forgotten, but they were never put to use. My sextant was also on board, with which I took the latitude twice only during the cruise, and on those occasions more for amusement than from necessity.

Our dinghy was eleven feet long; we had no room for it on deck, so we always towed it astern. It followed us thus all the way to Copenhagen and no accident befell it. This dinghy had a six-inch false keel, and sailed extremely well under her balance-lug. She was found very useful for ascending fiords and shallow rivers inaccessible to the yacht. A dinghy will tow in a far less erratic manner before a following sea if she is provided with a false keel. We were in the habit of putting a half-hundredweight of iron into her stern, to steady her when the weather was rough, with the result that she followed us as quietly as possible, not sheering wildly about and rushing furiously down upon us as is the wont of dinghies under such circumstances.

So much for the yacht, and now for the crew. Until almost the last moment I had no idea as to who was to be my companion. My wish had been to take friends with me and dispense with professional sailors; but though I found no lack of friends who would have liked to join me, none could spare the time for so long a voyage, especially at this early period of the summer.

I had no intention of shipping a yacht-sailor, for it is difficult to find among that somewhat spoilt class the right man for a foreign cruise in a small yacht. I knew of one John Wright, a young fellow who had been with me before, and who was the very man for my purpose; but the last I had heard of him was that he had sailed out of London before the mast on a vessel bound for India, Australia, or some other distant portion of the globe, and it was impossible to say when he might return.

So the *Falcon* lay off the "Doves Inn," her sails bent, ready for sea in all respects save that she had a captain only and no crew, when one afternoon in mid-May, when I was arranging things in the cabin, a messenger arrived to say that a young man wished to speak with me.

The young man proved to be none other than John Wright himself. He had landed in the docks that morning, having arrived from Alexandria in the very nick of time to sail with me.

John Wright has luckily had nothing to do with Cowes and yachts. His life is passed before the mast in foreign-going steamers and sailing-vessels, and for his fore-and-aft training he is indebted to Mistley barges and small coasting steamers on the North Sea —an excellent school. A yachting cruise of this sort was a novelty to him, and I believe he enjoyed it as much as I did myself, which is saying a good deal.

Provided with the best boat and best crew for my purpose, I anticipated a successful and pleasant holiday; and I was not disappointed.

As is usually the case when one wishes to get away, I found that business was likely to detain me in England until the end of the month; but I contrived to take the *Falcon* to the mouth of the Thames for a trial trip, so that if anything was wrong with the vessel we might discover and repair it at once.

On May the 13th Wright and myself were on board shortly after daybreak, getting all ready for the journey through London. We unstepped the mizen, lowered the mainmast on deck, took the bowsprit in, and, anchoring in the stream, waited for the beginning of the ebb, when the tugs with their strings of barges astern might be expected to pass us on their way from Brentford to Woolwich.

At about seven o'clock we recognised the " puffing-

I GET A NEW BOAT.

billy" *Sunbeam* coming round the corner opposite Chiswick, with three barges in tow. I hailed the skipper, came to terms with him, and he turned round to pick me up. We quickly got our anchor up, hove the tug the end of our grass-rope, and were soon towing at a rattling pace down stream under London's twenty bridges. Then breakfast was got under way, and we were quite ready for our hot coffee, for a strong and keen north-east wind was blowing. It felt and looked like December, and the weather was certainly as unsuitable as possible for small yacht sailing.

The day was still young when we reached Woolwich. Here the tug slipped us, and we let go our anchor off North Woolwich Gardens, close to the steam-boat pier, in the company of several schooners and barges; for this is a favourite anchorage for small coasters. We now raised our masts, set up the rigging, and made the *Falcon* look once more like a yacht. As we did not anticipate having to lower the masts again during the cruise, we took the precaution of frapping our forestay fall and also putting on a preventer fall—a very necessary precaution with a tabernacle-mast, the omission of which has caused many accidents.

When we had completed our work we found that there remained but an hour of ebb, then both tide and wind would be against us; so as it was clearly not worth our while to sail that day, it was decided to remain where we were until the morrow.

North Woolwich is a dismal and unlovely spot. A ferry steamer runs every few minutes to South Woolwich, but as this is an even still less inviting place I did not venture to cross the river.

A travelling circus proprietor had pitched his tent near the shore at North Woolwich, so in the evening I took a twopenny stall and sat through the performance. It blew very hard from the north-east, the rickety tent swayed in an alarming manner, as if about to fall and bury us at any moment. The wind, too, found its way within, and the climate became Siberian. Some of the performers were really clever, but it was not a very cheerful spectacle; the fair *artistes*, with blue noses, shivered in their thin tights, and the clown's teeth chattered so with cold that he could scarcely bring out his time-honoured jests. It would have been still more cheerless were it not for one comfortable rule of the establishment — the audience, and members of the company also when not performing, were permitted to smoke. We all availed ourselves of the permission, and, of course, under the enchantment of tobacco things seemed better at once.

To my surprise, I recognised among the troupe a clever acrobat whom I had last seen in Covent Garden Circus. This man, it seems, is so incurable a Bohemian in his tastes, that, though he can always command a salary which many a distinguished lawyer would envy, he loves to pass a large portion of the year in vagabondizing about the country with impecunious and ragged travelling companies of this description, living from hand to mouth, and often retiring supperless to bed after a hard night's work.

I GET A NEW BOAT. 13

And though he thus voluntarily endures so many privations, he informed me that he could not understand any sane person undertaking such a voyage as the one I meditated, in a small boat. This critic could see no eccentricity in his own uncomfortable way of taking his pleasure. This story has a moral which I submit to certain of my friends who are devoted to as arduous and not so healthy hobbies as my own, and who yet point contemptuously at the mote in my eye, quite heedless of their own beam—but this sounds confused and as if I was trying to pun.

CHAPTER II.

THE NEW BOAT LEAKS.

It was high water the next morning at seven o'clock; so we turned out of our snug berths, rather unwillingly I remember, to get under weigh. The strong north-east wind was still blowing and it was uncomfortably cold; the sky was heavy with snow-clouds, and a few flakes did fall in the afternoon. It was a strange day for mid-May, but we were destined to meet with plenty more or less foul weather in the course of this cruise. A friend wrote to me when I was in the Baltic and described it as being a real Jubilee summer at home. I tremble while I quote his words, for I know that dreadful penalties are inflicted by a Jubilee-satiated people on any who now utter that name; but be it remembered that I was away during the jollifications and did not do my share of the infinite Jubilee talk, so surely I may be pardoned for now writing the tabooed word.

But whatever the summer may have been, the

spring in England was a boisterous one, and it blew hard during the latter half of May. In June, while I was in the North Sea, gales and strong winds from the north followed each other in rapid succession; and lastly, when I reached the Baltic in midsummer, and the weather at home was the finest possible, the north-west wind still relentlessly pursued us; in Denmark, a proverbially windy country, the season was exceptionally stormy. In consequence of all this we were frequently weather-bound, as a rule in the least interesting harbours, for several days at a time; and, indeed, had it not been for our ill-luck in this respect the voyage would have been completed by a much earlier date.

It was the very day to test the yacht and reveal her faults. The wind was fresh, the lee-scuppers were generally under water, and there was a choppy sea in the lower reaches of the river. The boat behaved splendidly; she evidently turned to windward in a much smarter manner than she had done the previous year, and we felt that we had the right sort of craft under us.

We had reached the Lower Hope and were talking in rather a sanguine spirit, and congratulating ourselves on the improvement that had been effected in the vessel, when Wright happened to go below and light his pipe. As soon as he was in the cabin I heard him utter what may be politely called an exclamation of surprise, and one of anything but pleased surprise.

Leaving the tiller for a moment, I looked into the

cabin, and, to my dismay, beheld the water high above the floor, washing backwards and forwards over our beds, while the blankets and mattresses were floating to leeward. We were evidently leaking at a very great rate. Now the boat was quite tight when we left Hammersmith, so we could come to but one conclusion.

" She must be straining badly, Wright."

" I am afraid so, Sir."

" And after all these timbers have been put into her, too; what can it mean? "

We did not say much, but across both our minds flashed the horrible suspicion that the boat in which we had placed such confidence might be too rickety to stand much tumbling about in a sea-way and be quite unfit to cross the North Sea. It was strange, however, that she had shown no signs of this weakness before.

Then we set to work to pump her out. After some half-dozen strokes the pump choked. We pulled up the small hatch in the cabin floor that covers the pump-well and made a curious discovery. It would have been strange, indeed, had the pump worked properly, for the well was full of deal-shavings! That lazy scoundrel the Hammersmith self-called ship carpenter had evidently, after completing some work in the cabin, stowed away his shavings here to save himself the trouble of throwing them overboard.

If we had had that carpenter on board I think we should have first compelled him to eat his shavings and then have cast him into the sea to find his way to the nearest shore as he best could. Surely such a punishment would not have been too severe for a man who, out of sheer indolence, risks the lives of others in this fashion. I think Mr. Plimsoll would agree with me.

At last we succeeded in clearing the pump, and, as it was luckily a far more powerful one than is generally put into yachts of our size, we soon had the water out of her.

We were now in Sea Reach, and as the ebb was nearly done we ran into the little creek of Holy Haven in Canvey Island for the night, not feeling by any means so sanguine about the sea-worthiness of our boat as we had done on starting.

We let go our anchor opposite the coast-guard station, and proceeded to wring some of the water out of our mattresses and blankets and to hang them out to dry; but our beds, to put it mildly, were somewhat damp that night, as they were very often afterwards during this cruise.

We found that it was necessary to pump the boat out every four hours or so in order to keep the water from rising above the cabin floor; but it must be remembered that ours was a very shallow vessel and that our floorcloth would be wet (and the lee-bunk under water if we were sailing) when there were but a few gallons on board. Very uncomfortable is a leaky vessel, and, above all others, a shallow boat should be perfectly water-tight.

Holy Haven is the snuggest little harbour in all the Thames estuary for small craft. There are two houses opposite the anchorage, the coast-guard station and an old-fashioned inn whose eggs and bacon have comforted many a yachtsman. All around extends a flat country of marsh and pasture intersected by broad ditches, looking very much like a Dutch landscape; and the likeness is increased by the presence of quite a fleet of schuyts, for the creek is much frequented by the Dutch eel-boats, the reason being, so a Dutch skipper, whose statement may or may not be true, told me, that the Hollander eels will not live in any British waters save those of the muddy channel that surrounds Canvey Island.

I have heard that the dykes which protect Canvey Island from inundation were long since constructed by a Dutchman, very much after the fashion of those in his own country. Is it possible that the eels on this account imagine they are still in Holland, and so, not suffering from home-sickness, keep up their spirits and flourish here? The learned people who recently carried on a long correspondence in one of our leading reviews on the intelligence of brutes would do well to investigate this interesting subject.

We remained in Holy Haven for the night, and on the following morning I decided to take the *Falcon* to Rochester, where I could run her ashore and discover what was amiss with her.

So after breakfast we again put to sea in our sieve and sailed across the broad estuary of the Thames to

NORTH SHORE OF ECKERNFORDE FIORD.

the Medway. It was still cold, but constant exercise at the pump kept us warm.

In the Medway we overtook several barges bound for Rochester. Wright, who has sailed these seas before, recognised some of his old friends, and he saluted them in proper bargee fashion. Carried away by his pride at seeing our vessel leave one rather smart barge astern, he held up a rope's end to her skipper— a delicate way of bragging of one's own speed, understood by all mariners.

"So you've come down to shipping on board of a Dutch galli—hot at last, eh, Jack?" sang out the skipper by way of repartee, between two whiffs of his pipe.

There was, indeed, something Dutch in the *Falcon's* appearance, and a remark of this nature was often passed on us by facetious strangers.

There was a twinkle in Wright's eye as he gave his quid a twist and called out in reply: "You aint forgotten your fog-horn this time, have you, Jim?"

The crew of the barge roared with laughter at this sally, but I could not see the point of the joke till Wright explained.

"That chap, Jim, you see, Sir, was a terrible greenhorn when he first went to sea a few years back. Someone or other was always playing a trick on him. One evening the barge he was on was sailing by Sheerness, and the skipper, happening to look at the clock, saw it wanted a minute or so to nine. He remembered that a gun was always fired at Sheerness at nine; so, being a mischievous sort of chap, he sings out to the green hand, 'Hi! here Jim, come on deck at once and bring the fog-horn with you.' Jim tumbles up. 'Now blow that there fog-horn for your life,' cries the skipper. 'What for?' asks Jim, looking round. 'Don't ask what for, but blow, you lubber. It's the rule here. If a vessel don't salute Sheerness with her fog-horn as she passes they fire at her.' Jim, believing it all, takes the horn and blows like mad. 'Harder, harder!' cries the skipper, 'they can't hear that; they'll shoot us all if you aint louder.' So Jim was blowing away with all the wind he had, when suddenly off goes the nine o'clock gun, and he gives a yell, chucks the fog-horn on deck, and rushes below to hide from the cannon-balls. Oh, he was a green chap then! He's a bit smarter now, but that story of the fog-horn will always follow him."

We reached Rochester early in the afternoon and anchored among some other yachts not far below the bridge.

On the following morning we brought the *Falcon* alongside a boat-builder's yard at high tide, and at low water, when she was high and dry, we proceeded to examine her minutely. The usual crowd of yacht-sailors, carpenters, and nondescript nautical loafers that hangs about a ship-builder's yard was soon around us, ready to proffer gratuitous advice of more or less value—much of it of no value—advice, however, in all cases driven into the poor land-lubber of an amateur sailor by these learned professionals with language deliberate and dogmatic.

Each had a different infallible opinion of his own as to the cause of our vessel's leaking, but all agreed that she was not strained; she showed no signs of that serious fault. My own idea was that the tar, which had kept the water out of her during her last year's cruise, having been burnt off, and the varnish which had been put on in its place being insufficient to keep her tight, she was leaking all over her skin. It was easy to account for her not having taken in water at Hammersmith; for, while lying there, the mud had got into her seams and given her what sailors call a Blackwall caulking—very efficacious as long as a vessel remains stationary, but apt to wash out after half-an-hour's sailing.

Some of the wiseacres on the yard suggested that we should have her caulked throughout, but we knew better than that, for a diagonally-built boat—tightest of all boats when she is tight—is the most difficult to deal with when she is leaky. It is impossible to caulk her even in the most delicate manner without damaging her and forcing the two skins apart. Again, so beautifully constructed was our vessel, that it would have been impossible to insert even the smallest penknife between her close planking, far less a clumsy caulking tool.

At last the master shipwright of the yard, who had spoken little and listened less during the consultation over the invalid, but who had been employed in scientifically sounding with a mallet and closely examining every portion of the *Falcon's* bottom, as he crawled under her in the mud, gave his opinion.

"It's the old story," he said. "The boat isn't strained at all. She's as strong as when she was built. It's only along the garboard streak she leaks. She hasn't been caulked there for years. See here"—and he pulled out a bit of oakum that was decidedly rotten—"when they scraped the tow off this boat's bottom they scraped the caulking out too. It's just a little bit of stuff along her keel she wants, and I'll guarantee that she'll then be as dry as a drum's inside."

On hearing this the crew of the *Falcon* felt happy and sanguine again, his explanation seemed so probable a one. The garboard-streak, I must explain for the benefit of some readers, is the range of planks along a vessel's keel. In a diagonally-built boat this seam only is caulked.

So, having confidence in this wise man, I delivered the *Falcon* over to his care and took train to London, in perfect faith that I should return to find my vessel as tight as the tightest drum that was ever beat upon. But I am afraid that some of my readers will get very weary of reading about that leak. It was the great feature of the cruise, and one we would willingly have dispensed with. I have much to write yet concerning the many and fruitless attempts to cure it, until that happy day when, being hundreds of miles from home, with no professional by to doctor the poor vessel, we two amateurs took her in hand ourselves, with the result that we succeeded gloriously in effecting a complete and permanent cure of what seemed a hopelessly chronic complaint.

To stop a leak is easy enough when you have found your leak, but to find it is not always so easy as some would imagine. It is the diagnosis that distinguishes the great doctor. I think Wright and myself could now do a good business as quack leak-finders.

Business detained me in town until the 19th, when I bade London a final farewell and returned to Rochester. I found that our shipwright had completed his work and was confident that the leak was stopped. Wright, who had been living on board all the while, was not so confident.

"You see, Sir," he said, " we can't tell how she is yet. Lying here she's only afloat an hour each tide, so she hasn't time to leak much. I have had to pump her out, though, each day; but that may have been the rain-water that gets into her through the well, and it has been raining ever since you 've been away."

Oh, this Jubilee spring! A heavy gale of wind that commenced at south-west and shifted right round the compass now detained us at Rochester for four days. Not only did it blow, but it rained and hailed and snowed in turns, and for twenty-four hours the wind attained hurricane force. The papers were full of accounts of disasters at sea and on land.

Being thus weather-bound, and having nothing else to do, we anxiously observed the yacht's behaviour each day when the water was round her, and soon convinced ourselves that she leaked as much as ever.

Our shipwright, puzzled but energetic, determined not to be beaten, set to work again. Coming to the conclusion that some of the planking along the bilges had worked loose he screwed them up, and once more informed us that it was "impossible for the yacht to leak now."

On the 24th the weather improved somewhat and the wind shifted to the north. We sailed from Rochester in the afternoon and anchored off Port Victoria for the night.

Even as a man who receives a letter which he knows contains news of vital importance fears to open it and hesitates awhile, so were we for a long time afraid to break our suspense by looking into the cabin and learning the progress of our leak. We dared not hope that the shipwright had indeed been successful this time.

But after we had let go the anchor and stowed the sails I summoned sufficient courage, not indeed to look myself, but to ask Wright to do so.

He went below, and then I heard his voice declare the fatal news.

"The water is above the floor, Sir. She leaks as much as ever."

Upon this we became desperate and decided that as it was beyond the power of man to remedy this mysterious evil, we must make the best of it.

Though so serious a leak was likely to bring us a

good deal of discomfort, there was one thing certain, we could not abandon or even postpone our cruise on account of it. How that leak haunted us! We both suffered for weeks from a sort of leak-mania. By day we were ever watching to see if the water was coming in faster. By night we dreamt of giant leaks and choking pumps. We felt a morbid shame for this skeleton in our cupboard, and were terrified lest anyone should suspect its existence. In harbour we used to choose the dead of night, when no people were about, to work the pumps, and we would immediately stop the operation if anyone walked by, even as if we had been committing some heinous crime.

Port Victoria has a high-sounding name, but consists of a railway station, a usually deserted railway hotel, and nothing more. On either side of it is a desolate shore, and behind it extend the swamps of the Isle of Grain—a dismal place enough in all conscience; but luckily a ferry-steamer runs at frequent intervals to cheerful Sheerness on the opposite coast.

We were anchored close under the shore in the company of quite a fleet of weather-bound barges. I pulled off in the dinghy and landed on the railway pier. It was blowing and raining hard at the time, and only one human being was to be seen braving the elements; this was a coast-guard with a ruddy nose and a suspicious eye, carrying a telescope under his arm.

He scanned me curiously as I stepped on shore.

"What is the name of your vessel?" he asked.

"The *Falcon*, of London."

"Where from?"

"Rochester."

"Not from foreign?"

"No."

He seemed disappointed on hearing this.

"I thought you was a Dutch yacht by your build," he said. Then he walked by my side to the hotel, and in the course of conversation his suspicions seemed to vanish; he thawed and became communicative, as is the way of a mariner who anticipates beer.

"We are looking out," he explained, "for a cutter called the *Mary*. She passes herself off as a Dutch yacht, and has been suspected of smuggling. We have received information about her and think we'll catch her this time. I thought your vessel was the *Mary*."

It was interesting to be thus mistaken for a bold smuggler.

"And if my boat had been the *Mary* what would you have done?"

"Telegraphed to Sheerness, and they'd have come over and seized you."

After partaking of a pint of beer at my expense the guardian of the customs was quite reassured as to the *Falcon's* respectability. At the hotel bar were gathered together all the skippers of the fleet of weather-bound barges, sipping their respective drinks, and grumbling sorely at the villainous weather. Some of these were bound for Harwich and the North, and had been lying here for a fortnight waiting for a change. I joined this disconsolate conclave and did my share of reviling the elements until I found this amusement wax monotonous, when I returned on board and pumped the vessel out. This was a never-failing means of employing one's spare moments on the *Falcon*.

My intention was to sail for Harwich on the following morning.

Once or twice I awoke in the night and felt that the yacht was jumping about a good deal, while the wind was howling furiously.

At 2 A.M. I turned out on deck and looked around. It was a wild dawn. The wind had shifted to the north-east, and it was blowing half a gale at least. The rain was falling in torrents, and the broad estuary of the Medway was white with breaking waves. It was too chilly to stay long on deck, so I went below again and got under my warm blankets.

"How does it look, Sir?" asked Wright sleepily from his own berth.

"Worse than ever," I replied. "No starting for us to-day, so I'm turning into bed again."

And now, pursued by our usual ill-luck, we lay weather-bound off this dismal spot for four whole days more, tumbling about on the short seas in the peculiarly lively fashion that distinguishes this boat of mine.

The fleet of weather-bound barges was augmented

by daily arrivals till the hotel bar was almost inaccessible for the crowd of grumbling master-mariners who were mitigating their annoyance with strong waters. 'Twas an ill-wind, but it blew the "Victoria Hotel" good.

On the afternoon of Friday the 27th the weather improved and the glass began to rise with promising steadiness. I looked out at three o'clock on Saturday morning and found that it had become even too fine. Not a breath of air stirred the water, the sky was cloudless, but over the sea hung a light haze indicative of a sultry day.

It was high water and time to start, so I turned Wright out. We hoisted the useless sails, weighed anchor, and allowed the yacht to drift slowly out to sea with the ebb, while we gave her steerage-way occasionally with the sweeps, so as to avoid fouling buoys and anchored vessels. We were not alone, for the weather-bound barges also got under weigh, so too did a great number of fishing-boats, and we all floated lazily out of the estuary together. We saw a large fleet of yachts at anchor off Southend pier; for the first important race of the year was to be sailed—or drifted—this day. The course was to be from Southend to Harwich; so we were likely to see some of the sport, perhaps the finish, for we had seven hours' start of the competing vessels.

The sun rose higher and the heat became tropical; then a very feeble north-east wind sprang up and enabled us to tack slowly past the Nore. Near here we saw rising from the water the masts of a large vessel that had been run into and sunk a few days before. Around her hovered a crowd of fishing-boats and other small craft, whose crews were busy stripping the vessel's rigging. The scene reminded one of a pack of jackals gathering round a dead lion—not that I have ever seen this, by the way. Then the wind dropped altogether, and as often happens in a calm, all our fleet collected into a knot, drawn together by mutual attraction, like a flock of magnetic ducks in a washhand-basin—this I have seen, so the simile is legitimate. We all lay idly smoking on the decks of our respective vessels and conversed as we drifted across each other's bows, or came so close that we had to shove off with boat-hooks and take to the sweeps to prevent collision.

The bargee skippers grumbled at the calm with even more bitterness than they had reviled the gales which had detained them so long off Port Victoria. A bargee skipper is supposed to be the most inveterate grumbler of all seafaring men, but there was, indeed, some provocation on this occasion. Even on Charon's bark was never heard a chorus of more despairing and profane lamentation than that which rose all round us from these becalmed Billy-boys.

But at last a very light breeze sprang up from the south-west, giving us steerage-way and dispersing our fleet again. We set all the canvas possible on the *Falcon* to drive her along; for we wished to be in Harwich for Sunday. I think Wright was the more anxious of the two, for his home is at Mistley (near Harwich) and he looked forward to a holiday with his friends. We had a large tanned lug-sail on board, which we bent to a long boat-hook and set as a square sail on the opposite side to the mainsail. We even converted our jibs into water-sails; but do all we could, though we left the barges astern, we did not travel fast, for the wind was only sufficient to swear by.

At one o'clock we were met by a strong flood, and, as it was impossible to stem it, we let go our anchor on the shallows inside the Sheers lighthouse. Here we remained for nearly three hours, by which time the tide had covered the Maplin Sands. We got our anchor up again and sailed across the flat, thus cheating the strength of the current—an old bargee trick on this coast.

At high water the weather changed very suddenly. The wind shifted to the north-east and freshened quickly. It began to rain and look dirty, while, instead of the oppressive sultriness of the morning there was a chilliness as of November on the sea.

Our east coast is not a popular yachting-ground, in consequence of the paucity of good harbours; but on this day there was an unusually good show of pleasure vessels around us. These had evidently come out to see the race; but we could see nothing that looked like one of the competing vessels until late in the afternoon when we were near the Swin Middle lightship. We perceived a smart-looking yacht to windward overhauling us very rapidly.

"That's one of them at last, Sir," cried Wright.

There was no doubt about it. I looked at her through the glass.

"Yes, she's one of the fast ones too. What a pace she's going at!"

She was soon up to us and rushed by, as if we had been standing still. I have said that turning to windward is not the *Falcon's* strong point—and the yacht was sailing, I am afraid and ashamed to say how much, nearer the wind than ourselves.

"I never saw a vessel go like that before!" exclaimed my man, agape with wonder.

"Nor I. What can she be? and look at her mainsail! I have never seen so big a one in a yacht."

She was the only one of the racers in sight at the time and we saw none of the others afterwards, for the darkness fell before they came up. What could this mysterious clipper be so far ahead of them all?

Had I read the papers regularly while we lay off Port Victoria I should have guessed her identity. Not till I reached Harwich did I discover that this was no less than the renowned *Thistle*, the anticipated redeemer of the Queen's Cup, sailing her maiden race. If I remember rightly, she arrived at Harwich four hours before the second yacht.

As we had not the *Thistle* under us we knew that we could not reach Harwich that night. The tide would soon turn, and then the current as well as the wind would be against us, so it became necessary to find as snug a berth as is possible on this unprotected coast until morning.

At dusk we made out the Whittaker Spit buoy, so we tacked in towards the coast with the intention of bringing up in the Wallet, several of our old companions, the barges, following our example. It was a dirty evening, the north-east wind howled, and the drizzling rain fell steadily. The Wallet is an exposed anchorage, and a vessel brought up here is forced to get under weigh should it come on to blow hard, but we had no choice of stopping-places this night.

It was nearly dark as we passed the Spitway buoy, and the scene around was dismal in the extreme. The barges looked ghostly in the indistinct light. Above was a grey rainy sky; below was a grey tumbling sea of muddy water. The sense of cheerlessness was heightened by the bell-buoy which tolled out its warning in tones doleful as a funeral bell.

At last we let go our anchors in about four fathoms of water and rolled about uncomfortably all night. The yacht seemed to leak harder than ever, and we had to turn out twice and pump to prevent the water from drenching us as we lay in our bunks.

We got under weigh early the next morning and tacked down to Harwich against a fresh north-east wind. We let go our anchor in the harbour at mid-day, having been thirty-one hours from Sheerness, so this could not be called a smart voyage.

CHAPTER III.

ACROSS THE NORTH SEA.

THE harbour was crowded with fine yachts that had come in for the next day's (Whit Monday) regatta; so that dull and somewhat disagreeable place, Harwich, was more lively and attractive than usual.

My next port was to be Rotterdam; but on Tuesday a strong east-north-east wind was blowing, which put an attempt to cross the North Sea quite out of the question, so I determined to employ the time until a fair wind should spring up in again tackling that incorrigible leak. Wright told me that he knew of a good shore at Mistley whereon to beach a vessel, and that there we could ourselves examine the yacht at leisure and not be overmuch disturbed by the usual sage advice or—if you don't give him beer—would-be witty jeers of the 'long-shore loafer.

So on Whit Tuesday we ran up the pretty river Stour and put the yacht ashore at the top of high-water. The spot we selected was a short distance below Mistley. There were no houses very near; but a steep green bank of trees, ferns, and bushes sloped almost to the water's edge.

As we did not propose to commence operations until the following day, I set out to explore the neighbourhood, and I soon found that I had done right in leaving Harwich, a place with all the disadvantages and none of the advantages of a town, for this pleasant countryside. There is plenty of picturesque scenery about here, as the artists have long since discovered; and who could fail to be charmed with such jolly old-fashioned little towns as Mistley and its neighbour Maningtree? The author of *Our Village* would have loved to describe the life in these quiet places.

The two towns are joined by a road about a mile in length which follows the banks of the river. At high-water the Stour presents the appearance of an extensive lake, and at low-water—well, the least said about it the better, more than that on the broad muddy waste then disclosed may be gathered winkles, which, say the Mistley folk, are well known to be the best-flavoured in all England.

Mistley and Maningtree were well-to-do places in the old times. Important markets were held here, and the fine old inns, the " Thorn " for example, are relics of the days of posting. Formerly the river was crowded with shipping, now only an occasional barge ascends the winding Stour, and even yachts are rarely seen in these deserted harbours. It is, of course, the old story again. The railway has taken away the trade, the busy markets are held no more, and these towns are even as those dead cities of the Zuyder Zee which I was soon to visit. Fine houses, tenantless and falling to ruins, are frequent in Mauingtree High Street, and the old shops seem far too big for the business now carried on in them. The inhabitants themselves are old-fashioned in their habits, the energy and bustle of modern commerce are unknown to them, they take life in an easy way, though it must be confessed that no less than three lawyers extract a living out of Maningtree.

Bricks and beer are the principal productions of Maningtree and Mistley.

On the excellence of the beer I am qualified to give an opinion, for I passed a portion of the evening in the snug parlour of the "Packet Inn," where some of the elders of the town were hobnobbing over their tankards and churchwardens, and carrying on a pleasant gossip on sport, the prospects of the *Thistle*, the coming Jubilee, the Manchester cup, the cricket-club, and of course the local scandal, which seemed in some way to mix up with all the other topics of conversation and lend a piquant flavour to them.

I was awakened at a very early hour the following morning by tumbling out of my berth upon the floor. I rubbed my eyes, looked round, and perceived the cause. The ebb tide had left us high and dry, and the yacht was lying on her side at a very steep angle, so steep that it was impossible for anyone not constructed after the fashion of a fly to remain on my bunk.

I looked towards Wright; he was still sleeping soundly, for his bunk was on the other, and so lower side of the vessel. As the means of sleeping comfortably had been taken away from myself, I naturally felt much aggrieved that he should still be able to enjoy his slumbers, and I was on the point of waking him with a "Now, Wright, it's low water; let's have coffee and then to the leak," when, with an exclamation of consternation, he started up from his bunk with as much suddenness as I had tumbled out of mine. The reason was soon apparent. The water in the vessel—and there was plenty of it—had of course settled on his side, and was pouring over his blanket in a considerable stream, through the seams of the panelling.

As both our beds were now impracticable, one being perpendicular and the other a small pond, we turned out; and after that matutinal cup of coffee which everyone who goes to sea indulges in, we proceeded to wade through the mud round our vessel with bare feet, and inspect minutely every seam and nailhole, in search of the invisible leak. We discovered several places in her skin through which we thought that the water might possibly find admittance, and these we stopped with white cotton and putty, using pen-knives for caulking tools. We worked hard at low water for two days under a steady downpour of cold rain. The natives discovered our whereabouts, and several barge skippers and others stood round and criticised our work, but none of them could suggest any better measures than those we were taking.

On Saturday, the 4th of June, we had completed our work, so at high water we took the *Falcon* out into the mid-river and anchored there. At noon we pumped her quite dry, then we went on shore, and at three returned on board, in fear and trembling, to discover what had been the result of our labours.

I went into the cabin, pulled up one of the floorboards, and looked into the hold.

"Well, does she make any water now, Sir?" inquired Wright anxiously from the deck.

"Water! If anything, she is making it faster than ever."

So we had again failed utterly in our attack on the mysterious leak. We were very disgusted, and saw that we should have to trouble our heads no more about it, but sail away, leak and all. I knew that, though very uncomfortable, it was not dangerous. I had set my mind on a cruise in the Baltic, and it would have required a more serious obstacle than this to prevent me carrying out my design. Wright was of the same opinion and as obstinate as myself, but the barge skippers shook their heads when they heard where we were bound for. "Don't ye go, Jack," said one old friend of my man's; "ye'll never cross the North Sea in that little craft."

And now, after a spell of dirty weather, the glass began to rise. On turning out on the morning of the

6th of June we saw that a moderate wind was blowing from the south-west.

"The very breeze to carry us to Rotterdam, Wright," I cried. "I'll go on shore and find what the weather forecast in the papers is. If it's a good one, we'll sail down to Harwich this afternoon and cross the North Sea to-night."

The papers informed us that moderate south-west winds might be expected in the North Sea, but that the south cone was hoisted in Ireland.

"Which means that we must get across to Rotterdam before the bad weather comes over here," I said.

"It looks like a slant at last. Perhaps our luck has changed," remarked Wright, looking round at the sky with a hopeful expression.

We completed our provisioning by filling two large stone bottles with the excellent beer of Maningtree, and then ran down the Stour to Harwich before a spanking southerly breeze in about an hour. We passed the pier at 2 p.m., and having tacked out of the harbour, were soon tumbling about in the very choppy and uncomfortable sea which is so frequently met with off Harwich. The approaches to this port are known as the Pitching-Ground, the Rolling-Ground, and the Rough Channel, all three doing their very best to deserve their appellation, to which fact many a pale excursionist can testify.

When we were yet some distance from the Cork light-ship a change came over the weather, the sky became over-cast and wild in appearance, the wind freshened, and we seemed to be in for a strong blow.

We liked the look of things so little that at last, after some hesitation, we determined to return to Harwich for shelter. It always goes much against the grain to have to run back to a port one has just sailed from, and this was the only occasion on which we had to perform this manœuvre during our cruise.

Having let go the anchor, I sailed on shore in the dinghy and landed at Harwich pier. Here ancient mariners who had been watching the yacht, informed us that we had acted rightly in running home again, for very bad weather was coming. Said the coxswain of the life-boat to me: " A young chap belonging here, who is on board a barge bound up, wired to-day from Shields, 'barge detained by heavy gales,' so you know what to expect."

But my glass was not falling, and in spite of the prognostications of the ancient mariners—landsmen place too much reliance in them—I decided to see what the night should bring forth, and, if things looked no worse, to sail on the morrow.

Then I remembered having been told by someone that the Meteorological Office would, if applied to, telegraph a weather forecast for the sum of one shilling. I had never availed myself of this very useful arrangement before, so bethought myself to test it now.

I telegraphed: "What weather Harwich to Rotterdam to-morrow?" On calling at the telegraph-station in an hour's time, the following reply was handed to me: "Light S.W. breezes, fine sea, nearly smooth."

Then I went on board rejoicing, for I knew—though many an old sailor would ridicule the idea—that the official opinion of the clerk of the weather is more to be relied on than the wisdom of all the ancient mariners in England put together. So full of faith, and knowing that we should now, after our many delays, get away at last, we dined off our beef-steak and onions in a happy frame of mind, and fixed five o'clock the next morning as the time of our departure.

We got under weigh at the appointed hour on the 7th of June, and so far the predictions of the weather-prophet seemed to be entirely correct. It was a lovely morning, a moderate south-west wind was blowing, and the sky was almost cloudless. When we had beaten out of the harbour, we were able to set our tanned square-sail, and ran at a fine rate towards the Cork—running is the *Falcon's* strong point.

We passed the South Ship-Head buoy—marking the edge of that dangerous shoal, lying eight miles off the land, on which so many a vessel has been lost—at eight o'clock, and from this I took my "departure," steering an east by south course.

The distance from the entrance of Harwich harbour to the West Gate is rather over a hundred miles, so there was some chance of making a port before nightfall. The wind gradually freshened as the day advanced, and I observed that the aneroid in the cabin was steadily falling.

At mid-day I brought up my sextant to shoot the sun and found that we were exactly on our course.

The wind still freshened, and we were rushing through the water faster than ever.

" I don't like the sky now," said Wright ; " it looks very wild. It will blow to-night."

" Yes, we must carry on as much as we can, and try to get hold of the land before dark."

" It's a pity we didn't sail last night after all. We should have been in Rotterdam by now," remarked Wright.

I had been saying the same thing to myself, but as we were in the middle of the North Sea by this time, it was clear that we must run on, there could be no turning back now.

A steep high sea was following us, but the boat behaved splendidly. It must indeed be a rough sea before which these sharp-ended life-boats cannot run with safety ; they do not easily broach to.

" The weather-prophet is hardly accurate this time. I should hardly call this water almost smooth," I said, as we were looking at a small steamer steering west, and frantically pitching into the seas as she sent showers of water over her bows.

" Nor I, Sir. Just look at this roller coming at us now. What a whopper!—over she goes. Well done, little boat ! By George, she does behave well in a sea-way."

Still the wind freshened, and the sea rose till at six o'clock we had quite as much of both as we required. It was about this time that we came upon a fleet of Dutch fishermen, great tubby craft with lee-boards, which were rolling in a comfortable, lazy way that gave one the impression of their being quite safe, and very much at home in this sort of water.

We passed close to some of these boats and hailed the men, asking them how far off the land we were. I don't know whether they understood us, but they shrieked back replies which we certainly could not understand, so we ran on eastwards, hoping soon to see some signs of the coast.

It now began to blow so hard that we were compelled to take two reefs in our main-sail—we had taken in our square-sail some time since. To make matters worse, it became very thick; a heavy rain was falling, and there could be no doubt that we were in for a dirty night.

At eight we found ourselves in the midst of steep and dangerous-looking rollers, so we surmised that we were approaching the banks, and were in shallow water. Our lead proved this to be the case. There are few worse coasts than those of Holland; the shores are so low and destitute of land-marks, and have such perilous sands extending far seawards, that the mariner who approaches them in thick weather often has a very anxious time of it.

We saw that it would be exceedingly difficult for us to make a land-fall and distinguish the lights on such a night, so not daring to run in further towards the outlying shoals, we decided to lie to till morning.

With two-reefed main-sail and fore-sail to windward, the little boat behaved wonderfully well. Great seas with breaking crests thundered down upon her one after another, often seeming as if they must inevitably overwhelm us; but the *Falcon* rose to them all without fuss, with an easy motion as of a boat conscious of her seaworthiness. After we had watched her behaviour for a while, she imparted her confidence to us. We felt that it would need a much worse sea than any we were likely to encounter this night to endanger her. Besides, I still had sufficient faith in the clerk of the weather to believe that nothing very serious in the way of bad weather was coming. I must not forget to give due praise to the little dinghy who behaved very well; and though much more fussy than the *Falcon*, she never lost her head.

But there was some danger for us from big steamers on so obscure a night, so we lit our side lights and kept two-hour watches in turns.

No water came over the vessel, but plenty came through her. She leaked terribly, and we were pumping the whole while. Our arms ached for a week after this experience. The night was anything but a pleasant one; it rained, it blew, it was cold, and our position was rather an insecure one.

As I kept my watch in dripping oilies, pumping hard with one hand, holding on with the other, and peering through the obscurity on the look-out for those murderous nuisances the screw steamers, I became meditative.

I called to mind a luxurious friend of mine who had once—only once—slept out with me in an open boat on the Medway one chilly spring night. I was sleeping soundly on the bottom boards, when a melancholy voice calling out my name awakened me. I opened my eyes and beheld standing before me in the boat a spectral form shrouded with the white mist of the river. It was my friend, who, unable to sleep, had risen from his couch among the ballast.

" Well, what is it ? " I asked.

" My good friend," he said sadly, " do you call this pleasure ? "

The wretch had awakened me from my happy slumbers to put me this question!

" And now," I asked myself, " is this pleasure ? " My conscience replied in the decided negative. " Then what the dickens am I here for ? " and I called to mind many wise saws of the sea, such as : " A sailor's life is a dog's life," " Who'd sell a farm and go to sea ? " " What the dickens am I here for ? " I asked myself again, seeing that I might be safe and comfortable at home.

Then glancing round to see that no steamer was near, I dived below, had a tot of rum, lit a pipe, and returned on deck to my duties. Feeling more comfortable, I now found a satisfactory reply to my question. " This is not exactly pleasure," I told myself; " but such a night is an exception in a long cruise.

Bad weather now and then makes the pleasant days all the more enjoyable; besides, yachting would be no more exciting than a voyage on a Thames penny steamer if the weather was always fine. And now for that confounded pump again.

So passed the uncomfortable night. About an hour before dawn I turned into my bunk and fell asleep. Shortly afterwards Wright put his head into the cabin. "I can see a light, Sir," he said. "I thought it was a steamer's mast-head light at first, but it isn't; it's a flash light on the shore.

I tumbled on deck, and there surely enough to the eastward flashed out at regular intervals a white light, scarcely visible, for it was evidently a long way off.

I timed the rate of its appearance—three quick flashes every half minute—then went below, consulted the chart, and found that this was the Schouwen light-ship. We had therefore drifted considerably to the southward of our course during the night, and were much further from the land than I had thought. This light-ship is moored on the outlying shoals of the island of Schouwen and is more than twenty miles from the mouth of the Maas.

As we now knew our position, we let the fore-sheet draw and ran before the heavy seas towards the light. My intention had been to enter the Maas by the usual route, the Hook of Holland canal; but as we were so far to the southward of this, and as I wished to get into smoother water as quickly as possible, I decided to steer for the Slyk Gat to the north of Goeree island and make the harbour of Hellevoetsluis, whence we could reach the Maas by way of the Voorne Canal.

Before reaching the light-ship we sailed across the narrow Schouwen bank, where the water shoals suddenly from fourteen to four fathoms. On this we encountered a very troublesome sea, and we were much relieved when we got out of it into deeper water again.

From the light-ship our course to Goeree island was fifteen miles, east by south. The day broke cheerlessly. The wind had moderated somewhat, but the sea seemed as high as ever, the sky was full of dark clouds that were travelling at a great speed, and it was still so thick that we could not expect to discover the low coast of Holland until we were close upon it.

We ran on but perceived no buoys nor any sign of the land, and, as I did not know how the tide was setting across the banks, I was soon again rather uncertain as to our whereabouts. Far out to sea from Goeree Island stretches the dangerous Ooster Zand, on which there is only half a fathom of water in places, so we felt our way carefully with the lead. At last the water shoaled to two fathoms and still there were no landmarks visible. At this juncture it began to rain hard so that we could only see a few yards around us. It was now six o'clock.

As the water was still shoaling I bore away to sea a little, not liking to rush blindly over these dangerous banks in such weather. Suddenly there loomed out of the haze, close to us, a fine-looking Dutch sloop with polished oak sides and lee-boards. She was hove-to under a reefed main-sail, and the pilot flag was flying at her mast-head. Across her sail was inscribed in large black characters GOEREE.

Now it is against my principles to employ a pilot on a small yacht. A vessel drawing so little as three feet ought to find her own way everywhere; but on this occasion I broke my rule, hove-to, and, for the first and only time during this cruise, hoisted my Jack. After all, there was some excuse for taking a pilot under the circumstances. We had been tumbling about for twenty-four hours and were tired, the weather was bad, we were among dangerous shoals, and it was too thick to see the landmarks; but still I felt somewhat ashamed of myself as our signal went up.

The Dutchmen lowered their strong oak dingy and contrived to get a pilot on board of us very cleverly.

He threw into the cabin that oil-skin bundle which invariably represents a pilot's luggage, shook hands with me, and inquired where I wanted to go to.

"Hellevoetsluis," I replied.

"Right, Captain, I will take you there, and I shan't be long about it with this wind."

This man was a tremendous swell, resplendent in gold lace and brass buttons, and like all Dutch pilots he spoke English, of a sort, fluently. He took the helm and steered the same course we had been following ourselves.

"Capital boat to run before a sea this, Captain," he said after a few minutes, " but look, there is Goeree."

As he spoke the rain had ceased, the sky cleared a bit, and there, before us, about a mile away to leeward, suddenly appeared a low, pale-green shore with several hurrying wind-mills in the back-ground. Had the pilot appeared on the scene but five minutes later than he did we should have known our position and dispensed with his assistance.

We coasted by Goeree in smooth water, and now that we had escaped the dangers of the North Sea the weather began to improve. The storm-clouds disappeared and a bright sunshine lit up the fresh-looking green land.

We shook out our reefs and made good way against a strong tide. I need hardly say that we had to take an occasional jog at the pump, and our pilot observing this, made some rather sarcastic observations on our leaky condition. Presently we could distinguish the opposite coast of the island of Voorne, low also; its vegetation dazzling with the vivid colours of a humid climate. In rainy weather all this bright colouring is drowned in vapour, and the country assumes a most melancholy and sombre aspect; but a glimpse of sunshine will produce so sudden and marvellous a transformation on a Dutch landscape as is not to be witnessed even in our own moderately damp England.

Across the dykes of Voorne we perceived an enormous congregation of windmills.

"What do you have all these windmills for?" asked Wright.

"To pump de water off de land," replied our pilot; "if those was not always turning round, us Hollanders would soon all be drowned."

"Well, pilot," I said, "you were very severe just now about our boat leaking, but you must confess that your country leaks harder still. Your windmills are always pumping, just as they do on an old Norwegian timber-vessel."

He chuckled softly, and replied merely: "I think, Captain, I will take one little drop more of that rum."

The channel between the islands up which we were sailing now presented the appearance of a broad river. As a matter of fact it is a river, but what particular river I was quite unable to say off-hand when Wright put the question to me. Even after a study of the chart I was still undecided, for the Rhine, the Maas, the Schelde, and other rivers of the Netherlands, got so inextricably mixed up among the labyrinths of channels and canals of Zeeland that the mariner is justly entitled to take his choice. I therefore decided that I should like to be on the Maas, and informed Wright that was the name of the broad stream we were ascending.

The pilot did not contradict me. I suppose the Dutch themselves are far too wise a people to madden themselves with the disentanglement of their puzzling rivers. "Ah, Sirs," he exclaimed, "what a pretty country, what a pretty river!"

"Almost as muddy as the Thames, though," remarked Wright, looking down at the brown water.

"Dat is not the fault of de Dutch people," cried the patriotic pilot indignantly; "Dutch people hate dirt. Dis river comes from Germany. After much rain de water is filthy like dis. Germany, den, sends us all her dirt."

I thought of the first Napoleon's impudent apology for seizing Holland—that it was a country formed artificially of the alluvia of French rivers, and therefore belonged rightfully to France. But I kept this thought to myself; our Dutchman might not have liked it.

After sailing for about two hours under the pilot's charge he brought us alongside the quay of Hellevoetsluis, and for the first time in my life I set foot in Holland.

Hellevoetsluis was once an important fortress and seaport. British tourists of two generations ago knew it well, for the Harwich packet used to call here; but now there is not much life in the little place, and the arrival of a yacht from England seemed to be a sufficiently novel occurrence to attract much attention to us. I jumped on shore and a polite crowd guided me to the harbour-master's office, where I showed my papers, and paid the pilot his fee—twelve shillings. Then I returned to the yacht and found a great many people of all ranks, ages, and sexes, gazing at us from the quay, and discussing us in the curiously deliberate and unexcitable Dutch fashion. One who spoke English explained to me the sentiments of his fellows.

"These Holland people," he said, "think your boat too little to cross the North Sea. They not like to be passengers of you, not at all, by Jove."

I looked round Hellevoetsluis, which is like every other place in Holland, and I was struck by exactly the same things that first attract the attention of every stranger who lands in this country, and I, no doubt, made exactly the same remarks as every tourist does. I noticed that the crowd looked very much like an English crowd. I observed the clean streets and tidy little houses, the marvellous lock-gates of the canals, of bright oak, varnished and polished with loving care, as if they had been valuable old Chippendale sideboards at least—so different from the dirty tarred locks at home. Then I admired the schuyts and other craft, all of varnished oak to match the locks, with little windows having muslin curtains and flowers in pots, each with a clean family of many generations living on board—reminding one altogether more of life on a Thames house-boat than on a trading barge. Then I went into a *café* and approved of a glass of beer. But there was nothing very new in all this, and it has been described over and over again.

The wind was still fresh, and blew straight up the Voorne canal, so I thought it best not to waste such an opportunity, but to sail for Rotterdam at once. The following day might bring a head wind, and besides, Hellevoetsluis was not so particularly interesting a place as to make us loth to leave it.

So I again went to the harbour-master's office,

showed my register and paid the canal dues, which, as the *Falcon* is only three tons, amounted to twopence, or some such small sum.

We passed through the lock-gates, and, setting all sail, we ran before the wind up the perfectly straight canal. It was our first experience of a Dutch canal, and so we were excited and interested by the many novel sights; but I found that one soon wearies of the frightful monotony of the Dutch waterways, and after a few days I began to wonder how some yachtsmen wax so enthusiastic over Holland.

However, I thoroughly enjoyed this seven miles run up the Voorne canal. The smooth water, the sunny sky and green pastures were very pleasant after the dark and stormy North Sea. The quaint and cumbrous-looking, though handy native craft attracted much of our attention. At first we marvelled at their great apparent speed; but we soon found that there was more brag than real haste about them, and that we were being taken in by noise, for their bluff bows ploughed through the water with all the fuss and fury of a Puffing-Billy. The crews of these vessels looked at us with evident surprise as we passed. The skippers invariably asked where we were from. When we replied, from London, they as invariably made the same remark—it was an exclamation expressive of astonishment. I imagine from the sound of it that it was somewhat profane, so will not repeat it.

I had heard that on a Dutch canal one can always run full tilt at a bridge, and that the ever-watchful guardian will never fail to open it in time to let a vessel through. I felt rather nervous on trying this experiment at our first bridge. As we approached it, Wright blew the fog-horn lustily, and I ran on in faith. The man in charge of the bridge was sitting in an arm-chair at the door of his neat little cottage, with his back turned to us, smoking, with true Dutch phlegm, a portentous pipe. He made no response to our signal, he did not even turn his head. He smoked on apparently quite unconscious of our approach. Horrible thought, perhaps he was deaf! With great din of shouting and horn-blowing we rushed on before the strong wind—a smash seemed inevitable—when almost at the last moment this stolid fellow turned round to us, stretched his arms above his head and yawned; then he laid down his precious pipe carefully by his side, and, rising quite leisurely, proceeded to swing the bridge, and we passed through safely.

These bridge guardians on Dutch canals evidently take a pride in running very close shaves. It seems, however, that accidents very seldom occur; but these lifting and swinging bridges are beautifully constructed, and are set in motion with a wonderful ease and quickness.

We passed through the sluice at the end of the canal and were again on a broad tidal water.

"What river is this?" asked Wright.

Now I knew that this channel was undoubtedly one of the branches of the Maas; but having already told Wright that the stream we had left was called the

Maas, and not wishing to perplex myself or him with the complicated Dutch river puzzle, I diplomatically bethought myself to give the French equivalent for the Dutch name.

"This is the river Meuse," I replied.

But Wright's ear could not recognize the difference between my French and Dutch accent.

"I thought the other river was called that," he said.

I happened to be looking at the chart at the time, and there saw a capital way of getting out of my difficulty.

"Yes," I said, "but this is called the *New* Mass." Happily he asked for no further information.

We ascended the river against a strong ebb tide for fifteen miles. We passed the port of Schiedam, and saw the towers of that famous gin-making town about a mile inland. Shortly afterwards we perceived the city of Rotterdam before us, looking imposing with its lofty buildings and its vast quays. The river was crowded with every sort of craft, ranging from stately East-Indiamen to tiny fishing-boats.

We took in some of our canvas and sailed slowly on, looking round us for a suitable berth. After passing the public park we opened out a small harbour in which was tightly packed a great number of schuyts and other small coasters. This seemed to be the very place for us, so, lowering our sails, we allowed the yacht to shoot in, and made fast to a smart river-trader, laden with round cheeses, which lay alongside the quay.

ACROSS THE NORTH SEA. 55

On inquiry we found that this harbour was called the Veerhaven. There are many such in water-intersected Rotterdam; but, judging from what I saw, I should recommend this one to all small yachts. It is quieter than most of the havens, and though vessels moving in and out frequently compelled us to let go our warps and shift our berth so as to allow them room to pass, there was none of that fuss, shouting, and ill-temper which would accompany such manœuvres in a French harbour for instance.

Considering how crowded these Dutch waterways are, it is really astonishing how little a yachtsman cruising on them need fear damage to his vessel. The Dutchmen keep their own craft in such beautiful order that they treat all others with consideration. Though any of these strong oak schuyts could crush a slight yacht without herself feeling it, the Dutch sailor never fails to put out his fenders when there is chance of the slightest contact; even when he is forced to shove off in haste in order to avoid an accident, he is careful to thrust his boat-hook against your rigging or ironwork; he is as kind to your paint and varnish as you could be yourself.

These Hollanders are at home on the water if any people in the world are; and rough as they may be, they treat the boats of their neighbours with all the delicate caution of a china-maniac handling some invaluable old Sévres vase. These canals would be intolerable to the yachtsman were it not for the skill and care of these honest mariners, and they will get out of one's way so good-humouredly too; one will hear no oaths, perceive no excitement among them, even in moments of serious risk.

It was two o'clock in the afternoon when we reached Rotterdam, so we had been under weigh for thirty-three hours. We not unnaturally felt somewhat tired, and instead of at once going on shore to explore the town I turned into my bunk and slept till six, when I was awakened by the arrival of the harbour-master. This functionary, very polite, and clad in gorgeous uniform, examined my papers, saw that all was right, and informed me that I was at liberty to do what I pleased; so I sallied forth, refreshed by my rest, to "do" Rotterdam.

CHAPTER IV.

FROM ROTTERDAM TO AMSTERDAM.

ROTTERDAM is one of the most pleasant and interesting places I know, but I have no intention of describing its sights, or, for the matter of that, those of any other big city I visited in the course of this cruise; for are they not all written up in the books of Murray, Baedeker, and the rest?

I "did" some of the lions—not all, for lionizing is terribly hard work; and seeing that the average traveller, myself for instance, may have lived in London half his life and not have been compelled by public opinion to know one-tenth of the sights of his own capital, is it fair to expect him to lay himself out for the inspection of all the orthodox objects of interest in a foreign capital, in the space of a few days?

On the morning after our arrival a large number of the citizens of Rotterdam, who seemed to think that so small a vessel had no right to cross the North

Sea, came down to the quay-side to look at us. Among others was Mr. De Haas, the agent of the R.T.Y.C., who, recognizing the burgee of the club at my mast-head, introduced himself. I need not tell yachtsmen who know Rotterdam that this gentleman looked well after me during my stay. He supplied me with a store of Curaçoa, cigars, and Schiedam, whose excellent qualities made me many friends in the ports I visited. A good cellar is a capital passport by water as well as by land, and the hardness of even German officialism melts before this highest proof of respectability.

I, of course, took train to the Hague, that quaint, painfully-clean, and perhaps rather dull capital, which seems so peaceful with its lakes, quiet canals, and many green trees. A soothing influence is about the place which seems even to affect the rushing tourist; here he flits from sight to sight with less hurry than is his wont. I actually saw one nodding in a seat in the Plein, while that awful red book, which is the badge of all hi tribe, and which, like a malignant spirit, is ever with him, allowing him no rest, but driving on the weary wretch from lion to lion, lay idle on his lap.

In the way of sights I contented myself with a stroll through the picture-galleries of the Mauritsluis; after which I slummed the town, looking at the shops, the people, the *cafés*, the barges on the canals; for, being a Philistine, I take some interest in the live people of a country and their ways.

While exploring the Mauritsluis I remembered that the collection included Paul Potter's famous Bull; so I referred to my Baedeker (I, too, carry with me the scarlet familiar, and very useful, nay necessary, he is if kept in his place and not allowed to become a tyrant master), and found that the number of the picture was 111. I discovered the room in which the master-piece is kept; there I saw before me a gigantic gold frame, at the foot of which was a tablet with the number 111 inscribed on it—there could be no mistake about that—but within the frame I could distinguish nothing but inky blackness. I came nearer; there, indeed, was the frame and the black back of it, but the celebrated bull had gone. So I left the gallery in disappointment, and was walking through the court-yard which surrounds the Mauritsluis when I perceived a considerable crowd assembled. Concluding that I had fallen on a street row, and curious to see what a Dutch row was like, I approached, and lo! there was the lost bull after all. The picture had been brought out into the open air so that a photographer could take the noble animal's likeness; it seemed rather a casual way of treating so priceless a gem.

I remained three days at Rotterdam, and could have stayed much longer without being bored. As a traveller is expected to describe some features of the towns he visits, and as I have declined to allude to Rotterdam's lions, I will make a few remarks on the facilities for eating in this city—a subject of interest to most male readers:—The chief *cafés* are splendid palaces, and the restaurants are as good as any I know. Dutch dishes have weird names, and are often compounded of what the English consider to be incompatible elements; but those I tried—and I went in for an experimental course—seemed to me to be excellent. Here is one for example: I had entered a *café* for a snack at lunch-time, and on looking down the bill of fare read the item "Wienersnitzel." "That sounds as if it ought to be good," I said to myself, so pronouncing it after the light of nature, I called for one. When my Wienersnitzel was put in front of me, I, first of all, noticed that its odour was delicious; then I placed a morsel in my mouth, its taste came up to its odour. Then I proceeded to analyse its contents, and as far as I could make out, the lowest layer of a Wienersnitzel consists of juicy veal steaks and slices of lemon-peel; the next layer is composed of sardines; then come sliced gherkins, capers, and divers mysteries; a delicate sauce flavours the whole, and the result is a gastronomic dream.

During this cruise I was in the habit of living on board my vessel to a greater extent than most yachtsmen do, and I generally contented myself with Wright's plain but wholesome cooking. But, hungry after knowledge, I made a rule of indulging in one big dinner at a first-class restaurant in each new country I visited. I made a confident of a friend of mine resident in Rotterdam, who knew his way about that city and understood what dining meant. So he piloted me to the right place, and we dined together at the

Café Riche, which commands a pleasant view over the river. This establishment is not frequented by British tourists but by native gentlemen; so it has not yet been spoilt, as nearly all the famous Paris restaurants have been. The proprietors here still find it to their interests to please their habitual customers. I trust that the excursionists will not have found this place out before I next visit Rotterdam, for I intend to dine there again.

Mr. Tourist, when you next find yourself in Rotterdam, I should advise you—that is, if Madame Tourist will not object—to visit the Tivoli Spielgarden, which is a sort of Cremorne, a few miles outside the city, and you will certainly be surprised and amused at the quaint, rough, good-natured, frankly, and almost innocently immodest way in which the Hollanders take their pleasure. After this you will better understand those famous old paintings of carousing boors which you have been gazing at in the galleries.

Hither the lover of the lower middle class brings his beamy and, to English eyes, not altogether lovely sweetheart. This is a place of boisterous merriment; there are swings, rifle-shooting, and boating on an extensive lake, and, in short, all the fun of the fair. I noticed that Dutch maidens are much given to slapping the faces of their swains in public, not in wrath, but to restrain their boorish ardour; and the slaps were delivered with all the sturdy lasses' strength. The lovers seem to take it all in very good part, even when they were felled to the ground, which occasionally happened. The courtship of Dutch boors is evidently as rough an amusement as football with us. The dancing was grotesque and after Jan Steen.

The Dutch are our cousins. I entertained no doubt of this, and I almost fancied myself at home again when I saw these Dutch servant-girls and other plebeian damsels from the town here dressed in their Sunday best. All the outrageously bad taste and gaudy draggletailedness of English girls of the same degree were exactly reproduced. But the drunken ruffianism that would have attended such a gathering in England was altogether absent; so I felt no longer at home, and realised that I was a stranger in an alien land.

To one who has never visited this country before, the road to Hillegersberg, the village in which the Spielgarden is situated, is also interesting, for it is a very typical Dutch highway. It is paved with brick and bordered on either side by a broad ditch and an avenue of trees—the latter, of course, all of one size and shape, to satisfy the Dutch love of symmetry. On the way I passed many villas, each surrounded with a brimming moat, and having a draw-bridge across the ditch to afford communication with the road. Each orderly garden displayed an almost tropical gorgeousness of bright blossoms, and the name of each villa was conspicuously painted on the door or designed on the lawn in large letters of flowering plants, all quaint names suggestive of steady Dutch contentment, such as "Rest after labour," "Competence and leisure."

Occasionally, too, on the side of the road were extensive ponds, or rather lakes, bordered with sedge, reminding me of Norfolk Broads. There were pleasant pastures also, where, among the rich deep grass of Holland, the sleek kine grazed. This combination of blue sky, tender green vegetation, rippling water, and comfortable homesteads, the keen pure air and the song of many singing birds, made me in love with cheerful Holland. The Dutch genius was apparent everywhere. These people have set themselves to make beautiful landscapes out of reclaimed mud, and they have succeeded.

And now, having done Rotterdam, I had to decide whither to go next.

The object of this cruise was to explore the Baltic and not the Dutch canals; I should not have touched at Holland at all were it not that her inland waters enabled me to cheat the North Sea. So I wished to cross the country as quickly as possible, and consulted my charts in order to discover which was my nearest route to the Dollart, where the region of canals terminates and the open ocean has to be braved once more. I decided to go by river and canal to Amsterdam, thence cross the Zuider Zee to Zwartsluis, from which I could reach Delfzyl by way of Meppel, Assen, and Groningen. The total distance from Hellevoetsluis to Delfzyl, by the route I followed is, 234 miles.

The people of Rotterdam, on hearing that I intended to take my boat to the furthest extremity of their country, informed me that it was absolutely necessary that I should engage a pilot, and what was more, one of the English-speaking pilots, of whom there is no lack here. Many of these men called on me, each laden with glowing certificates from English yachtsmen. These testimonials satisfied me that a Dutch river-pilot must be little short of an angel. But in spite of this I would not be persuaded; I could not for the life of me see wherein lay the necessity of shipping a pilot on so small a vessel as the *Falcon*. Each fellow shook his head when I told him this, recited a formidable catalogue of the dangers I was about to court, and prophesied that terrible disasters would result from my pig-headed obstinacy.

However, we contrived to cross Holland without a pilot and without understanding a word of the language, and also without meeting with the slightest accident. It is true that once or twice we completely lost ourselves amid the intricate network of canals which is found in every large Dutch town, when we would sail and punt disconsolately up and down mysterious drains and wild slums, whose inhabitants could not or would not understand our questions; but these were but amusing incidents, and we always contrived to emerge somewhere at last.

A portion of the great bridge which spans the Maas at Rotterdam is swung at certain times so as to allow vessels to pass through. I was informed that it was thus opened every morning at 5 o'clock, so we turned out at an early hour on Sunday the 12th of June, pushed our way out of the crowded Veerhaven, and, setting all sail to woo a very light south-west breeze, drifted up to the bridge. We passed through just before it was closed, and, in the company of a number of schuyts—all of which, to our gratification, we easily outstripped—we sailed up the broad muddy river. The flood soon overtook us, and though there was but little wind, the current carried us along at a good pace.

Our immediate destination was the town of Gouda, which is about eighteen miles from Rotterdam by water, situated on the river Ijsel, a branch of the Maas. At Gouda, so my map informed me, we should have to leave the tidal river and work our way by one of the canals—there seemed to be several to choose from—to Amsterdam. The Ijsel joins the Maas about four or five miles above Rotterdam, so, not having the faintest idea as to how large it would prove to be, I kept a sharp look-out for any stream that might appear on the port hand.

At last, after running some way up the Maas, we opened out what looked like a rather narrow creek. I hesitated, doubtful as to whether this could be my river. I noticed that though many small traders were ascending and descending the Maas, no craft of any description were to be seen on this tributary. A schuyt happened to be sailing close to me. "Is that the Ijsel?" I cried, pointing to the opening.

The skipper spoke not a word but shook his head, evidently not understanding me. Doubtless my pronunciation of the name Ijsel was incorrect, and little wonder seeing how it is spelt.

"Is that the way to Gouda?" I cried again, mumbling the first words of the sentence, but bringing out "Gouda" very loudly and distinctly.

A gleam of intelligence lit up the worthy Hollander's stolid features. "Yah, yah, Gouda," he shouted as he sailed by.

So I turned the yacht into the unpronounceable river, and the wind now freshening we made good progress, running, reaching, and tacking in turns; for the Ijsel is very winding. We had the whole river to ourselves, not another vessel was upon it. We were thankful for this, as the channel was often a very narrow one. Sunday is the best day for yacht-sailing on a Dutch canal or river, for nine out of ten Dutch skippers will not sail on a Sunday, so there is plenty of room and no crowd. Strict Sabbatarians will say that I might have followed the example of these good men with advantage; but I shall soon have to describe the Dutch skipper's manner of passing his Sunday.

It was a dull day with drizzling rain at intervals. The scenery we passed was not interesting and there was little life on the banks. There were the usual half-flooded pastures, clumps of trees and numberless windmills that compose a Dutch landscape. We sailed by the scarlet-roofed villages of Ouderkerk, Berkenwoude and Gouderak; one of these was *en fête*, covered with bunting and crowded with holiday-makers who cheered us as we ran by.

At about eleven o'clock a more considerable settlement opened out before us. That, we thought, must be Gouda at last. When we came nearer we perceived the lock gates of the canals communicating with the river, and we saw masts rising among the houses in every direction, showing that a great number of canal boats were resting here for the Sunday.

We lowered our sails and came alongside the quay. A crowd of men soon gathered round, who did not speak, but looked at us with evident wonder. "Is this Gouda?" I asked of a fat little man, who might have been a mate of a ship from his appearance, and who had caught and made fast our warp when we threw it on shore.

"Yes, this is Gouda; and what are you?" he replied in English. He spoke politely, and the seemingly rude abruptness of the speech was evidently due to his limited acquaintance with our language.

I explained that we were bound for Amsterdam.

Then by a curious mixture of Dutch, broken English and signs he gradually, and not without much difficulty, led me to understand that it was not worth our while attempting to go farther that day, as the wind was contrary and the canal too narrow to allow of tacking, and that if we waited till the following morning he would tow us to Amsterdam.

As his statement seemed to be hardly a disinterested one, I had a look at the canal myself, and had to confess that he was right; for it was very narrow to begin with, and the vessels were packed so densely on either side of it that there was scarcely left a free channel of twelve feet in breadth.

"Head wind morrow, too, captain," said my friend, scanning the heavens.

"What are you going to tow us with?" I asked.

"Come," he said, and he beckoned me to follow him.

So leaving Wright in charge of the yacht I accompanied the Dutchman, through many clean, well-paved streets, by the side of many canals crowded with craft, and over many swing bridges, till we came to a small steam-tug that lay along the bank of one of the principal canals.

"Mine," he said proudly, pointing to the vessel and then to his breast. "Mine. Me captain, owner, all one."

I followed him on board the steamer and into the cabin, a wonderfully comfortable and smart one for a mere "puffing-billy." Here we found the mate, who was also engineer, cook, and general factotum, dressed in his Sunday clothes, drinking gin in solitude. This mate, a tall, lean, and comical-looking chap, who had evidently knocked about the world a good deal, spoke English much better than his skipper, having served long in English ships, so he now acted as our interpreter.

The tug was to start for Amsterdam at three o'clock the next morning with a string of schuyts in tow. "The captain says he will tow you there for half an English pound," explained the mate, "and out of that he will pay all the canal and bridge dues."

As Amsterdam is at least forty miles from Gouda by water, this seemed anything but an extortionate charge, and knowing that we might occupy several days in working the yacht up ourselves, should the head wind continue, I closed with him at once.

The captain seemed to be rather proud of our acquaintance, and had evidently made up his mind to take us entirely under his charge during our stay at Gouda. In the first place, so that we should not escape him, he woke up the lock-keeper, who, as business was dull, was taking his Sunday afternoon nap, made him open the gates for us and we passed out of the river into the canal. Then he boarded the *Falcon* and piloted us through the intricate net-work of canals to the centre of the town where his tug lay and lashed us firmly alongside of her. This, we said to ourselves, was far better than lying by the quay side, as we should not be worried by the usual crowd of inquisitive spectators—but we did not know what was before us.

So far all was well, and we were very much obliged to the captain for his kindness; but he soon showed the cloven hoof, and turned out to be the most horrible bore we were destined to encounter during the whole of this cruise. However, the poor fellow was evidently well-meaning, and I found myself in the unpleasant predicament of being unable to shake him off without displaying the grossest ingratitude.

Having, as I said, secured us alongside his vessel he and his mate came into our cabin and made themselves quite at home. Dutchman of the lower class possess little of the instinct of politeness, do not know when they are intruding and never take a hint. These two men calmly helped themselves to cigars, gin, and any other stores they found about our cabin; not that they had the slightest intention of sponging upon us, for they brought us eggs, a large Gouda cheese, a quantity of beer, and some vegetables out of the steamer, informing us that later on we should all dine together on board the *Falcon*, the mate cooking some dishes, Wright the others, so that it should be a regular Anglo-Dutch repast, and combine all the respective merits of the two cuisines. We could do nothing with the fellows, they forced us to receive from them quite as much as they took from us. "We are well at home on your boat," said the mate, "you make yourself at home just same way on board us, as if we were all brothers; take what you want from us, we have plenty good stores."

These two worthies had no doubt passed the morning in steady beer soaking, and now, I discovered to my dismay, they were gradually becoming, not exactly drunk, but imbecile. Their conversation was limited to suggestions of more drinks and praise of each other. The following little bit of dialogue was repeated a hundred times at least in the course of the day: — "This captain very good man," the mate would say, "best captain I ever sailed with." "And dis man," would return the captain, "de best cook, de best mate, de best engineer in de Nederlands." "And we are two very good friends," the mate would go on. "We work hard and make plenty money all week and get drunk together all Sunday."

So as to get rid of them I suggested that I was going to take a stroll round the town. "Dat's so," exclaimed the mate. "Captain go with you and show you round; I go with your man show him round. Two captains go together, two cooks go together. Dat is de good way; and after enough walk we will all come back dine together."

This was not exactly what we wanted, but what were we to do? I considered the question, and remembering that we were under obligations to these men—that our vessel was made fast to theirs (the only decent berth left in the crowded canal), that we were to be towed by them at three on the following morning, and that, as far as we knew, they were the only people in the town who understood English—I felt that we were clearly at their mercy, and that our best policy was to resign ourselves with good grace to our fate.

I therefore gave my consent to the proposal. First of all, the little fat skipper and myself sallied forth; and shortly afterwards Wright went off with the tall, lean mate. I may mention that my own build is rather like that of the Dutch mate, and that Wright is as short and beamy as was the Dutch skipper, so the contrast between the two parties must have been somewhat amusing, and indeed jeering remarks were made upon us by some rude little boys as we passed.

My friend the skipper's idea of showing a stranger round his native town was to take me into all the public-houses where he was known, and their name was legion, and treat all his open-mouthed acquaintances to beer and to what sounded like a very flattering history of my life. I noticed that in every instance this history ended with the same words uttered in a proud and defiant manner. After puzzling my brain awhile I came to the conclusion that their meaning was: "And he is under my charge." I was so with a vengeance.

I was becoming very weary of this state of bondage when at last we entered a *café*, which the captain told me was his favourite one, as it belonged to his brother-in-law. Here luckily he tarried so long that beer and the heat of the day overcame him, so that he fell asleep over the table at which we were sitting. Now was my opportunity for escape. I succeeded in stealing out of the *café* on tip-toe without awaking my jailor, then I fled down the street. I was free at last!

There are several lions to be visited in Gouda, and among others, so Baedeker informed me, is the Groote Kerk, a grand old church, built in the fifteenth century, which contains forty-two very beautiful stained-glass windows. I found my way thither, entered, and after recovering from my first surprise at finding that it is the custom for Dutchmen to keep their hats on in church, I passed some time in admiring the windows, which appeared to me to be by far the finest specimens of stained glass I had ever seen.

Gouda is a town of about 1,800 inhabitants, and I think it is more cut up by canals than any town I saw in Holland. As every canal in it looks exactly like another, and as all the avenues of trees and the houses that border the canals are after one pattern, it is the easiest place to lose oneself in that I know of. I lost myself several times before I discovered the *Falcon* again, and, as it was, I only came upon her by accident, for I had no idea what canal or street to enquire for, even if the people could have understood me.

I crossed the deck of the tug, jumped on to the yacht, and then found, to my disgust, that I was locked out of my cabin. Wright had taken the key with him when he had gone off for his walk with the mate, and neither of them had returned. So in a state of great indignation I sat on the deck in the sun, smoking and glaring sulkily at the crowd of citizens who were staring at the yacht from the opposite bank of the canal.

At about seven o'clock in the evening Wright returned alone and disarmed my anger by explaining the cause of his delay. He, too, was highly indignant at the way he had been treated by his companion the lean mate. It seems that this thirsty Dutchman had behaved in very much the same manner as his skipper. He had taken Wright from *café* to *café*, and had become idiotically tipsy, so that my man, finding that he could do nothing with the fellow, and seeing that dinner-time was near, deserted him, even as I had deserted the fat captain. But the *café* in which Wright had left the recumbent mate must have been in some remote portion of the town, for he told me that he had been wandering about from canal to canal in search of the yacht for quite an hour, that he had not met a soul who could understand English, and was beginning to despair of finding the *Falcon* at all before nightfall, when he suddenly recognized the red and black funnel of the tug and made for it.

I need not say that the international dinner did not come off that night; we did not wait for the two Hollanders, but dined alone. As we had to be up at daybreak we turned in early. At about ten we heard the skipper return to his vessel, bringing with him some half-dozen elated friends, and for the rest of the night there was a hideous noise of Dutch carousing on the tug. The skipper did not at all approve of our absence from the merry party. He came on board of us several times and shouted to us through the cabin hatch: "Come have beer and Hollands with us. Plenty fun on board us."

The last time he thus visited us—it was about 2 A.M.—I lost my temper and flew out of my bunk at him, with language loud and expressive. But he did not seem to understand the strongest hint that I wished to be left alone. Some of his friends, however, must have been more sober than himself, for they dragged him back to his own vessel, and, I believe, prevented him from boarding us again.

Shortly before 3 A.M., I was awakened by the whistle of the steam-tug sounding shrilly in my ear. I came on deck and beheld standing on the bridge the sturdy Dutch captain, now quite sober, with all his wits about him, giving his orders like a man; his mate, who seemed to have been suddenly transformed from a drunken scoundrel into a respectable and intelligent officer, stood by his side. I was amazed, I rubbed my eyes. Was it possible that after carousing for a day and a night two men could turn out and look so fit at three in the morning? But so it was, and the captain, who might have been a teetotaller for years from his appearance, took four schuyts and the *Falcon* in tow and started for Amsterdam. He stood at his wheel and steered eight hours right off without being relieved, and very skilfully he steered too, through the crowded and narrow canals. There could be no doubt about his being a very tough double Dutchman indeed; he accordingly rose again in my estimation.

We were towed by the steamer from 3 A.M. to 2 P.M. Our speed was not great, and the numerous locks caused constant delays. It was, however, an interesting journey, more so, I think, than any other we undertook on the Dutch canals.

It was a hot cloudless day and the scenery looked its best. We traversed a rich agricultural district. Extensive pastures, on which browsed great herds of cattle, bordered the dykes. Comfortable farm-houses nestling in clumps of trees dotted the landscapes, and occasionally we passed some picturesque little village, always having an air of cheerful prosperity about it. Of these a place called Boskoop especially struck me for its quaint prettiness. This village was surrounded with fruit trees and intersected by avenues of fine chestnuts in full bloom; its houses were of bright red brick and glazed tiles, its quays and bridges of beautifully polished dark oak. There was here such a wealth of rich colouring, so harmonious in tone, glowing under the blue sky, that, beholding, one understood how it was that the old Dutch landscape painters never went far from home for inspiration.

Monday is the busiest day of the week on the Dutch waterways, and our canal, crowded with craft steaming, towing with horses, and sailing, presented a very animated appearance. Sturdy peasants in blouses and wooden shoes came off from every farm in clumsy boats to sell cheeses, vegetables, and buckets of sour milk to the crews of the passing vessels. The canal was one long floating market. We bought a quantity of sour milk for threepence. This mixed with sugar is a cool and pleasant summer drink that I can recommend to the teetotallers as a far more wholesome and palatable beverage than any their ingenuity has yet discovered.

Though I had as yet seen so little of the country I found that I was already becoming conscious of an uncomfortable restraint in the presence of all the scrupulous cleanliness of Holland. This Dutch love of cleanliness is a fidgety mania. I soon felt as one does when one is staying in the home of some prim old maid, who snarls and looks daggers if a book is not replaced in exactly the same spot on the table whence it was lifted, or a newspaper not neatly refolded after being read. I soon began to long for the comfortable case of dirt again. I could never make myself really at home in a land where, I believe, the very pigs deny themselves the luxury of a mud bath in their horror of a soiled coat.

At last we came out of the canal into the Oude Rijn, the main channel of the Rhine, by which that river, with volume much diminished by the numerous pilfering canals that cross it, finds its way to the German Ocean. Instead of following the shortest route to Amsterdam, our captain now towed us down the river for several miles in the direction of Leyden, and, leaving the Rhine opposite the town of Alfen, steamed up a canal that passes through the Haarlemmer Meer. I was afterwards told that his object in selecting this circuitous course was to avoid the higher tolls which have to be paid on the direct canal. I was glad that his economy carried us in this unexpected direction, for it enabled me to see an interesting and very characteristic portion of Holland.

The aspect of the country changed as we left the Rhine to the southward. The land became less fertile, large patches of black morass were to be seen here and there amid the pastures. Then we steamed across an extensive lake, which, I believe, is called the Brasemeer, a splendid sheet of water for small boat sailing, no Norfolk Broad could compare with it. Shortly after leaving the lake we entered the Haarlemmer Meer, which is one of the best specimens of a Polder, or reclaimed morass, in Holland. This, I learnt from Baedeker, was once a lake eighteen miles in length, nine in breadth, which was formed in the fifteenth century by the overflow of the Rhine, and afterwards increased so considerably as to imperil the towns of Amsterdam, Haarlem, Leyden, and Utrecht. The operations for draining it were commenced in 1840, and completed in 1853. It now supports a population of upwards of 10,000.

I went up to my mast-head so as to look over the canal dykes, and command a good view of the vast polder. I beheld stretching to the horizon a plain of amazing fertility cut into regular squares by canals, dykes, and rows of trees. Each square had its snug farm-house. The huge chimneys of the engines that had pumped the water from the lake, and hundreds of windmills, were scattered over this rather monotonous landscape. I seemed to be looking at a gigantic chess-board, even such a one as Alice played upon with the eccentric White Queen in Wonderland, and the chimneys and windmills might have been the pieces. This plain was far below the level of the canal.

At last we saw the domes and steeples of Amsterdam rising in the distance, and at 2 P.M. the tug reached her destination, which, we were not very pleased to discover, was not the port of Amsterdam, but some suburb (I believe it is called Overtoum) quite five miles from the centre of the city. We slipped our tow-line, and brought up alongside the quay.

"We go no farther," said the captain, when he came on board of us to claim his six guilders.

"But how is this? We are not in Amsterdam," I expostulated.

"No, but it is only one half hour down there," he said, pointing to a very narrow canal which was so crowded with dredgers, lighters, and other craft of that description that it was difficult to see how we were to work our way through.

Refusing the assistance of a man who wished to pilot us, and who forthwith began to curse us, we now started on what proved to be rather an extraordinary journey. For four hours and more we punted, shoved along with boat-hooks, occasionally sailed under our mainsail, and in short, progressed in some manner or other, through a labyrinth of narrow canals, some of them mere ditches, very malodorous and bordered by slums of rickety houses inhabited by what I should imagine was the lowest population of suburban Amsterdam. I was lamenting just now over the lack of dirt in Holland, but I found more than I wanted in these districts. I have no idea how many drawbridges and swing-bridges, we passed through, and how many times we became completely bewildered and lost ourselves amid the network of ditches. On one occasion we came to a *cul-de-sac*, or rather the canal passed through a subterranean channel, a pitch-dark hole under the slums, into which we shrank from venturing.

Most of the men we saw on the banks were rough hang-dog looking fellows, who were loafing about with their hands in their pockets, as if they had no work to do. I think the criminal classes and Socialists of Amsterdam must hail from this quarter of the town. The Dutch people are generally well-disposed and polite to strangers, but here they either scowled at us in silence, or jeered at us, and encouraged the little boys to throw stones at us. I inquired the way to Amsterdam of several people; they either stared or laughed at me, but none replied. I suppose that as I was already in Amsterdam—though not the part I wanted—the question sounded ridiculous to them, even as if someone on the Pimlico canal should ask his way to London.

Even the bridge guardians seemed to object to strange vessels. They overcharged us, and kept us waiting an unconscionable time before they would open to us. It was, in short, a most disagreeable journey, and I was not sorry when we at last reached a more respectable quarter of the town, where the canals were bordered by broad boulevards and fine shops. We were again amongst civilized beings who understood our queries, and replied to them politely.

We ultimately emerged from the canals into what is called the Timber Dock, passed through a last lock, and were once more on broad water, the Y, which forms the harbour of Amsterdam. We sailed down the front of the city before a fresh breeze, and seeing at last what looked like a good berth, made the yacht fast alongside a jetty on the Ruyter Kade, in front of a cheerful *café* much frequented in the evening, known as the *café* Czar Peter.

CHAPTER V.

ON THE ZUIDER ZEE.

My stay in Amsterdam was short; I arrived on Monday evening, and was off again on Wednesday afternoon. The weather was very hot, and well adapted for seeing the sights of the commercial capital of Holland and smelling the smells of its canals. As these canals, or "Grachten," crossing each other like a spider's web in concentric circles and diametric lines, divide the city into nearly a hundred separate islands, it is impossible to get out of the way of their noisome exhalations; and yet Amsterdam is, I believe, a very healthy place. It is evidently not the stink that kills.

I found much to interest me in this Northern Venice (I am not sure, by the way, that this title has not been copyrighted for Stockholm). Its general appearance is more strikingly original than that of Rotterdam. Built, as it is, entirely on piles, and having no more solid foundation than sand and mud, its houses in their uneven subsidence lean out of the perpendicular at all manner of angles, some hanging over the streets, some falling backwards. There was one large building just in front of where the *Falcon* was lying, which had sunk so far into the bowels of the earth, that its gates and ground-floor windows had completely disappeared. While returning on board late at night, I came upon one broad straight street of lofty toppling houses. The street was paved, and had no doubt once been level, but now the ground was split by great cracks, and rose in hillocks or fell in deep hollows. The rays of the moon fell on the white walls; there was not a soul besides myself in the street, and all was quite still. The effect was strangely weird. It would not have required a great effort of the imagination to suppose oneself in some city over which an earthquake shock had passed, and which had been deserted by its inhabitants. I believe that even in London men returning home late after a dinner occasionally come across streets which present this same tottering and wavy appearance. To ward off any imputation that I had dined too well, I may mention that I passed through the same street on the following morning, and that it then appeared to me no otherwise than it did overnight.

Amsterdam is, I think, the only dirty place in Holland: not that it is very dirty—it would be considered a clean city in most countries—but it is quite foul in comparison with other towns in this morbidly cleanly land. The Jewish quarter, which is well worth strolling through, is the dirtiest portion of the city. Here the picturesque slovenliness and filth of the East appeal to eye and nose. These squalid streets and alleys, with their numberless fried-fish shops and old-clothes stores, are thronged with a crowd of unwashed but often singularly beautiful people of decided Hebrew type. The very schuyts that trade on the canals of this district seemed to me to be wanting in the usual Dutch polish, and looked dirty. But there is quite as much wealth as dirt in the Jewish quarter. The Jews have always been an important body in this tolerant city. Here dwell the famous diamond merchants and polishers of Amsterdam, and the numerous fine synagogues, rich in golden vessels, attest the prosperity of the chosen people.

On Tuesday, while exploring the Ryks Museum, I fell in with a friend, and in accordance with my rule already explained, I took him with me to discover what Amsterdam could produce in the way of a good dinner. We tried the Bible Hotel, and were satisfied with the result. We also visited some of the principal *cafés*, which being vast, magnificently decorated and lit with the electric light, are even finer than those of Rotterdam.

On Wednesday the 15th of June we started at 2 P.M. for the Zuider Zee. As we were getting under weigh we saw a large steam yacht coming in, flying the R.T.Y.C. burgee. We were told that she was the *Rionag na Mara*.

The Y or harbour of Amsterdam is an inlet of

6 *

the Zuider Zee. In order to protect the city and its canals from an incroach of the sea, a huge dam has been constructed across the Y at Schellingwoud. This dam (I quote Baedeker) is one and a quarter miles in length, and has five locks, the largest of which is 110 yards in length, and 22 in width. There are fifty-six ponderous lock-gates, the two heaviest of which weigh thirty-four tons each. This will give some idea of the gigantic scale on which work of this description is done in Holland.

It was a very hot day with a cloudless sky and a light wind. We drifted slowly to the great dam, and entered one of the locks in the company of several traders. The outer gate was opened, we passed through, and were afloat at last on the Zuider Zee. We were glad to be free of the tedious canals for a time, and to cruise once more on broad water.

What small amount of wind there was came right aft, and we contrived, to the gratification of our pride, to run away from all the schuyts. As we came out of the estuary of the Y, the view of the Zuider Zee was a singular one. The heat had produced a thin haze, which did not obscure but surrounded objects with a golden atmosphere. Seawards only the horizon was not visible; there the sky and water mingled in a beautiful sunlit mist that Turner would have loved to paint, while distant fishing-vessels seemed to be floating in the air. Along the shore we were following, stretched as far as the eye could see the massive grass-grown dyke; above which rose here and there red roof-tops, steeples, and trees. Farther still a tall church-spire stood out of the waters, like an island; the low land round it being beneath the horizon; this, from its bearings, I took to be the church at Hoorn.

I had started from Amsterdam without troubling my head as to what port I should put into for the night, for my chart showed me that there was a large choice of harbours all round the Zuider Zee. True that most of these are silting up, and can only admit fishing-boats and such small fry, but then the draught of the *Falcon* is under three feet, a fact we were grateful for when on this very shallow sea, where the greatest depth in the centre is a little over two fathoms.

We steered to the northward, keeping close under the shore in about six feet of water. The wind, still very light, now headed us, so it was evident that we should not get far before nightfall. At about 6 o'clock we opened out the little island of Marken. Between this and the mainland is a channel two miles broad, with only four feet of water in it, and at the head of a small bay opposite the island is the town of Monnikendam, which is about fifteen miles from Amsterdam by water. I decided to bring up at this place for the night, so we sailed into the bay, where the water gradually shoaled till we had only two feet under us—a foot less than our own draught; but we contrived to drive the yacht on with oars and quant through the deep mud, which was almost as yielding as the water. This, we discovered, was a common method of navigating the Zuider Zee; there is no possibility of foundering under such circumstances.

The little town presented a pretty picture on this quiet summer's evening, with its quaint gabled houses, its background of green trees, and its flat-bottomed fishing-craft, lying alongside the quay or the canal—of course it has its canal, what Dutch village has not? There came to us from the shore the sweet scent of new-mown hay, and the sound of cackling hens and lowing cattle, and noise of children just let loose from school, that sounded pleasant and homely to our ears.

We pushed on through the soft mud till we reached the quay, which was already crowded with wondering people, and here we stuck comfortably in the slime, with only a foot or so of water round us, so that it was scarcely necessary to take warps on shore. This night our weary pump had a rest, for her bed of mud gave the *Falcon* an excellent Blackwall caulking.

No sooner were we alongside than a man came down to the quay, and spoke volubly to us for some time. We could not understand him at all, so he tried signs, and showing us a handful of stuivers, pointed to the yacht. Had he taken a fancy to our vessel, and was he making a bid for her?

Evidently Wright took this view, for he called out indignantly, "It isn't enough, Mynheer." The man stared at him for a moment, then despairing of our intelligence, he hurried off, and soon returned with a pompous little fellow in spectacles, who, I believe, was the schoolmaster. He was able to speak a little of a language which he called English. I don't know what it was, but it sounded stranger to our ears than the other man's Dutch.

I do not know how it was managed, but between these two individuals and various members of the crowd, who occasionally put in their suggestions, our dull brains did eventually grasp the idea they were so anxious to convey to us. We understood that the first speaker was the harbour-master and that he wanted our wharfage fee, four stuivers. I gave him his fourpence and he departed happy. I think this was the only port we visited in the course of the cruise in which we did not come across someone who spoke English.

We found the small boys somewhat of a nuisance in Monnikendam; but this was nothing to what was before us. As I shall shortly have to explain, the shores of the Zuider Zee produce in large quantities the most troublesome urchins of all Europe. Happily, it is the custom to pack them off early to bed, so at any rate we were able to sleep comfortably through the night. On the following morning we were awakened by a familiar sound on the quay above us, the cry of the milkman—they call it "mulk" here—so we turned out and bought a bucket-full. In every Dutch port the vendors of milk and eels, and often the butchers as well, would thus visit us at an early hour to solicit our custom.

On studying the chart I perceived a dot right in the middle of the Zuider Zee, and which represented the little island of Urk. A lonely island on the sea he happens to be navigating always has a fascination for a yachtsman, so, having before me as a further inducement the fact of its lying on my way to Zwartsluis, I decided to sail for Urk. The morning was sultry and calm, and there was no wind at all until 11 a.m., when a light air sprang up, but it was right ahead. Seeing that it was not possible to reach Urk that day, and having had enough of Monnikendam, and its boys, we punted the yacht through the mud out of the bay and made for the opposite island of Marken, which was visible about three miles distant. Every tourist who goes to Amsterdam is obliged to visit Marken. This is one of the rules laid down in the tyrant guide books and it must be obeyed. In vain I rose in revolt against this law and tried to sail elsewhere. The wind, which was in league with Baedeker, would not have it so, and I had to submit and go perforce to Marken.

The island possesses a small artificial harbour with not more than four feet of water, which, however, is quite enough for its fishing-boats and for our yacht. We tacked across the channel, entered the harbour and made fast to the quay, which, to our surprise, was deserted. Were there, then, no boys in happy Marken?

I looked round me and saw that there were only two or three houses near the quay, for the village is towards the middle of the island. Marken is inhabited by a race of hardy fishing folk, the most primitive people in Holland, who still go about in the costume in fashion with their forefathers three hundred years ago. The island has been much written up of late, is often visited by tourists, and has, therefore, become a recognized show place, and its inhabitants run the risk of losing their simplicity and being considerably spoilt.

The natives soon found us out, and first of all the harbour-master came down to us for his wharfage fee of two stuivers per ton. I then left Wright in charge of the yacht and proceeded to explore the island on foot. Marken is rather more than two miles long. It consists of flat pasture-land intersected by little ditches, and it is, of course, surrounded with a dyke. There is a church and a neat little village of tiny old wooden houses huddled up close to each other, with no streets between them, but narrow paths only, a plan conducive to cosiness in the long hard winters. The men were away fishing, so I only came across women and girls, who were all dressed in the picturesque and becoming style of their great-great-grandmothers, and several of whom, though built much after the model of the native schuyts, having their greatest beam at the waist, were decidedly pretty. The girls of Marken have beautifully fresh and clear complexions, and many a one of these fair plump faces, with its honest blue eyes, and golden curls falling coquettishly on either side of the close-fitting skull-cap, would have made a very pretty picture indeed.

I returned to the yacht and found that a schuyt had come into the harbour with a party of Dutch tourists from Amsterdam, who were being personally conducted by what seemed to be a native Cook on a small scale. And now I saw that the primitive islanders had acquired some of the tricks of civilization, even such as are practised by the simple mountaineers of Switzerland. For no sooner had the tourists stepped on shore than down trotted to the quay-side three pretty little maids of eight or nine, with their yellow curls flying behind them. They were not dressed in their every-day clothes, but in the gorgeous Sunday costume peculiar to the island. They had not even completed their toilet before starting from home, for they were assisting each other to arrange a ribbon here, or haul taut a refractory lace there, as they came along. They seemed very much amused and very proud of their finery as they stood hand in hand in a row on the quay, blushing and smiling archly and looking up occasionally with shy eyes at the strangers of the city. The little humbugs! It was so obvious that their mothers had hastily dressed them up, and sent them down for the inspection of the innocent tourists, as specimens of the famous Marken medieval costume, on the chance of earning a few stuivers; and the children certainly did not return empty-handed to their shrewd mammas.

Later on some of the fishing-boats came in, manned by sturdy, clean-shaven men, whose dress, if not so splendid, was as old-fashioned as that of the women. They wore tight-fitting black jackets, black skull-caps and black knickerbockers of true Dutch voluminousness, while their well-stockinged feet were thrust into loose sabots. Save for the sabots it was a very Oriental-looking get up, and its like can be seen in any Turkish city.

In the evening, after we had finished our dinner, I believe that all the girls in Marken were down at the quay-side, drawing buckets of water to carry home for that last general wash-up of everything, which is never neglected in a Dutch establishment. They stood on the wharf chatting and laughing and peeping into our cabin with the curiosity of their sex, as fresh-featured, pleasant-looking a lot of blonde lasses as one could wish to see, and very smart too in their bright-coloured frocks and snowy linen.

I did not mind the girls. I may as well confess that I rather liked their presence; but by and by school broke up, and down to the quay-side ran all the naughty boys of Marken. We suffered a terrible persecution at their hands, so that the tender-hearted girls pitied us and rebuked, but to no effect, their unruly brothers. The Hollanders spoil their children, never punish them, and allow them—provided they don't play the truant from school, for education is a serious business in this country—to do pretty well as they like. Should a stranger—my authority is one of our consuls over here—take it upon himself to spank one of these little rascals, for throwing stones at him or otherwise misbehaving himself, the whole of the parents of the locality would rise in a body and seek that stranger's blood. A Corsican vendetta would be child's play to what he might expect. If you value your life, put up with insult, robbery, blows, torture at the hands of a Hollander infant, but do not venture to chastise him. Of all the children in Europe the Dutch child is most to be feared. Now the Zuider Zee child is the most terrible of Dutch children, and the Marken child the most terrible of the Zuider Zee, and hence of the whole species. Our position can, therefore, be imagined by any father of a large family.

These small ruffians stood on the quay and reviled us in unknown tongues, they hurled stones at us and also bricks from a convenient stack—bricks are very dear in Marken and are imported here by sea, and yet the owner of those bricks, who happened to be standing by, contented himself with a timid remonstrance, but dared take no stronger measures.

As we could not defend ourselves we dissimulated, pretending to be altogether unconscious of what was going on; then, as our persecutors waxed bolder, we smiled at them with an affectation of amiability we were far from feeling, for infanticide was in our hearts. But the most pathetic smile fails to move the ruthless Marken boy to mercy.

At last a fisherman who spoke a few words of English took compassion on us. He came on board.

"I vill show you vere you was better go," he said, "not to have bad children alongside. Dey vas very dam here, de children."

This good Samaritan piloted us to the other side of the harbour, where we lay moored to some stakes.

"You stop better here," he said, "not many boys throw so long as this was."

But some few of them could throw as far, nevertheless, and worried us occasionally; and let me warn yachtsmen who visit Marken that the boys are not sent early to bed here, as they are in most Dutch villages, but are permitted to stay up and annoy the poor foreigner half the night. Some people pay blackmail to these brigands, but that makes matters worse unless it be done in a scientific manner. Had I been able to speak Dutch, I should have picked out some half-dozen of the strongest boys and offered to give them sixpence each on the morrow in consideration of their thrashing the other boys and keeping them quiet during our stay. I mentioned this to Wright.

"It's a very good plan, Sir," he said; "and then, after we'd set them all fighting like Kilkenny cats, we could sail away to-morrow morning without paying them their sixpences."

That would have been a sweet revenge, indeed, for all our ill-treatment at the hands of the children of Marken, but alas! we knew no Dutch, and found it impossible to make delusive promises in pantomime.

But I must do Marken the justice of saying that its women are charming and its men kindly honest fellows, somewhat subdued in manner, perhaps, and sad-visaged; but what else can be expected of a people who are groaning under the heartless tyranny of an infant democracy?

The wind howled dismally through the night, and

on turning out the next morning we found that a fresh
north-east breeze was blowing. We set all sail and
escaped from the island before its demon boys had left
their beds. My intention on starting was to cross the
Zuider Zee to Urk, but when we got clear of the lea
of Marken we encountered a very choppy sea; the
water was leaping up round us, not into waves, but
into pyramidic lumps like sugar-loaves. Urk was dead
to windward of us, and we first put the *Falcon* on the
port tack.

"She don't seem to be making much way against
this lop," remarked Wright, after a while, and she
certainly was not.

"It doesn't look much like getting to Urk to-day,"
I replied; "we'll go about. She'll just lay up the
coast on the other tack, and we can put into Hoorn or
some other port if the sea and wind don't go down.
We'll be well to windward at Hoorn, and if the wind
is in the same direction to-morrow we can fetch Urk
easily from there."

So we put the *Falcon* on the starboard tack and followed the coast to the northward, travelling very
slowly, for each of the short steep seas slapped the
yacht violently in the nose and almost stopped her
way altogether. However, we staggered along somehow, with much more noise and motion than speed,
our decks constantly wet, and we came to the conclusion that if a moderate breeze like this can raise so
nasty a sea on the shallow Zuider Zee it must be a very
uncomfortable piece of water when a strong gale is

blowing. It has the reputation of being so. Luckily the currents are feeble, the rise and fall of the tide being almost imperceptible hereabouts, else this would be a very dangerous sea indeed.

After two hours or so the wind headed us so that we had to tack, and the sea became so confused that we missed stays several times in getting about. We stumbled on—that is the best term to describe the boat's motion on this day—through the muddy water, past the monotonous stretches of the dykes, until about 1 P.M., when we perceived the town of Hoorn before us, almost hidden by the branches of its many trees tossing in the gusty wind. We passed through one of the two channels that lead to the harbour, and made fast to the quay close to the picturesque old Water Tower, which dominates the town and serves as a landmark to vessels far out to sea.

The usual crowd gathered on the quay above us, and an old woman commenced to address us. She became quite angry when she found that we could not understand her, and she began to scream at us at the top of her voice, heedless of the fact that we were not deaf but merely ignorant of her language. Had it been a man we should have jumped at the conclusion that this was the harbour-master demanding his fee; but what could this irate lady want with us?

Having failed utterly to explain herself, she suddenly ceased her clamour and beckoned me with her bony hand to follow her. Her air of authority was such that I dared not refuse; I crawled on to the quay and did her bidding with a sinking heart. She led me through the street in silence till we reached a small house. The door was open. Again she beckoned. I hesitated. Then she seized me by the hand and dragged me in. A crowd of inquisitive boys had followed us, so she slammed the door in their faces, and I was left alone with this mysterious woman. Her next proceeding was to unlock the drawer of a fine old carved oak bureau, of which I envied her even in that moment of trepidation. From this she took out a small book, which, without saying a word, she placed in my hand. I opened it at the title-page, and lo! it proved to be a French-Dutch dictionary! It was shrewd of the old lady to have thought of so excellent an interpreter between us.

I consulted the pages and pointed out to her the Dutch equivalents for the words "What want you with me?"

She opened the book in her turn, and, following her finger with my eyes, I read in succession the two words *huit sous*.

A light broke on my dull intelligence. I hastily turned over the dictionary again and showed her the uncouth Dutch word that stood for harbour-master. "Ja Ja!" she cried, laughing and slapping me on the back. We understood each other at last; this was the harbour-mistress after all, so I paid her the fourpence and she allowed me to depart.

Hoorn is one of the pleasantest-looking towns I saw in Holland. It is pierced by numerous canals, all crowded with craft and bordered by avenues of fine trees. In its streets are many quaint old gabled houses, and it has preserved all its original mediæval appearance without being by any means a sleepy and stagnant place, for it is a garrison town and its public ways are full of life and colour.

And yet Hoorn is one of the famous dead cities of the Zuider Zee. I was prepared to see ruined houses and grass-grown deserted streets, but there was nothing of the kind in this tidy busy settlement; it is the most lively "dead city" imaginable. As for the grass-grown streets—tourists in these regions, whose imaginations run away with them after reading Havard, sometimes speak of these—I doubt that they exist in the deadest Dutch city. True that at Urk, which is not a dead city, I saw a tuft of grass in one of the streets. I stood and looked at it in wonder; how could neat Dutchmen tolerate such an eye-sore ? Now there happened to be a native sitting in front of his shop, smoking his huge pipe placidly. His eye followed mine ; he saw the dreadful thing, started, blushed deeply, and hurrying to it plucked it up by the roots. Then he looked at me sadly, as one who should say : "I would not for many barrels of herrings that you, a stranger, had seen this thing."

But though what remains of Hoorn is alive enough, especially its boys, it is a genuine dead city, for it was once a far more considerable and important place, being the ancient capital of North Holland ; and Cape Horn, which was first doubled by Schouten, was named by him after his native town, then a flourishing seaport.

I looked into my Baedeker and there read that in 1573 a naval engagement took place off Hoorn between the Dutch and Spaniards, when the admiral in command of the latter was taken prisoner. Late in the afternoon I was sitting on deck smoking, and as I gazed across the yellow Zuider Zee I was thinking how ridiculous it seemed to associate the idea of a naval action with that shallow water—only eight feet deep in the neighbourhood of Hoorn—when I saw a sight which made me leap to my feet and rub my eyes. Was I dreaming or was I looking at phantoms? For I beheld two men-of-war making straight for the harbour. One was a full-rigged ship and the other a very beamy iron-plated gunboat, with no masts to speak of. The ship was of very old-fashioned build, the other an ugly modern steamer; they approached slowly side by side, good representatives of the old and new styles. The ship furled her sails and came to an anchor off the entrance of the harbour, the gunboat steamed right in and brought up alongside the quay opposite us. These vessels had doubtlessly been constructed expressly for the Zuider Zee defence, and must have a very light draught. The clumsy ship stuck fast in the mud when she got under weigh the following morning, but the gunboat tugged her off again. Possibly the former always accompanies the latter for this purpose.

I have made no mention of our pump lately, but it

must not be supposed that it was at all idle, for the Blackwall caulking of Monnickendam had been washed out in a very short space of time by the choppy waves of the Zuider Zee. This very necessary apparatus had got completely out of order, its india-rubber valves were worn away by much friction, and on this day it definitely refused to pump at all. Now ours was not an ordinary or garden pump—which is as good as any and is easily put to rights—but a patent arrangement, and therefore exceedingly difficult to mend. I doubted whether the tinkers of Hoorn could restore it to its pristine condition, so I thought it best to take the job in hand myself, and, instead of repairing it, convert it into an entirely new pump on the good old garden system. I cut a valve-plate out of a piece of hard wood, and then, as I required leather to complete my job, I sallied forth to procure some.

I soon found a cobbler's shop, entered, and endeavoured to explain my wants—a piece of hard leather for a valve and a soft piece with which to serve the piston.

"Some leather like this, please," I said, pointing to the sole of my boot. The cobbler put on his spectacles, seized my foot, and closely examined the boot, evidently under the impression that I wanted him to repair it. But as there was nothing amiss with it, he looked puzzled and shrugged his shoulders. "Vor de pomp of de ship," I cried; this ought to be good Dutch if it is not.

He seemed to understand me at last, and, motioning to me to wait for him, he went into an inner room and shortly returned, bearing in his arms a great load of every description of foot-covering, ranging from a dandy's patent-leather chaussure to a fisherman's sabot. He threw them on the floor before me with a gesture that said "Take your choice."

"No, no!" I said, shaking my head.

"Then what the deuce do you want?" he cried impatiently.

I don't know Dutch, but I could swear that was the signification of his words.

I was about to retire in despair when I noticed that a policeman was standing in the doorway smiling grimly to himself. Our eyes met.

"What is it you want, Sir?" he asked in English.

An interpreter had arrived very opportunely on the scene, and now the cobbler and myself were able to carry on our negotiations. This policeman had been for many years in the employment of the General Steam Navigation Company, hence his acquaintance with our language. Having procured the leather, I set to work before an admiring crowd, and soon put the pump to rights again.

On the following morning, Saturday, the 18th of June, we started at 8 P.M. for Urk. This island is only twenty-five English miles from Hoorn, but we were so unfortunate with our wind that we must have sailed three times that distance.

The weather was glorious, and only a few small

APPROACH TO THE ISLAND OF URK.

fleecy clouds, very high up, crossed the blue sky. At first the wind was north-west, but it did not remain long in that favourable direction; it gradually freshened up and blew right in our teeth. We put the yacht first on one tack, then on the other; but whenever we went about the wind would veer round also and head us. We were pursued by Vanderdecken's ill-luck; however, it was very pleasant sailing, and the sea, though choppy, was not nearly so rough as on the previous day.

At mid-day we were in the centre of the Zuider Zee and out of sight of land. I brought up my sextant and took the latitude, an operation, I imagine, very rarely performed on these waters.

Later on the atmosphere became very clear, so that we were able to distinguish in several directions the summits of far-off steeples and the isolated tops of trees. It was exactly as if we were looking over a country that had been submerged by an immense flood, for no land was anywhere visible.

In the afternoon the wind dropped and there was only a slight ripple on the Zuider Zee. We progressed very slowly until about four o'clock, when we perceived on the horizon, right ahead of us, a group of red lumps which we knew must be the roofs of Urk.

As we approached it, the tiny island—its size is not quite a third that of Marken—presented a curious appearance. There rose, seemingly straight out of the sea itself, a row of little houses dominated by a church and lighthouse. To the right of this village was a dense forest of pole masts, each with its long pennant streaming to the breeze, showing where the fishing smacks were lying in the commodious haven. And the whole of the shallow tideless sea was dotted with a vast number of other schuyts, all making for this harbour as fast as they were able with sail and oar.

Urk, diminutive though it be, is a most important fishing-station, and a population of upwards of two thousand is here supported solely by this industry. This was the very day to see Urk at its liveliest, as all the fishermen flock home on Saturday and stay in port till Sunday night. The scene reminded one of a hive on a summer's evening into which all the working bees are hurrying laden with the spoil of the day.

As the harbour seemed to be already full to its mouth I did not care to venture within, for I feared that the boats that came in after me would block up all the available space and prevent my getting out till Monday. Again I preferred to rely on the mercy of an open roadstead than to risk persecution at the hands of diabolical boys; so our anchor was let go some fifty yards from the shore in about eight feet of water. We found that the bottom consisted of hard sand and gravel. This considerably surprised us, for we did not expect to find stones anywhere on the muddy Zuider Zee. I thought that we had anchored over the remains of some ruined dyke or flood-destroyed village—there are many such in Dutch waters. But I believe that Urk is one of the few places in this half-liquid land where the solid earth that lies beneath asserts itself and sends forth stony offshoots to the surface.

As we had only tinned meats on board I went on shore in the dinghy to buy stores. I pulled between the piers into the harbour and was astonished to see so many fine oak fishing-boats lying in tiers along the quays. The letters on their bows told me that they all belonged to Urk. I do not think that any other place of its size in Europe can boast of so large a fleet.

On landing I found myself the centre of an admiring crowd of what appeared to me to be the strongest and healthiest people I had ever come across. The men, in their baggy trousers, tight jackets, and broad belts, looked like a race of giants, possessed too of hard and wiry frames that few giants are blessed with. The buxom women were proportionately tall and broad, and the children were far too robust to be otherwise than terribly naughty. When I looked at the boys I was glad that I had left the *Falcon* outside.

The men seemed well disposed to strangers. Many of these sturdy fishermen had fraternized with our sailors on the Doggerbank and understood something of English. Two or three of them piloted me to a little shop where every commodity that the people of Urk require can be purchased. But fresh meat is evidently not considered a necessary here; for they all shook their heads and laughed good-naturedly when I spoke of it. I could have as much salt pork as I liked, but beef was an unknown luxury. Just then, very opportunely, a hen began to cackle, and the sound inspired me to ask for eggs. The good lady of the shop sold me a large number for tenpence; but they were the smallest eggs I have ever seen. I met some of the fowls in the street and saw they were proportionate in size to their island, which the men certainly are not. I now bade Urk farewell, a proceeding that lasted some while, for all those who had joined in the procession that had followed me round the village considered themselves to be my friends and came up to shake hands at parting.

During the night the wind blew on shore so that we tumbled about at our anchorage a good deal. The sky was wild and crossed with mares' tails, and, to all appearance, we were in for an unquiet night. The wind moaned dismally, as it always does in Holland on very small provocation. In this country a stranger finds his meteorologic wisdom much at fault at first; for the weather has a habit of looking worse than it really is, especially when there is any north in the wind; then, even in midsummer, there comes suddenly over a fine sunny day a chilliness, a hazy bleakness, a wintry howling of wind that dismays the imagination and leads one to believe that a storm is imminent.

On the following morning (Sunday, June 16th) we resumed our voyage across the Zuider Zee immediately after breakfast. Bad weather had not followed the threatening signs of the previous evening. It was another sultry, cloudless, and almost calm day, and the light wind was again right in our teeth.

We tacked in an easterly direction, intending to sail round the north end of the island of Schokland, which lay between us and our destination, the entrance of Zwarte Water.

For two hours we saw no signs of the land towards which we were sailing; then we perceived a line of yellow sand-hills to the north of us—the mainland near Lemmer. But ahead of us, towards the rising sun, there was a dazzling glare on the water, and a mirage which prevented us from distinguishing anything, save here and there a phantom-like schuyt greatly magnified by the heated atmosphere and appearing to be floating in mid-air. There was a considerable ripple on the sea round us; but it was difficult to say how it was caused. The surface of the shallow Zuider Zee seems to be sensitive to the slightest breath of air. So feeble was the wind that, after tacking with flapping sails for nearly four hours, we had not left Urk more than two miles astern, and the only sound to be heard on this quiet Sunday morning was the persistent cackling of the hens of that island.

But about mid-day a nice north-west breeze sprang up, and, setting our tanned square-sail, we began to bowl along at a good rate. At last we sighted that commonest landmark of the Zuider Zee, a steeple, bearing south-east, and we ran down towards it under the impression that it belonged to the church of Schokland. But we were mistaken, for Schokland

and its low buildings were not yet visible above the horizon, and we were really looking right over the island at some lofty town spire on the mainland far beyond. After running on some way farther we saw three small hummocks, like three separate islands, ahead. Then as we approached we perceived a low sandy coast connecting these three hillocks, and we now had no doubt that this was the island of Schokland before us.

This island is very narrow, but it is three miles long. It seemed to be an almost barren sand-bank, with few houses on it, and not many fishing-boats in its small harbour.

We gave the north corner a wide berth, for the water is very shallow round Schokland, and, indeed, there is but little more than six feet anywhere between it and the mainland. Having passed the point we sailed into an extraordinary labyrinth of tall sticks that puzzled us a good deal. At first we thought they were intended as marks for the different channels; but we soon decided that there were far too many of them for that purpose. These sticks were planted close together in double rows which stretched across the water in every direction as far as the eye could see, like so many streets. There must have been some thousands of them in sight. They were doubtlessly the stakes to which the fishermen attach their nets or lines; but it seemed strange to find such crowds of them stuck right across the fairway of vessels.

We could now plainly distinguish the mainland, and

we made out the Kraggenburg lighthouse ahead of us. The Zwarte Water river empties itself into a very shallow bay, across which, from the mouth of the river, a deep channel, known as the Zwolsche Diep, had been dredged for four miles out to sea. This channel is bordered on one side by a pier, at the end of which is the Kraggenburg lighthouse, and on the other side by a submerged embankment of stone marked by big beacons. The wind was now freshening every moment and a nasty sea was rising; but we ran on merrily under all canvas, and at last rushed suddenly into smooth water under the pier-head, and we had done with the Zuider Zee.

CHAPTER VI.

TO THE DOLLART.

WE sailed up the long straight cutting into the winding river here flowing through marshy flats, and, running on before the strong wind, we soon reached the little town of Zwartsluis. Here we had to leave the river and pass through a lock-gate into the canal. The lock-keeper's lodge was some little distance from the lock. I called upon him and found him sleeping in a chair in his garden.

I woke him gently, and then found that I was unable to explain to him what I required, for he understood no English. But a little crowd had gathered round us, and one intelligent man made a proposition to the lock-keeper which for some time the latter received with stolid silence. I was able to make out that the man was urging the official to try me with French, a language he professed to understand.

But the lock-keeper was diffident, and some time passed before he yielded to the entreaties of the crowd; then he took his pipe from his mouth and said to me, "Parle Français, Mynheer?"

On this I commenced to explain volubly in French what I was, and to ask him if he would let the *Falcon* through the lock, whether there were tugs starting for Groningen on the morrow, and many other things. He listened solemnly. At last I was silent and waited for his reply.

"Faché, parle mal Français," he said, bringing out the words with difficulty.

He was a fraud, and knew a dozen words of French at the outside, though it seemed that he had passed himself off as a linguist among the simple people of Zwartsluis. But through our agency he now stood discovered, and his friends did not spare him. They chaffed him unmercifully as he sulkily walked down and opened the lock-gate for us.

We passed through the sluice, and, despairing of obtaining any information from the natives of Zwartsluis, we hoisted our canvas once more and sailed on.

A long canal journey was now before us, the distance to Delfzijl being about eighty miles. As far as the town of Meppel, which we reached before sunset, the canal was broad—the broadest we had yet seen in Holland—but shallow reed-beds bordered it, and we got on shore once or twice when tacking in the reaches where the wind headed us.

We passed through the lock of Meppel and brought up in the middle of the town for the night, alongside a large schuyt laden with the red cannon-ball Dutch cheeses with which we are familiar in England. We thus had a formidable bulwark between us and the naughty boys; and luckily for us the skipper of the schuyt was a surly man, who would allow no youngster to cross his deck.

After dinner I put myself in shore-going togs and procceded to explore Meppel. It was a lovely summer's evening and the little town looked its best. Crowds in their Sunday clothes thronged the pleasant avenues that bordered the canals. And what cheerful-looking, well-fed, well-dressed crowds they were! There were no signs of any sordid struggle for existence among this people. I began to wonder if beggars and paupers existed in Holland outside the big cities. Poor, but shrewdly thrifty and industrious, these brave Hollanders make a wonderful show of comfortable prosperity.

In one of the canals I came across a little steamer called the *Cupido*. She was very fat, was painted pink, and had quite a cherub-like appearance, so she was well named. Her skipper told me that he was bound for Assen at six o'clock on the morrow, and he offered to tow us there for fifteen guilders. This I considered to be too much, as the distance was only thirty miles; but he explained that his vessel was a cargo boat and not a tug, and that we should delay him a good deal at the locks, of which, he said, there were many. After some discussion, he agreed to take us in tow for twelve guilders—about a pound.

When I returned on board, the inevitable English-speaking Dutchman called on us. This time he came in the shape of a young policeman who had been to sea and retired as mate at the age of twenty-two. Nearly every Dutchman seems to have been a sailor in his time, but I was puzzled to find that so many had served as officers. Wright entertained a great contempt for these ex-mates.

"I know the chaps," he would say, "they don't need tickets (certificates) in this country, and I've often seen a lad of sixteen years old the mate of a Dutch vessel. When a boy leaves school his family send him to sea for one voyage, just to rub him up before he starts on his trade, and he calls himself a mate ever afterwards."

I believe that my man's remarks were just; and again, out of the thousands of Dutch sailors to be found on English ships how few are otherwise than very young men ? A Hollander seaman is a stay-at-home fellow at heart, and only navigates the high seas from necessity. He serves on foreign-going vessels for as short a period as he is able ; then he returns to his beloved lowland with a bag full of savings, either to settle down to his father's trade or to purchase a share in a schuyt, in which to earn his living on home waters as fisherman or canal-carrier. Those ancient British shellbacks whom one so often comes across on our ships, old reprobates who have knocked about the oceans for half a century and have never put by a stuiver, are rare among this provident race.

We rose at six on the following morning, to lay in a

stock of bread, beef, and beer, but the *Cupido* did not get under weigh till ten. The sky was cloudless, but a strong head-wind was blowing, so I was not sorry that I had engaged a tug, for the canal was far too narrow to have allowed of the *Falcon's* tacking.

Before we started the steamer's skipper offered to carry our dinghy on his deck, as she would be in the way if we towed her through the locks. He sent four men to lift her on board. They seized her, and proceeded to raise her with so much energy that she gave a jump in the air, and two of them losing their balance fell on their backs. They rose, gazed at the boat with intense astonishment, and then burst out laughing. Accustomed only to their own clumsy and very heavily-built boats, they had not conceived it possible that any dinghy could be so light as ours.

We passed through many swing-bridges and locks. These last were very small; in several of them there was but just space for the steamer and the *Falcon* to lie; while in one lock we were squeezed so tightly together as the water rose, that the dead-eyes of our shrouds were driven into our bulwarks by the *Cupido's* covering-board.

This canal cannot be recommended to yachtsmen; it is one of the narrowest and shallowest in Holland. A yacht's paint is sure to suffer considerably in its locks, while collisions with schuyts are very likely to occur, for in many places there is not room for two of the larger canal-boats to pass each other. We took soundings occasionally in the centre of the canal and found that the average depth was under five feet.

We travelled up-hill all this day, and at each sluice we were raised about six feet. The aspect of the country gradually changed as we advanced inland; the rich well-watered pastures disappeared, and unfertile wastes of furze and sombre heath, on which goats only browsed, took their place. We passed many lagoons bordered by clumps of dark pines, while on the port hand a range of desolate sand-hills stretched along the horizon. The landscape had lost the usual Dutch characteristics—a pleasant change, however, after the oppressive culture and richness of Lower Holland, but the population and the houses were painfully Dutch in their inordinate tidiness and cleanliness.

We were not sorry to be out of the Zuider Zee this afternoon, for it began to blow a gale from the north-east, so that the lagoons were lashed into foam. The gray clouds rushed across the sky, and the bleak moors looked as they might well do in November instead of June, while the temperature fell until we shivered with cold. Those who revile the climate of England as changeable should visit the countries to the east of the North Sea.

This was by no means a dull journey, for we were traversing a remote portion of Holland inhabited by a primitive people, and the costumes of the peasants we saw on the banks of the canal were often very quaint and picturesque. Many of the women wore gold helmets, as they do in the neighbouring province of

Friesland. It was a curious thing, too, to see a swell in frock coat and tall hat driving a dog tandem along the tow-path. The animals were evidently well broken in and travelled at a great pace. We saw a goodly number of dog-carts (in the literal sense of the term) in this part of the country, but I believe that the practice of harnessing dogs is forbidden by law in many provinces of Holland, as it is in England.

About half-way to Assen we passed a village called Dreuerberg. Here I was told I had to present myself at the office of the canal superintendent to pay the dues for the whole route. These amounted to about twopence halfpenny. The superintendent, who was also burgomaster, spoke tolerable English and excellent French. He came on board and had a yarn with me while we were passing through the lock. He told me that he had never before heard of an English yacht on this canal. The people certainly seemed more astonished at our appearance than they did anywhere else in Holland.

Among the crowd that saw us through the lock was a very ancient mariner, who spoke to me in a queer sort of Dutch-Yankee-English. He told me that he had lived in America and had served for many years in the English navy, but that he had left the sea fifty years ago and had never spoken to an Englishman since. He stood on the bank as we were going through the lock and commenced to spin a fearfully tough and interminable yarn which was incomprehensible, but had something to do with Vera Cruz, sharks, and pirates. He had not finished his tale when the tug steamed away with us, and we left the poor old chap leaning on his stick looking wistfully after us, for he had now used up what was most probably his last opportunity of exercising his long latent English.

At about six in the evening we steamed down a straight avenue of trees, at the end of which was visible a bridge, and behind this a steeple and a glimpse of red-tiled houses.

"There is Assen," shouted the skipper of the *Cupido* from his bridge.

The tug lay alongside the quay in the middle of the town, and we remained outside of her for the night, thus cheating the boys again.

Assen is a very pleasant little place nestling in the middle of an extensive wood. It is pierced by avenues of fine trees, and the green foliage of chesnuts, blending with the scarlet tiles of houses and the rich tones of the oaken schuyts and lock-gates, produces a cheerful wealth of colour.

At one extremity of the town is a beautiful park well stocked with deer, where many paths wind among the great trees and the meadows of deep grass and brilliant flowers. Hither I strolled after dinner. The wind had dropped, and a warm summer's evening had succeeded the chilly afternoon. It was the longest day but one of the year, so there was no real darkness at night. I do not remember to have ever heard so vast a chorus of singing-birds as was ringing overhead. This was evidently the favourite haunt of birds, and

8 *

also, naturally, a favourite promenade of the young lovers of Assen, of whom I met a great many walking in shy couples through the glades.

On my return I found that Wright had chummed up with the skipper of a canal-boat who had been to sea in his youth and spoke English. He invited me to visit his vessel, which lay tightly wedged in a crowd of similar craft. His own schuyt was called the *Contentment*, and true Dutchman that he was he had his wife and six children living with him on board. The family name might well have been Contentment too, for I never came across people of more cheerful well-fed appearance. He told me that the boat was his own; he had bought her fourteen years ago, when he married, and she had been his home ever since. He was not only his own owner and captain, but he was his own merchant as well. He served no one and carried no other man's freight, for he made his living by sailing up the canals into remote country districts and there buying cheeses, onions, and potatoes from the farmers to retail in the towns at a considerable profit. While he lay at Assen his deck was converted into a small shop, connected with the shore by a gangway, and his plump wife, when not washing or scrubbing something or other, or looking after the children, sold the cargo by pennyworths from behind an extemporized counter in front of the binnacle.

He took me into his cabin, which, though small, was wonderfully comfortable, and looked very picturesque, with its dark oak panelling, carved cornice, and little windows with white curtains. I need not say that all was scrupulously clean; and though the woman must have plenty of work continuously on her hands, she had found time to cultivate a pretty flower garden in a green and vermilion painted balcony which overhung the stern. I rather envied this man. Independent, free from worry, his every simple want supplied, his occupation varied and healthy, and having all his worldly goods and interests gathered together on board of his stout oak ship, he surely ought to be happy if any man can be. I told him so.

"You are right, Mynheer, I am a fortunate man, but there is my poor brother, now. He has a finer vessel than this and plenty of money, but he is not happy; he is not fat like me, but thin and bald and miserable."

"And how is that?" I asked.

"He has a she-cat for a wife," was the reply.

To be confined for life within the narrow space of a schuyt in the company of a shrew must indeed be a martyrdom. The skipper was selling his cheese at twopence a pound; we invested in some and found it very good. He told us that no steamer would start on the following day in the direction of Groningen; so we anticipated a canal journey without assistance, a tedious task should the wind remain in its present quarter.

I was enjoying a last pipe on deck, and was just about to turn in, when a young man in a blouse hailed me from the quay. He had a great deal to say for himself, and he was very anxious that I should understand him, but I could not follow his voluble Dutch. Still he persisted; so, seeing that he must have some important communication to make, I invited him to come on board. He entered our cabin and tried hard in every possible way to express himself.

There was one word, *paard*, which he constantly repeated with anxious emphasis. What on earth could *paard* signify? For this was evidently the key to his mystery. At last, seeing a piece of paper on the table, he seized it and proceeded to draw some strange diagrams on it with the charred end of a match. Wright and myself examined his work with puzzled interest. It was an oblong figure supported on four pedestals, with an irregular excrescence at one of the upper corners.

"It's an arm-chair," said Wright.

"Or it might be a sheep," I ventured doubtfully. "Possibly he is a butcher and wants to sell us some mutton."

The young Dutchman was becoming wild with impatience at our stupidity. Snatching up the match again, he drew a horizontal line from the figure—we watched him in suspense—and at the end of the line he sketched what we thought might be intended for a boat.

"Ah! of course! I know what he's after, Sir," suddenly exclaimed Wright. "He's got a horse and wants to tow us to-morrow."

And that was exactly what he did want. Having

now discovered that *paard* — I don't vouch for the spelling—is Dutch for horse, we soon, by sign and diagram, came to terms with him, and he undertook to tow us to Groningen at eight in the morning for four guilders. No sooner had we arranged matters thus satisfactorily than another young man appeared on the scene, and offered to tow us there for three guilders. On this a noisy discussion ensued between the rivals. Wishing to get rid of them and go to bed, I intervened, and explained that I had engaged the first comer, so was not now in a position to entertain lower tenders. When I made this clear to them the first *paard* owner patted me on the back with surprised approval, as much as to say, "So you are that rare thing, an honest man, O Englishman!" At every lock we passed the next day he told the bystanders the tale of my probity, and they gazed with wonder at the man who had sacrificed a guilder to his principles. How they would have despised me had they known that it was more a question of sleepiness than principles!

Punctually at eight our friend appeared with his tow-line and horse, a big strong black animal like those used at funerals at home. I noticed that nearly all the canal horses were of this description, and I believe that great numbers are exported from here for our undertaking trade.

The wind was northerly and the day was bleak and sunless. The Noord Willem's canal, as this is called, took us through an infertile country of dark heaths and thorny copses, only relieved here and there by the golden blossoms of the gorse. We also passed sandy wastes and swamps, where the sole industry seemed to be the cutting of peat. The villages were small and far between.

Our tow-man, whom, as we could not pronounce his name, we called Hans, bestrode his horse and trotted along at a good pace. He had an old French horn slung on his shoulder, on which he attempted to sound a military call when we approached a swing-bridge or lock. We found towing with a horse far more comfortable than following a steamer, especially in the sluices. The canal was still narrower and shallower than that of the day before, so that the craft sailing before the wind had to haul their booms amidships in order to pass us. The schuyts which were bound in the same direction as ourselves did not attempt to sail, but were laboriously towed against the strong wind by the wives and children, while the papas steered and meditatively smoked their long pipes.

" How you like this country, Sir ? " called out one of the fat skippers thus taking his ease, as we passed his vessel.

" Very much, captain—fine country."

" Ah, but you should have brought your vife and the young 'uns, like me; then they would have towed you, and so you not have to pay for tow-horse."

We had been ascending all the previous day; this day we were going down-hill again, for there was a fall of ten feet or so at each lock. The canal dues amounted to about twopence, and yet a friend told me that I should find these heavy in Holland. Possibly the pilot-interpreter he employed could, if he chose, explain this difference between our experiences. But I believe that most of these fellows are thoroughly trustworthy.

It was the 21st of June, the longest day of the year, and at home the Jubilee was in full swing. All Dutchmen read the papers, and those we met were taking great interest in the doings in London; they seemed to wonder that we were so unpatriotic as to be abroad at the time. We passed a canal barge towing down stream; she was carrying a large holiday party. When they saw our ensign their band struck up "God Save the Queen," and they shouted "Hurrah! Queen Victoria!" We returned the salute of the jolly Dutchmen, and they went by us singing, laughing, waving flags, drinking deep flagons of beer. It was a typical Dutch scene—the straight canal with its dyke, the numerous windmills, the red roofs here and there, and that Teniers-like crowd of revelling peasants on the clumsy oaken barge.

Later on there sailed by us a beamy little centre-board yacht flying the German flag. A gentleman and lady composed her crew. I afterwards heard that this was a young Hamburgher and his wife who had navigated their vessel by themselves all the way from that port. There were several things about the *Falcon* that surprised the Hollanders, but they seemed to wonder most that I had not a wife on board. A vessel without its *vrouw* seemed a melancholy thing in their eyes, and they evidently pitied me for my forlorn condition.

At two o'clock the spires of Groningen hove in sight, and at four Hans had brought us to the sluice-gate at the entrance of the town and bade us farewell.

We passed through the lock into the harbour which is formed by the artificial deepening and widening of the two rivers that traverse the town. This commodious haven is upwards of a mile in length, and we had to quant from its eastern to its western extremity before we could find a berth; for where it flows along the south side of the city it is bordered by well-kept lawns, public gardens, and the principal boulevards, so that there is no quay to which one may make fast. It took us quite an hour to reach the commercial portion of the harbour, for five bridges, across which all the traffic of Groningen is carried, had to open to us in succession, and we were delayed for a considerable time at each.

But at last we got out of the fashionable quarter and reached the Ooster Haven, where several square-rigged vessels and schooners lay alongside the broad quays. It was pleasant to behold sea-going ships again. We made fast to the quay bordered by stores and great warehouses, and the usual crowd soon gathered round us; but we were not molested. It is only on the Zuider Zee that the boys are so very objectionable.

I liked the look of Groningen, so I decided not to

travel on the following day but to remain and explore the city. The next morning a pleasant, English-speaking, retired sea-captain found me out and offered to accompany me round the town. After visiting the main streets and squares we went to the Plantaage, a very pretty park that was laid out three years ago on the sight of the dismantled fortifications.

"There is a fine hill in the Plantaage," said my companion, "and from the summit of it you will be able to see the country for a great distance around."

It interested me greatly to hear that there was such a thing as a hill in Holland.

"But where is it?" I asked, looking round the interminable plain, "I can see no hill."

"It is just over there; but you cannot see it, for it is hidden by that bush."

I ascended this fine hill, which proved to be an artificial mound not twenty feet in height. But the natives are very proud of it, and speak of it as if it were some huge mountain. As an instance of how successfully a Groningener is deceived by his admiration for it, I may mention that my companion heaved a deep sigh, mopped his face, and dropped exhausted into a chair—thoughtfully placed there by the corporation for this object — when he reached the summit. But to do this eminence justice it must be allowed that it is beyond dispute above the level of the sea.

Of all clean Holland surely there is no cleaner city than Groningen. It contains fifty thousand inhabitants, and all of them seem well-to-do. No smoky factories disfigure it; no pallid and poverty-stricken people are to be seen in its bright streets. It is the centre of a rich agricultural district, and the trade in grain and other country produce seems to occupy all the energies of its citizens. The huge Groote Market is a model market-place. No litter of straw and cabbage leaves is permitted here; the very eggs are carefully washed in the farm-houses before they are brought into town.

The municipality of Groningen certainly does its work well. Everything is admirably ordered here, and large sums are expended each year on improvements of all sorts, including the laying out of beautiful and extensive public gardens. A very army of labourers is constantly employed in keeping all up to the Groningen standard of smartness—a very high standard; one fears to walk its streets with muddy feet. But what is most extraordinary is that with all this great expenditure of public funds, the rate-payers seem to be contented and proud of their corporation. Here no rumours of jobbery and corruption are floating about; no cry for economy is raised. The art of local self-government must indeed be well understood in Holland.

In the evening the sea-captain and myself crossed the river to a lovely wood of oaks and other trees, which is the favourite promenade of the citizens. Broad drives and winding paths traverse this wood, and *cafés* and milk-houses are scattered through it. The people were here in their thousands, for it happened to be the occasion of the children's annual festival. All the public-school children of Groningen were gathered together in the wood to sing glees and hymns under the leadership of their respective masters. The prizes were afterwards distributed by a pleasant-looking gentleman, who, I believe, was burgomaster of the town. All the mammas of Groningen were, of course, here, knitting industriously and gazing at their offspring with proud eyes. Many of the fathers were also standing by smoking, with a look of stolid approval on their faces. It was a pretty sight, and though I do not altogether appreciate the Dutch style of beauty, I could not but allow that these plump, rosy, bright, and highly-polished (I am not speaking of their manners) infants were very pleasant to look upon. At sunset they sang the national anthem lustily and the ceremony was over; then the woods rang with the childish laughter and merry chattering of the innumerable scholars returning homeward.

At six on the following morning, the 23rd of June, the wind being right ahead, I arranged with a man to tow us with his horse to Delfzyl. There are sixteen draw-bridges on this canal, but we paid a guilder and a half at Groningen before starting which franked us for the lot, and we were presented with a tin medal as big as a soup-plate, which we hung in our rigging as a sign to the bridge officials that we had duly settled the fees.

This is a fine canal, broad, straight, and deep, and

it is navigable for sea-going vessels. Among other craft we passed a good-sized barque on the way.

Peter, our tow-man, had been to sea and spoke a little English, but the conversation between us was limited and somewhat jerky. He had visited several English ports, and, being an observant traveller, he favoured us with a succession of pithy comparisons between Dutch and English ways, such as, "Tobacco cheap in Holland, dear in England"; "Gin good here, bad in your country"; "Holland clean place, Cardiff dirty place"; "Drunken Dutchman a quiet man, but London docks on Saturday night, oh much row!" But honest Peter was a good-hearted fellow, and it flashed across his mind that it was cruel and impolite to thus hurt a stranger's feelings by pointing out his country's faults, so he racked his brain to find something complimentary to say about England. For some time he could think of nothing in our favour, but at last the sight of a draw-bridge inspired him. "Dat," he exclaimed, "is a poor small bridge, but Bristol has a very big bridge." He shouted out all these remarks to us in a stentorian voice, for his tow-line was long and he was far ahead of us.

We reached Delfzyl at about mid-day. At the entrance of the town we found the only lock on the canal, a gigantic one this; and on the other side of it flowed the tidal waters of the North Sea. Having passed through the sluice we entered the harbour, enclosed by a breakwater, beyond which spread the estuary of the river Ems, here five miles broad, looking very rough and white with foam, for the wind was still strong. Across this we saw the low, wooded coast of Germany.

We had now traversed Holland and had done with her canals, and the next stage of our journey was to be a coasting voyage on the North Sea.

CHAPTER VII.

THE FRISIAN ISLANDS.

DELFZYL is an uninteresting little seaport, and I had seen all I wished to see of it in half an hour, so I decided to sail across the bay of Heligoland to the Eider river at four on the following morning. But the elements would not have it so, and we remained here weather-bound for six days. I was impatient at this waste of time, but it would have been madness to have attempted a long voyage on this dangerous coast with a stormy north-west wind blowing in our teeth.

Delfzyl is protected from the sea by a lofty grass-grown dyke. Outside this is the harbour, from which the roofs only of the town are visible. We lay alongside an old hulk, on board which lived a man, his wife, and a large family of children. The youngsters took the very greatest interest in us during our stay and almost wept when we went away. At first they were shy, but we introduced ourselves on the morning after our arrival by presenting one of the boys, a sturdy little chap of four, with a piece of bread and marmalade. His brothers and sisters crowded round him. He stood holding the unfamiliar food in his hand, eyeing it suspiciously, afraid to taste it, till his elder sister, a pretty flaxen-haired girl of seventeen, timidly bit off a mouthful to reassure him, and, having expressed her approval of this new luxury, returned it to him. He had acquired a very decided taste for marmalade before we sailed.

An acquaintance having been once struck up, these children would never let us alone. The rigging of toy boats, the repairing of hoops and dolls for them, and the supplying of jam and biscuits became no unimportant portion of our day's work. The smallest boy became a nuisance; he used to rise at daybreak and awake us with loud cries of "Ma-an, ma-an!" in order that we might play with him. We of course quite won the heart of the plump mother of the brood, who brought us frequent presents of milk and eggs. The eldest daughter was very anxious to acquire our language, and, as she leant over the bulwarks of her floating home, would point to various articles and ask the English names for them. She acquired a long vocabulary in those six days.

Besides these we picked up several friends among the English-speaking ex-sea-captains, who, as publicans and store-keepers, composed the aristocracy of Delfzyl. Two of these were nearly always with us; they often stayed out late at night in order to converse with us, and succeeded in making the innocent *Falcon* a terror to their wives, who were no doubt very glad when the English yacht sailed away and so left their husbands to fall back again into the old domestic groove. Both of these rollicking dogs were dreadfully henpecked, but each unconscious of his own thraldom chaffed the other mercilessly on the subject, and each would tell me in private of the other's pusillanimous obedience to his *vrouw*. One of these old sailors kept an inn, cultivated a farm with his own hands, and supplied coasting steamers with coals, so was an exceedingly busy person though he did contrive to waste so much time with us. The other, a portly gentleman, was water-clerk to a firm of ship-brokers. His duty consisted of standing on the dyke and gazing seaward through a long telescope for vessels that never came —at least none came while we were there—but he was still busier than the other, and when he called on us he insisted on hurrying away every five minutes to his post of observation for another inspection of the deserted offing. There was only one square-rigged vessel in the harbour, an Italian barque from Pensacola. Her chain was padlocked to a buoy, as she was detained by the authorities for some offence or other against Dutch law. Her skipper, a pleasant young Neapolitan, also joined our circle.

For days the rain fell in torrents and the north-east wind howled across the sea and the flat lands. Occasionally the glass would rise a little and the weather show signs of improvement, but only for a few hours, then down would drop the mercury again and the wind would freshen to a gale. "It's almost like the north-east trades here," said one old skipper to me; "the wind is generally in this quarter with us from March till August"—which was not an encouraging bit of information for us.

Thanks to my friends, the time passed cheerily enough despite the foul weather. One evening the two henpecked Dutchmen sneaked away from their wives and took me for a walk along a straight road very carefully paved with red bricks and bordered by broad ditches, to the neighbouring village of Appingedam, an ancient place with narrow canals over which hang some very picturesque old gabled houses. They brought me to the parlour of an antique tavern whose walls were panelled with carved oak black with age. It was just the quaint hostelry one sees in the old Dutch pictures, and the Dutch roistering after the good old style was not wanting.

Chief of the cronies here assembled over long pipes and brimming mugs was the village doctor, who was just such a man as one would expect a Dutch doctor to be—stout, pedantic, and jovial. Here too was another character, a wild old sailor, quite six feet and a half in height and broad in proportion. He had served on many a British ship and spoke English well. He was now dressed rather smartly in tweed dittos; for a small fortune had recently been left him and he was running through it, so he said, at the rate of fifty shillings a day. The Italian captain had offered to ship him as carpenter at five pounds ten shillings a month, but he refused this.

"I won't go to sea as long as I have a stuiver left," he said. "That's my way. When I've spent all my money I'll go to Cardiff and ship for what I can get, but not till then."

He was the only thriftless Dutchman I came across. He had mixed so much with the British shell-backs that he aped their reckless ways. But like most imitators he overdid the thing and practised in a deliberate fashion, which spoiled all the effect, what poor Jack does out of the natural devilry of his disposition. He had picked up a great fluency of profane language in our ports; if his native Low Dutch was lower than his English it must have attained great depths.

My friend who combined the avocations of publican, farmer, and coal-merchant, took a great fancy to our dinghy. We sailed about the inner harbour together, and he was astonished at her speed under canvas. "She sails like a man," he cried repeatedly. So enamoured did he become of the boat, that he did his utmost to persuade me to sell her to him. True Dutchman that he was he did not care to part with his money, but he offered me a variety of his possessions in exchange for her. He proposed to fill my lockers with gin and beer, and, finding this did not tempt me, he proffered me a large musical box. Fowls, sheep, and potatoes I could have acquired in profusion had I chosen; but I would not part with the dinghy, knowing that I could not have found another that would have suited my purpose.

Even the pleasures of Delfzyl began to pall on us, and we anxiously watched the glass and sky for a sign of weather sufficiently fine to allow us to sail away. On the 28th it blew harder than ever. Furious rain squalls swept across the sky, and a heavy sea was rolling into the bay so that the yacht tumbled about a little even in the sheltered harbour. As I sat in the cabin after breakfast smoking, in despair and wondering whether we should ever get further that summer, a happy idea occurred to me—why not occupy this idle time by once more trying to discover where that mysterious leak of ours was situated? For the leak, though I have not alluded to it lately, was as lively as ever.

I laid my plans before Wright, and we set to work. We raised the flooring, took all the ballast out of the yacht and laid it on a raft which happened to be alongside of us. This laborious and very dirty task over, we pumped, baled, and mopped until nearly all the water was out of the hold, and then sure enough the cause of all the mischief was revealed at last. From a hole in the middle of the keelson forward there spouted up a small but constant jet of water. It was not strange that we had not discovered this when we prosecuted our minute examinations of the outside of the vessel; for this hole—no doubt intended for a bolt which some knavish Hammersmith carpenter had omitted to drive in—pierced the false keel, and was, therefore, invisible from without. A wooden plug soon stopped the leak, and we were contented with our day's work. The pump had a much easier time of it after this.

Of my two henpecked friends the publican was the most so, but he found an excellent excuse for neglecting the company of his spouse for that of the English yachtsman. He had contracted to coal a coasting steamer which was being expected in port at any moment during our stay, and which never turned up after all. He brought the coals on an old lighter of his own and moored her close to us. The leaking of the *Falcon* at her worst was nothing to the leaking of this lighter. She would have gone down in half an hour if left alone, so two of his men were constantly pumping her out, while he sat on the *Falcon's* deck and saw that they did their work properly.

On the 27th the glass rose and the weather showed signs of improving. It was hardly good enough yet to venture out to sea, but I bethought myself of sailing across the comparatively sheltered bay to the old Hanoverian city of Emden, about twelve miles distant. I suggested to the publican that he should come with us. He was delighted at the prospect.

"But I must go and spin some yarn to my wife," he explained. "You come with me. She won't raise objections if you are present."

So I accompanied the poor wretch to his house. His wife, not a sweet-tempered woman, frowned savagely at me when she perceived me.

"My angel," he said, "I am to pilot this English captain to Emden, and I have to call on Herr Smit, the wine merchant there, and bargain with him for some more of that excellent *kirshwasser* of his."

I don't suppose she believed a word he said; but after a little grumbling in guttural Dutch she let him go. Then an animated discussion ensued, he imploring, she refusing, some favour. I made out that he was asking her to give him some pocket-money to spend on the journey, but he did not succeed in getting anything out of his better-half. "While I call her out of the way you take some money out of the till," he said to me in English. But I dreaded the consequences of discovery and refused to help him.

Fearing lest his men should neglect the pump while he was away, he proceeded to caulk the lighter before starting, in an original manner. The men held his feet while he hung over the side and thrust handfuls of coal into the seams. To my surprise he succeeded in almost completely stopping the inflow of water.

It was still early morning when we got under weigh. We sailed across the shallow flats and opened out the great circular pool of the Dollart; and now we had to pick our way from beacon to beacon carefully, for the navigation is encumbered by great sandbanks which dry at low tide. The Dollart is a piece of water one hundred and twenty square miles in extent, produced by a terrible inundation in the thirteenth century. We were sailing over the buried towns and villages of what was once a fertile plain.

A canal rather more than a mile in length connects Emden with the Dollart. We had to bring up at the mouth of the canal to report ourselves at the custom-house. This was my first visit to Germany, and I had heard so much of German officialism that I dreaded this experience. But I found these officers exceedingly pleasant and polite. It was their duty to search our vessel and put our stores under seal before allowing us to proceed up the canal. Hearing that I proposed to return to Delfzyl that evening, they advised me to leave the yacht with them and ascend the canal in the dinghy, thereby saving myself the above formalities. We accordingly moored the *Falcon* in front of the custom-house and sailed in the boat to the old city whose steeples and steep red roofs were visible ahead of us.

For the first time in my life I stepped ashore on the Fatherland, but the first sight that met my eyes called up strange memories. A company of Prussian infantry was marching by the quay where we landed. I had seen plenty of those uniforms seventeen years before in sunny France.

I was delighted with Emden. It is possibly more like a Dutch than a German town, but it does not possess the more objectionable Dutch characteristics. True it is surrounded by huge dykes and intersected by many canals—for East Friesland of which it is the capital is as flat and watery a region as any portion of Holland—but there was a refreshing untidiness and dirtiness that told me I was indeed in a new country untrammelled by the tyranny of Dutch cleanliness. The canal banks were ragged and unkempt, green alders and rank weeds had been allowed to grow here and there in the crannies of the old walls, the ancient gabled houses that overhung the water were rickety and agreeably slovenly. How dreadful all this must appear to a Dutch eye! I even saw a spider—that creature so loathsome to the Dutch—hanging unmolested from the great oak beam of one antique tavern we visited.

There is much to see in this picturesque mediæval town. We visited the Rathhaus, a grand building three hundred years old, which contains an interesting collection of antique weapons and armour, mostly relics of the thirty years' war. The suits of armour contain automatic wooden warriors with the most grotesque faces, who, when the grim old lady who is custodian of the museum pulls the strings, commence to blow discordant trumpets, beat drums, brandish battle-axes, and lunge with pike and sword in a manner my companion thought very imposing. A collection of more modern arms has been recently added to these —a quantity of chassepots, standards bearing the imperial eagles of France, metrailleuses, and other trophies of Germany's greatest war.

On our return to the *Falcon* we found that Wright had prepared an excellent dinner for us. In the evening we beat back to Delfzyl across a very choppy sea, for the wind had veered to the north-west.

On the 29th of June I turned out at daybreak and

found that a fresh north-north-west wind was driving heavy rain-clouds across the North Sea. It looked dirty; but I had come to despair of fine weather, so I decided to push on somewhere.

My chart showed me that I should find no harbour into which I could run for shelter between the Ems and the Eider, unless I went considerably out of my way up one of the rivers. Up to the mouth of the Jade, the East Frisian islands border the mainland; but the channels inside the islands cannot be navigated with safety by a stranger. In many places these channels are left quite dry by the falling tide, so that a man can walk dry-shod from the islands to the Hanoverian coast.

But as my chart indicated a well-buoyed route as far as the island of Norderney, the most fashionable of German watering-places, I made for this place, with the intention of bringing up there for the night should the weather continue to look unfavourable.

We got under weigh as half-past six and tacked down the eastern Ems, carefully picking up buoy after buoy, and sounding with boat-hook when we approached the shoals, for the *Falcon* would probably have broken up had she gone aground with the sea that was running. At last, though surrounded by sand-banks, we were out of sight of land, and the thick rain made it difficult for us to distinguish the buoys, which are placed at intervals of about a mile. At mid-day, it being about high water, we saw a street of booms stretching away on our starboard hand. I took it for granted that this must mark the Bants Balg, a channel that crosses the Koper sands and leads to Norderney. We accordingly left the Ems, and now, having the wind right aft, ran at a good speed, keeping close to the booms, and feeling very uncertain as to where we were going. The water shoaled till we had only four feet under us in the middle of the channel, and the sands were showing in patches on either side of us; but of land there was still no sign. We were now luckily in perfectly smooth water, else we should have felt somewhat anxious. The tide was evidently falling, and it seemed as if we should soon be left high and dry in the middle of this sandy wilderness; but to our relief we saw a native flat-bottomed coaster lying at anchor some way ahead. We ran down to her and let go our anchor close to her, in three feet of water.

In half an hour the water left us lying on the hard sand, and we could have walked, had we known how to avoid the quicksands, either to the island of Juist or to the mainland. The skipper of the coaster spoke English. He told us that this was an excellent place to bring up in during low water, and that a gale of wind could not hurt us.

I was anxious to ascertain whether I was in the right channel, but, not wishing to display my ignorance of my whereabouts, I obtained the information indirectly.

"Where are you bound for, skipper?" I asked.

"For Norderney, captain."

It was as I had hoped, and, as I saw that the channel was not very distinctly marked further on, I determined to let my friend the coaster get ahead of me and thus serve as my pilot.

The atmosphere had been thick all the morning, but now it cleared somewhat, and out of a rift in the black rain-clouds the sun shone out feebly for a short space, revealing to us the strange nature of the place we were in. All round us vast mud-banks and dreary sands stretched for leagues, broken only by narrow creeks and pools of water, which, to judge from the numerous whiskered faces that were ever and anon rising above the surface, must have been alive with seals. On our right, appearing like a low black line, was the dyke that protected the land of Hanover. And ahead of us, some seven miles away, gleamed the yellow sand dunes of Norderney, above which towered a great lighthouse two hundred feet in height, a most important landmark to vessels that approach this perilous coast. To the left of us loomed dimly the shores of the island of Juist, while between Juist and Norderney there glittered a bright white line—the foam of the open North Sea.

The aspect of these waste flat lands ever contending with the stormy seas was inexpressibly melancholy. The only sounds were the distant roar of waves and the wild cries of innumerable sea-birds that were searching for fish on the wet sands. But we were able to see all this only for a few minutes; then the blue rift in the clouds closed again, and the falling rain soon obscured the distance in universal gray.

At three o'clock the tide had risen sufficiently to float us, so we got up anchor and sailed on again. The coaster, whose draught was heavier than ours, did not get under weigh for some time afterwards. After having proceeded about a mile we came to a portion of the channel which was not indicated by booms, and, as we did not know the landmarks, we soon lost our road and ran hard aground.

"The tide's making fast and we'll soon be off again," I said to Wright, "but we'll wait now until the schuyt overtakes us. We will let her show us the way."

When the Dutchman came up we allowed him to pass us, and, as we could outsail him easily, we triced up our tack and stowed the mizen so as to let him keep the lead. It was lucky that we did this, for we had now to cross the opening between the two islands and were exposed to the sea that was rolling in from the ocean. It rained and blew harder than ever, and we were evidently in for another dirty night. I came to the conclusion that it would have been difficult for a stranger to have picked his way across these banks in such weather.

We took short tacks between shoals on which a nasty sea was breaking. Our consort kept his boat-hook sounding all the time, and went about as soon as he found himself in eight feet of water. We followed his example. The old skipper knew what he was about; as soon as he calculated that the tide had risen high enough, he left the circuitous channel, and, bearing away, steered a straight course across the now covered sands to Norderney light. We understood the meaning of this change of course on his part, and, thinking that we could now dispense with his pilotage, we basely decided to desert him; so, hauling down our tack, we soon left him far astern. The wind was now on our quarter and we rushed along, wallowing in the steep beam seas with only six feet of water under our keel.

At last we were under the lee of the island and in smooth water, and at 6 P.M. we rounded the pier into a broad shallow bay, where we brought up among a crowd of small craft. The night was a wild one and the cold wind howled across the dreary dunes. We were glad to be in so snug a harbour and we enjoyed our dinner and grog and pipe afterwards, and we turned in with a comfortable sense of security which seemed all the sweeter when we thought of what it was like outside.

We had not yet done with our ill-luck, for we were weather-bound here for three days. We were lying at the very edge of the channel, which is so steep, that though our anchor was in only five feet of water there were five fathoms under the yacht's keel.

The next morning was bleak and windy. I looked round me and saw that the island was composed of serrated sand-hills which looked like mountains after the low countries I had left, and the only vegetation on them was the wiry sea-grass. A few years back the population of this bleak spot consisted of two or three hundred fishermen; and the only buildings save their huts were the lighthouse, the lifeboat station, and the ice signal which informs vessels at sea whether the rivers and channels of the coast are free or blocked with ice. Every island and promontory of the main possesses one of these ice signals, which made us realise that we had been travelling north into inclement climates.

But the desolate little island has now become Germany's principal watering-place, and as many as fifteen thousand people have visited it in one summer. It has been well chosen as a holiday resort, for the climate is as healthy and bracing as any in the world; the keen fresh wind of the North Sea is ever sweeping over these barren sand-hills; appetites that have flagged in the cities become voracious in Norderney, and dyspepsia vanishes. In accordance with the new system of treating consumption the German doctors send their patients who have weak chests to pass the winter here.

I close-reefed the dinghy's sail and steered for the end of the long pier that has been built across the sands and shoals to the edge of the deep water. From the end of the pier a walk of nearly a mile brought me to the bathing village where I had been informed that I should find *cafés*, casinos, theatres, and all the fun of Trouville or Dieppe. I had been looking forward to a little luxury and dissipation here after my late simple life, but I was to be sadly disappointed. I found myself in a town that was evidently intended exclusively for holiday folk. Every building that was not a *café*, hotel, or music-hall was a lodging-house. I strolled through the streets; some were of deep loose sand, some were paved with brick, but all consisted of little wooden houses with red roofs and gaily-painted verandahs, in which stood tables and chairs after the fashion of a *café*, and outside each was a board bearing the inscription "LOGIS." There was unlimited accommodation—everyone let lodgings —but where were the lodgers? There were many places of amusement and signs of revelry, but where were the revellers? In the course of my walk I only came across a few fishwives and bare-footed children, who gazed at me curiously as I passed.

It was possible that I had turned out at too early an hour; the fashionable visitors of whom I had heard so much might be still in bed. So I lunched on board and then returned to the town, but was dismayed to find the streets as empty as before. I now became depressed and began to dislike Norderney intensely. It seemed a ghastly thing to come across a city of concert-halls and spacious *cafés*—a city that had evidently been dedicated to luxury and pleasure—thus lying silent, deserted, and empty under the stormy sky, even as if some plague had ravaged it. Trouville is a dismal place in mid-winter, but it is cheerful to Norderney in the end of June. On this cold coast the bathing season is not so early as it is with us, and this year the summer weather was exceptionally late in coming, therefore few visitors had yet arrived. I entered the principal *café* and made a noise to attract the waiters, but no one came to me, so I got disgusted with the queen of German watering-places, in comparison with which the dead cities of the Zuider Zee are very much alive, and left its desolate streets to explore the sand-hills that surround it.

I reached the summit of one of the highest dunes and commanded a view of the whole island. It appeared to be very barren; even the tough sea-grass could only take root here and there. Magnificent sands, that doubtlessly serve as play-ground to thousands of German children in the later summer, stretched far out from the north of the town, and beyond these were the white-capped waves of the North Sea. The miles of desert sands and the stormy ocean looked bleak under the leaden sky; but after all, it was a more cheerful scene than the deserted pleasure-town, with its suggestion of impossible dissipation.

The following day, July the 1st, was cold and squally, and we could hear the breakers thundering as loudly as ever beyond the sand-hills. I did not go on shore this day, but cruised in the dinghy under the lee of the island. I now observed that Norderney was making some attempts to wake up for the season. Two passenger steamers touched at the pier and landed half a dozen people. A long string of cabs was drawn up at the pier-end to convey the visitors to the town; the day's business amounted to about one fare to four cabmen.

On Saturday, the 2nd of July, I awoke early and immediately felt that a change had come to the weather. The sun was shining brightly into the cabin and it was quite warm. A big blue-bottle was buzzing round my head and I welcomed him as a harbinger of summer. I jumped on deck and looked round. I found to my delight that the wind was in the right direction, west by south, and all seemed to favour our departure, except the barometer, which I saw was falling. Had our luck indeed changed at last, and were we to fetch the mouth of the Eider this day, and so have done with this detestable North Sea?

As it would not be high water till nearly nine o'clock I went on shore and ascended the sand-hills to the storm signal station, so as to see how our course lay through the sand-banks that encumber the navigation of the channel between Juist and Norderney. The sea was beautifully calm and blue. I could distinguish the white and red beacons that mark the passage across the bar; and the broken water showed me where the shoals were situated. I saw that the indications on my chart were entirely misleading, as I had anticipated; for the sands on this coast are constantly shifting, so that a stranger can place no reliance on the recorded bearings and soundings.

After my recent experiences of the climate I somewhat mistrusted so glorious a morning and scarcely dared hope that we were to sail at last. I returned on board; we ate our breakfast; and then, even as we were getting all ready for sea, a sudden change came on the scene. First we perceived black clouds rising rapidly above the dunes, then round rushed the wind in a trice to its old quarter, north-west, coming with a violent squall. In almost less time than it takes to describe it, summer had given place to winter again and the treacherous wind howled over the sea, which, unruffled and blue a moment before, now tumbled in dark waves capped with white foam.

We reviled our ill-luck and despaired of finding summer in these latitudes; but the weather cannot always be vile, even on the coast of Friesland, and late in the afternoon it began to fine down. I turned out several times during the night to inspect the sky. It looked well, but the glass was still falling. At sunrise a light south-west wind sprang up, and at high water, half-past nine, we hoisted our canvas and put to sea, determined to get to some new port for a change, even if we did not succeed in at once reaching the Eider, which was still upwards of eighty miles distant.

We sailed round the west side of the island, crossed the bar, and now, having the wind almost right aft, we set our square-sail and steered eastward along the sandy dunes. But our progress was very slow. We seemed to have reached a climate of extremes only, and the cold stormy weather had suddenly given place to a sultry calm. At times the wind fell away altogether and we drifted on with the tide, our sails flapping idly. There was not a cloud in the sky, but we did not trust this fair appearance. Such intense heat was likely to be succceded by strong wind; the glass was steadily falling, and a long swell was rolling in from the north, the usual forerunner of a gale from that quarter. We had so far been treated in so treacherous a manner by the North Sea that it had established a sort of funk in us, and we were always dreading bad weather, not, as it turned out, without good reason.

Other ominous signs were not wanting. Large shoals of porpoises were blowing and gambolling round us in a way the mariner dislikes, and the heated shore quivered in mirage; the glaring sand-hills, bare save for the bluish sea-grass which grew scantily here and there, looked hot and arid as the coast of Africa. There were no signs of life on shore, and the only sounds were the melancholy and ox-like bellowing of the whistle buoy at the end of the bar and the murmuring of the waves breaking on the beach.

At dinner-time we discovered that the water we had taken on board at Delfzyl was commencing to stink—Dutch water is usually full of impurities and will not keep long—so, not wishing to add typhoid to our other grievances, we condemned the water to be used for tea and coffee only, while we drank soda-water, of which I had laid in a small store in view of the probable sea-sickness of some friends who were to have sailed down the Thames with us.

At four in the afternoon we were still off the centre of the island, having only made six miles in seven hours. We now found that the tide was setting us back to whence we had come, so we took to the sweeps, pulled to the shore until we reached the three fathom soundings and let go our anchor. At six o'clock a light northerly wind sprang up—a direction that made us suspect mischief—and we got under weigh again. Cheating the tide by keeping as near as possible to the shore we contrived to sail by Norderney at last, and we came abreast of the next of these desolate Frisian islands, Baltrum.

At eight the wind once more died away, and our lead, which we used as a ground log, showed us that the tide was sweeping us towards the shoals of the Accumer Ee; so we came to an anchor two miles from the shore, off the Baltrum lifeboat station. The sun set in a red haze that was reflected on the sand-hills, making them appear strangely beautiful. Thousands of black duck and porpoises were around us, and we saw many seals; but as there was nothing good to eat among them we spared these creatures and did not bring the gun on deck.

From our anchorage we could see the islands of Norderney, Baltrum, and Langeoog. These Frisian islands have queer names; the others are called Schiermonnikoog, Bosch, Rottum, Spiekeroog, and Wangeroog, from which one can form an idea of what an elegant dialect the old Frisian is. These islands are all much alike, sandy, barren, and surrounded by dangerous shoals. Each has its lifeboat station—the lifeboats have plenty to do on this coast—and each has its gigantic beacon of a peculiar form, so that the mariner far out to sea can distinguish one island from another.

We kept watch and watch during the night, for I wished to get away as soon as there was any wind. We did not feel secure at this exposed anchorage. If it should come on to blow again from the north-west, as the falling glass foretold, we would be on a lee-shore with no port near at hand to which we could run; for, as I have before said, the channels between the islands cannot be safely attempted by a stranger in broad daylight, and at night it would be impossible to find one's way in. Wright took the first watch and I relieved him at midnight. At 3 A.M. a light breeze came up from the south, so I awoke my man and we got under weigh again.

This day, July 4th, was much like the previous one, calm, sultry, and cloudless. We crept by Langeoog and Spiekeroog, and at eight o'clock we saw looming through the heat haze right ahead of us what first appeared to be a ship, but soon proved to be the lofty steeple of a church. This was all that was visible of the distant shore, and we knew that it was upon the island of Wangeroog, the most eastern of the group. The wind now headed us, but we tacked slowly on until the tide turned and obliged us to let go our anchor. It then became quite calm. At this rate the voyage promised to be a prolonged one, but the glass

THE FRISIAN ISLANDS. 151

was still steadily falling, so I knew that we should have more wind than we wanted later on.

The water hereabouts was very clear, and as we lay at anchor we saw several large skate swimming beneath us. We were anxious to secure some of these for dinner, but had no lines on board, and an attempt to harpoon them proved futile, as might have been expected. But the multitudes of sea-fowl were evidently having an excellent morning's sport among the fishes.

At two o'clock there was the faintest possible northeast wind, so we got up anchor and proceeded. The glass had now gone down another half inch since the morning, so it was certain that we should soon have a blow. I therefore consulted my chart with the view of finding some sheltered anchorage which I could make before nightfall. Under the circumstances I did not wish to remain another night at sea. We were near the great bay formed by the estuaries of the Jade and Weser; but there are no harbours on these broad rivers until either Wilhelmshaven or Bremen is reached, and both these places were far out of our course. However, my chart showed me that the channel inside the islands communicates with the mouth of the Jade close to the east end of Wangeroog by a creek called the Blaue Balge. If I could find my way into this creek I could lie there safely for the night, under the lee of the island, and sail on the next morning, should the weather be propitious. It was worth trying.

We passed Wangeroog and entered the great bay; with the exception of the small sandy island behind us no land was visible, but buoys and beacons were everywhere round us indicating the passages among the labyrinthine sandbanks that here dry for several hundreds of square miles at low water. We made for the buoys that show the entrance to the Jade. The Germans have an excellent system of buoyage, so that it is impossible for the mariner to mistake his whereabouts. On entering a channel from the sea all the buoys on the starboard side are marked with consecutive letters of the alphabet, all those on the port hand with figures. At sunset we came to the buoy marked E, and it was opposite this, according to my chart, that the Blaue Balge joined the Jade.

Following the directions of the chart I now left the deep river and sailed boldly in towards the creek. But we soon found ourselves in a very unpleasant position. Sounding as we went we could discover no trace of the channel. The water shoaled rapidly, and we perceived that we were being swept by a furious cross current, broadside on, towards the shallows. The water was tumbling in races and overfalls all round us. We should have needed half a gale of wind to stem such a tide, and it was almost calm; so the only thing to be done was to hurriedly let go our anchor before we were driven aground, and wait for high water.

These were spring tides, and I do not remember to have ever experienced before so rapid a current, even

THE FRISIAN ISLANDS. 153

in the river Seine, and it is bad enough there. The yacht rolled about violently to her anchor, while the water foamed and hissed and whirled by us in a way that almost made one feel dizzy to contemplate. Had our anchor dragged it is very probable that the *Falcon* would have been lost.

The glass was still falling, and at ten o'clock a violent thunderstorm broke over us accompanied by vivid forked lightning and a tropical downpour of rain. The wind now freshened up and the sky had a very wild appearance. I was anxious to get away from our exposed position, so at midnight, it being high water, we weighed anchor and once more attempted to enter the Blaue Balge. The chart told me that there was a depth of five fathoms in this channel at low water; but as I sailed on the water gradually shoaled until there were only two fathoms under us. There was evidently something wrong somewhere. We could distinguish, about a mile ahead of us, the riding lights of two small craft that were brought up snugly in the Balje under the lee of Wangeroog.

We envied them their security and would have much liked to have been lying alongside of them. But the water shoaled until we only had four feet, so, not daring to run on farther, we put the yacht's head round, and, much disappointed, beat out again towards the deeper water within the Jade buoys. I afterwards discovered that my chart was entirely wrong, that the creek had long since shifted its position, and that the bearings I had followed would have taken me on to the sands, where the yacht would most probably have broken up. This was a lesson to me to avoid the swatch-ways and shallow channels, and trust only to the main waterways frequented by large vessels, and therefore well-buoyed. It does not do to play tricks with such a coast as this.

CHAPTER VIII.

FROM THE JADE TO THE EIDER.

ONCE again in the deep water of the Jade, we let go our anchor close to the letter E buoy, and here passed a very uncomfortable night. The wind was blowing straight in from the ocean, and when it met the ebbing tide, which was quite as furious as the flood had been, a very nasty sea got up, in which the yacht pitched, rolled, and strained at her anchor with violent jerks as if she would be pulled to pieces.

I turned out of my bunk several times to see how we were getting on. The anchor was holding well, but the sky had a stormy appearance and the northwest wind was howling again after its old fashion. Our faithful barometer had not gone down for nothing. I was glad indeed that we were not lying at our anchorage of the previous night at the back of Norderney. For there was now little cause for anxiety; we had the Jade under our lee, well marked by buoys by day and lightships by night, so that if it should become too rough to remain where we were we could always make for shelter.

The glass dropped another two tenths in the night, and on the following morning, July 5th, the sky looked so bad that I saw we should have to run up the Jade to Wilhelmshaven and wait there till the weather improved. This port is twenty miles up the bay. I did not like to go so far out of my course, but it could not be helped, for the breaking seas of the Jade are dangerous in a north-west gale, and that a gale from that quarter would soon overtake us I had little doubt.

At six o'clock the tide began to flow, so we got up anchor and set all sail. It rained in torrents and blew harder every minute. Soon the squalls became so violent, with promise of worse coming, that we had to close reef the mainsail. We rushed along over the tumbling waves, picking our way from buoy to buoy. At first we could see no signs of land, but numerous gigantic beacons of grotesque form rose from the submerged sands as a warning to vessels. Later on we perceived on our starboard hand the low coast of the Duchy of Oldenburg, about two miles distant, and four miles away on our port hand stretched the great sands of Hoher Weg, which divide the Jade from the Weser, but which are covered at high water, so that then there is no dry land between the channel we were following and the coast of Hanover fifteen miles away.

The Jade is generally described as a river on the

charts, but it is nothing of the sort. It is a long bay opening out at its head into a broad shallow gulf, resembling the Dollart, and like this last was produced by a mighty inundation centuries ago. The channel narrows into a neck at the entrance of this gulf, and it is on the west side of the neck that Wilhelmshaven is situated.

At ten o'clock we saw the harbour in front of us; two large men-of-war lay at anchor in the roads. Of the town itself we could distinguish little save the massive dykes that surround it, and the gates that open to the great docks within. When we were not half a mile off, a stinging torrent of rain drove down the bay, obscuring everything, and then the gale broke on us with all its fury.

"It strikes me that we have got here none too soon, Wright," I shouted.

"No, Sir. We're just in time as usual," he replied.

"Just in time" became a regular catch-word with us this summer; for though we were very unlucky in encountering a lot of bad weather, we had a wonderful knack of always reaching a snug port just as the weather was becoming dangerously troublesome.

When we were near the town we perceived two piers close together. Under the impression that we were entering the harbour we luffed up between these and lowered our sails. We now found ourselves in a very small haven surrounded by deserted quays, with a dock gate at the end of it. But there was no shelter, for the waves were rolling into this haven and dashing against its lofty walls. This was clearly no safe place for us to remain in, so we hoisted the foresail as hastily as we could with the object of running out again before the wind should drive us against the stone quays.

At this juncture a man clad in oils appeared above us and motioned to us to get outside and steer to the right. We followed his advice, and after nearly fouling one of the pier ends we escaped from this *cul-de-sac*, which, I afterwards discovered, was the entrance of one of the man-of-war docks. A hundred yards or so farther on we opened out another harbour, in which the water was quite smooth. We sailed in and made fast to some stakes at its inner end. Our work was over for the day; and though wet and weary we were very hungry, and felt very contented and jovial, now that we had at last found a safe berth, after having passed fifty somewhat anxious hours at sea. We had taken no breakfast before sailing, so the first thing we now did was to open a tin of beef and a bottle of pickled onions and do justice to a square meal.

After this we looked around us. The harbour we were in did not present a cheerful appearance. It was surrounded, not by quays and buildings, but by muddy waste ground strewn with old railway iron and timbers; behind this were grassy dykes which prevented us from seeing what lay beyond. The harbour contained two deserted lighters only, and no human being was in sight, save one small girl who was milking a sheep on one of the dykes. This desolation puzzled me extremely, for were we not in Wilhelmshaven, the second war harbour of all Germany, and her chief naval station on the North Sea?

I went on shore and walked up the dyke, so as to command a view of the scenery and discover what manner of place this was which we had now reached. I looked down on several cheerless rain-swept docks of considerable size, in which some men-of-war were lying, but the only people to be seen were a few disconsolate sentries in caped great coats, struggling with the wind and rain. Beyond the docks I perceived the red roofs of the town, so I walked towards it.

I conscientiously explored the city of Wilhelmshaven, and, making all due allowance for the inclement weather, I came to the conclusion that this was one of the most depressing and cheerless-looking places I had ever visited.

In this city everything is new and useful, but little is beautiful as yet. It has been planned on a large scale; its brick-paved streets are broad, straight, and very clean, but empty of people. The public buildings are imposing. I came across a post-office big enough for London and a spacious naval hospital. There are also great open places where parks and gardens are being laid out. But there is something very cold and dreary in the appearance of this young and inchoate settlement, which is yet far too vast for its present population; many of its chief streets have only been sketched out, having a building every hundred yards and desert spaces between.

In another forty years or so, when Wilhelmshaven is fully grown and has a sufficiency of inhabitants to fill it, it will no doubt be a pleasant and magnificent city; but I believe that even Dido's Carthage, despite the pious Eneas' polite expressions of admiration for it, could not have appeared a very inviting place while the carpenters and masons were still at work on its half-finished walls and temples.

Wilhelmshaven is as yet but the skeleton of a town, and to a stranger seems sadly wanting in life and colour. It is a great war-station and nothing more; a camp of soldiers, sailors, and dockyard officials, who all attend to their work in the uncompromising German fashion. That air of roistering jollity that invariably pervades a British garrison town is altogether wanting here. The strict discipline of the German service and the impecuniosity of the average German recruit prevent anything of the sort. This is a very serious place indeed, where there is much work and very little play.

The history of Wilhelmshaven explains the character of the town. About thirty years since, the Prussians, anxious to acquire a naval station on the North Sea and possessing no territory on that coast, purchased what was then little more than a mere mud-bank on the Jade, from the Grand Duke of Oldenburg. It was very far from being the best site for the purpose, but it was the only one in the market, so the best was made of it. Land was reclaimed, dykes were constructed, and docks excavated at an enormous cost. On one occasion, at least, great embankments and works over which months of labour had been expended were swept away before their completion, by storm and flood. The Prussians have been steadily working here for thirty years, and there is much to be done yet before this becomes, what it certainly will be some day, one of the strongest places in Europe.

The Eider and Elbe canal and the canal from Wilhelmshaven to the Weser and Elbe will be completed in a few years. The German gunboats will then be able to steam from the Baltic to this port without putting to sea. Another important ship canal, that from Wilhelmshaven to Emden, will be open in a few months. It will thus soon be possible for a yacht to travel all the way from Ostend to the Baltic by river and canal, and the Danish fiords will then no doubt become a favourite cruising-ground of the Corinthian sailor.

When I returned to the yacht I found an amiable-looking giant in a green uniform vainly but patiently attempting to make himself intelligible to Wright. I saw that he was a custom-house officer, and though I understood nothing else of his discourse, I managed to catch the word *zollhaus*, which I knew was German for custom-house, so I presumed that he wanted me to go on shore with my papers and report myself to the authorities. I motioned to him to lead the way, and he took me to an office where sat several intelligent-looking gentlemen in uniforms and spectacles. I produced my register and Admiralty warrant; but not a word did any of them know of English, so I was unable to give them the information about myself which they required.

"Do any of you gentlemen speak French?" I inquired in that language.

They shook their heads and smiled. I found that Germans in their own country generally exhibit amusement when asked that question.

Then one of the superintendents of the department took me with him all over the town, and we called upon several merchants, store-keepers, and others in the hope of finding an interpreter of some sort. It was all in vain, and we returned to the custom-house to report our failure. Next they sent out messengers in all directions, with the result that at last a petty naval officer was discovered who understood English. Through him I explained who and what I was and how I had run into the harbour for shelter. Upon which I was told that I could stay in Wilhelmshaven as long as I liked, and that I had no dues to pay.

Now I have heard a great deal about the rude and overbearing manners of Prussian officials, and surely this was an occasion on which I might fairly have expected some unpleasantness. I put these officers to a good deal of trouble, and I must have been a horrid nuisance to them; but they showed no signs of impatience and were as courteous as possible all the while. I had plenty more experience of German officialism in the course of this voyage, and I am inclined to believe that the British opinion on this subject is about as well-founded a prejudice as the French theory of our Smithfield wife-market.

An ex-man-of-war's-man, who spoke English well, found us out in the course of the afternoon. He told us that he was now a *schleusenwarter*, which I suppose signifies a dock-watchman. He was a very decent fellow and was of great use to us during our stay, showing us where the best stores were, acting as interpreter, and so on. He was no novice at this work, for when the British squadron was at Wilhelmshaven in '86 he took charge of all the stewards and piloted them in their marketings.

He took me round the town and showed me all that there was to be seen. Being a German, he was of course a well-instructed man; he had the history of Wilhelmshaven at his finger's ends and was better than any guide-book. He pointed out to me some old man-of-war hulks that had been purchased from the English Government, among others the *Renown*, which had last seen service in the Crimean War, and to my surprise he related to me her whole previous career. This well-informed person, when off duty, used to come on board of us in the evening and yarn over his pipe. He was well up in all the latest English news. He described to us the Jubilee festivities and the yacht race round the British Isles; he discoursed to us on the Irish Question. Germans belonging to classes which with us know and care nothing about what is

11 *

going on in other countries than their own, take a lively interest in the current history of the entire world, and, what is more, can discuss foreign matters with intelligence. This dock-watchman had followed the careers of our principal statesmen and he knew quite as much about our ex-premier's policy as most Englishmen do; but this is after all a doubtful compliment to his knowledge.

But the subject which he had read up most carefully of late, and of which he was never weary of talking, was the Jubilee. He and all the other Germans I came across appeared to be excessively gratified at the way in which the Crown Prince had been received in England. Even the most insignificant German papers were printing long quotations from the English press which testified to the popularity of their future king with our people. The result is that a most kindly feeling towards us has been aroused. I found the same favourable impression in Denmark and Holland. The Jubilee has brought about much goodwill and sympathy between the races nearest allied to us and ourselves, and there can be little doubt that it has served a far higher purpose than that of a mere costly pageant, as some foolish cynics would have us believe it.

I was told that the deserted harbour in which the *Falcon* was lying was the old Torpedo Haven, now abandoned on account of the rapidity with which it silts up and the consequent heavy dredging expenses. But this is the only tidal harbour here that affords shelter from all winds, and vessels drawing more than

five feet have either to remain at anchor outside
or to enter the docks and pay heavy dues. At low
water the *Falcon* was here left high and dry for several
hours.

For three days it blew a whole gale of wind from
north-west to north-east, so we once again remained
weather-bound in port, reviling our persistent ill-luck.
Readers will begin to look on Wright and myself as a
couple of very timid mariners, so often do I chronicle
delays in consequence of foul weather and so much
have I to say about the perils of the North Sea. But
this was an exceptionally stormy season on this coast,
and to show that we did not shirk the open sea without good reason I may mention that while we were in
Wilhelmshaven there was lying at anchor off the back
of the town, where shelter is afforded from off-sea
winds, a considerable fleet of coasters weather-bound
like ourselves. Many of these schooners and ketches
had been here nearly a month, and as the skippers and
crews are generally part owners and share profits, they
would not be inclined to lose freights by unnecessary
delay. These vessels were all far bigger than the
Falcon, and though Wright and myself should be the
last to say so, were most probably quite as weatherly
craft as our own. Some had leeboards like the Dutchmen and hailed from the Elbe and Weser, others were
of deeper draught and heavier tonnage, that traded
between the Baltic and North Sea by way of the Eider
Canal.

The dock-watchman, who was a Hanoverian, told

me that the wind usually blows from the sea on this bleak coast during the winter, spring, and early summer, and that the only fine and warm season is the autumn, when south and south-west winds prevail.

On the evening of the 7th the wind moderated and one of the weather-bound schooners got under weigh. I was about to follow her example, but the watchman dissuaded me from doing so.

"She is a stranger," he said, "and has never been here before. Her skipper belongs to Lubeck. He is making a mistake and you will see that he won't be able to get outside. He will be obliged to run back here to-night."

My friend was quite correct in his surmise; the wind freshened again in the afternoon, and on the following morning we saw the schooner lying at her old anchorage.

"You can't feel in here how hard it is blowing at sea," he explained, "but I know what it is doing by the height of the water outside the dock-gate. So long as there is a strong wind from this quarter in the North Sea the water is piled up in the Jade."

But on the 8th the weather improved considerably and the glass rose steadily. At mid-day the clouds were travelling from the south-west, so once more I was impatient to be off.

"Not to-day, Captain," said our mentor. "To-morrow you can sail. You must always give the sea twenty-four hours to calm down before you start for the Eider from here. You have to cross the banks, where the water is very rough unless the deep sea outside is almost smooth."

A glance at the chart showed me that this was a precaution not to be overlooked. Sailing from the Jade to the Eider one is always in very shallow water though out of sight of land, and the tides are very strong; so the sea breaks dangerously, on very little provocation, over these extensive shoals and ever-shifting channels.

At three o'clock on the morning of the 9th of July I turned out and saw that the wind was south-east and that the day was breaking with an appearance that promised fine weather; but the glass had fallen two tenths in the night and was still going down.

However, the wind was fair for the present and off shore, and I knew that if we wasted this chance we might have to wait a week or more for another one; so I decided on an attempt to fetch the port of Tonning on the Eider before the bad weather came on again. This was a run of only eighty English miles, and with ordinary luck we ought to accomplish it before dusk. I awoke Wright and we got under weigh at once.

This was a somewhat curious voyage, for after we left the Jade we saw no land until we were well into the estuary of the Eider, and yet we never were in more than two fathoms of water, often in very much less, and were at times crossing shallows which are left high and dry at low tide. Our route was very well marked by buoys and beacons and the sky was clear, in fact too clear, for when the sun's rays do fall powerfully on these cold waters a thin haze rises, accompanied by a peculiarly dazzling glare that makes it difficult to distinguish any object until one is close to it.

Our luck seemed to have changed at last, for this day we experienced neither calm nor storm, but a fresh and favourable breeze which carried us along at a good pace. As there was no rough water on the banks, we were enabled to shorten our distance considerably by cutting great corners across the sands at high water, and we were generally quite out of the track of other vessels. From the mouth of the Jade we steered for the tower on the Rother shoals, a signal-station standing among the quicksands off the mouth of the Weser. Great difficulties were overcome in the construction of this tower; after many endeavours the engineers almost despaired of finding solid ground, and on one occasion, after it was supposed that a substantial foundation had been prepared, the whole of the massive masonry sank bodily into the treacherous bottom.

From here we sailed across the mouth of the Elbe, where we crossed the path of many craft of all nations and sizes, that were bound to and from Hamburg and other ports of that mighty stream. We could trace the channel by the double procession of craft, but of the land itself nothing could yet be seen.

Thence, feeling our way with the lead, we passed over the sands by the Suder Piep and the Norder Piep, and at 3 P.M. we reached the beacons at the mouth of the Eider, and, altering our course, steered from buoy to buoy towards the shore. Soon we saw land ahead of us, no longer low and flat, but the undulating hills of Schleswig.

For some hours we had heard distant thunder, the glass had fallen a good deal more since the morning, and now dark clouds were rising over the sea. We were almost in sight of our port, but it began to look as if we were destined not to get in there after all, and I began to think of Vanderdecken again; for the channel we had to follow across the shoals now began to take a south-easterly direction, so that we had to tack, and as the tide was running out strongly we could make no way and soon found that we were going astern.

It was a very exposed place to anchor in and bad weather was coming on, but there was no help for it.

" Our usual luck, Wright," I cried. " Down with the head-sails. We'll have to bring up here till the tide turns, or rather till to-morrow, for we can't find our way up the Eider in the dark."

And now a remarkable thing happened. Even as I spoke, and as Wright was about to take in the jib, there came a terrific peal of thunder.

" Hullo!" he cried. " Look out, Sir; here it comes."

I turned round and perceived a squall of wind and rain rushing across the sea towards us with a hissing sound.

" Scandalize the mainsail, Wright!"

No sooner said than it was done, and the next moment the squall was on us and we were scudding fast before it. The squall was from the south-west, which I knew was a fair wind for us to Tonning. Here was, indeed, a piece of luck. We had carried the southeast wind behind us all the way up the coast, and now, at the very moment when we had to alter our course, round had run the wind to the direction we needed to drive us up the estuary against the tide.

We felt very jubilant. The wind freshened and the sea got up and another dirty night was evidently coming on, but we cared nothing for all that now. Every gust was hurrying us towards safe shelter; the storm was exactly what we wanted. Soon we had sand-banks dry or just awash on either side of us, and the channel became narrow and winding, so that the water was almost smooth.

"We're just in time, as usual, Sir," cried Wright, laughing, as he looked back towards the open sea we had left behind us, already leaping in angry white-capped waves.

We were, indeed, just in time; had we been an hour or so later we should have found it highly unpleasant, if not dangerous, on those perilous shoals.

At last we passed the sands and had genuine dry land on either side of us, with green hills, trees, and houses, and at five o'clock we came to an anchor in Tonning roads after a fourteen hours' pleasant voyage.

It rained so hard that I did not go on shore that evening to explore the town. The yacht tumbled about a good deal during the night, for these roads are quite exposed to the south-west wind, and the sea, though broken by the shoals outside, was very choppy. But we heeded not the weather now; we thoroughly enjoyed our dinner of bacon and potatoes, and smoked our pipes afterwards in a very happy frame of mind; for at last we had done with our persistent foe the North Sea. We were practically in the Baltic; we were no more to be weather-bound in dismal places for days at a time; in short, our troubles were over and our real and enjoyable cruise was to commence.

CHAPTER IX.

KIEL BAY.

WHEN I awoke the next morning, after dreaming that I was lying weather-bound for ages in some desolate bay of Friesland, and realised where I was, I experienced a keen sense of relief and satisfaction. It was Sunday the 10th of July, a hot and fine day; but as there was no longer any necessity for making use of every rare spell of decent weather, and as, moreover, the wind was still south-west, and therefore unfavourable for the ascent of the river, I decided to take a holiday and remain where I was till the morrow.

We brought up our wet clothes and bedding and hung them up to dry in the sun, and after breakfast I set sail in the dinghy and went forth to explore. I perceived an English steamer discharging coal on the other side of the river, so I first sailed over to her in the hope of borrowing some home papers. She hailed from the Tyne and had a Scotch captain and a crew of big Geordies. The captain lent me several papers a fortnight old and then accompanied me on shore.

Tonning is a pleasant-looking, old-fashioned town of 4,000 inhabitants, who show more traces of Danish blood than I had expected to find in the south of Schleswig. Most of its houses seem to have been built about two hundred years ago, and many of them have gardens full of fine roses, which were now in full bloom. Nearly everyone we met spoke English, but none of the custom-house officers could do so; curiously enough I found this to be the case in all the German ports I visited.

We entered a *café* in the quaint old market-place. We found no one in it, but soon a tall, graceful, and very good-looking young lady came in to serve us with beakers of Rendsburg beer. The skipper and myself were expressing our admiration of this very charming person and remarking upon the great superiority, in point of figure, of the women of Denmark over their sisters in the Teutonic and the other Scandinavian nations, when her eyes flashed with a lively amusement, and she said, with a quiet smile, " I understand what you say, gentlemen."

I do not think she was offended at the very respectful praise we had been giving expression to. She was the daughter of the host, who now appeared on the scene, a jolly old chap who had fought as an officer against Prussia in 1864. She was a well-educated girl, and had been a governess in good families both in London and Brighton. Her English friends had sent her the Jubilee numbers of the *Graphic* and *Illustrated London News*, which she was able to lend us. She said that Tonning was a very quiet town, but that in the autumn steamers left here several times a week with cattle fattened on the surrounding marshes, for England. But this trade, she told us, was now falling off, as meat had become so cheap in England that it did not pay to export it. This was, indeed, news to me, and I made a note to talk the matter over with my very affable but not little-charging butcher on my return to London. When we rose with reluctance to bid farewell to our agreeable hostess, she took us into the garden and presented us each with a bouquet of magnificent roses.

In the afternoon Wright and myself called at a butcher's, a baker's, and a grocer's to lay in stores. In each we were served by young women who had acquired the English language in London. It seems as if it is the custom for all the girls of Tonning to complete their education in our country.

In the night there was half a gale of wind from the south-west and heavy rain, so we again tumbled about merrily at our anchorage.

The next stage of our journey was a pleasant and interesting sail up the river Eider and the Schleswig-Holstein canal to the Bay of Kiel. This waterway between the North Sea and the Baltic, whereby the long and stormy voyage round the Skaw is avoided, is unfortunately not practicable for vessels of much more than one hundred tons burden, for the river is very winding and of little depth, and the evershifting sand-banks that obstruct the mouth of the Eider cannot be crossed by any but shallow craft. No vessel of more than ten feet draught can take this short cut across the peninsula. But the new canal, now in course of construction, from the Eider to the Elbe, will admit even large men-of-war, and is destined to be one of the most important shipcanals in the world.

The distance from the mouth of the Eider to Kiel Bay is, as the crow flies, rather more than fifty miles, but so tortuous is the route by river and canal that I imagine it must be double that distance. The canal itself is only twenty miles long and joins the river about six miles above Rendsburg. The tide flows as far as this last-mentioned town, where the first sluice is met. There are altogether six sluices, each one hundred feet long, and the greatest altitude attained is twenty-five feet above the level of the Baltic.

At mid-day, July 11th, when the flood was just beginning to make, we weighed anchor. Our luck had indeed changed. The wind had followed us all the way up the coast from Wilhelmshaven, had then considerably altered its direction to help us up to Tonning, and now it turned round to the north-west—the fairest wind possible for a vessel bound from here to Rendsburg.

It blew hard and the squalls were often severe. We scudded along fast and soon reached the little town of Friedrichstadt, where a railway-bridge spans the river. This bridge, the only one between the sea and Rendsburg, is built at a sharp bend of the river, and the tide runs under it with great velocity and in an oblique direction, so that sailing-vessels have difficulty in passing safely through the narrow opening left by the swinging portion of the bridge. In consequence of this, the railway company is compelled to keep a tug always ready under steam to help vessels through free of charge. The bridge was open when we approached, and as we had the wind right aft we did not need the steam-boat's services.

After sailing some miles through a monotonous flat country of marshy pasture, we entered a region of low hills, among which the river, now much narrower, took a very winding course. The scenery appeared very charming after the artificial level landscapes of Holland. We were no longer hemmed in by regular dykes, but the woods and grassy slopes came down to the water's edge. Comfortable-looking old farmhouses, with high thatched roofs, nestled among the beech trees and called to mind the homesteads of our own west country. This was evidently a rich pastoral district, and the people appeared happy and well-to-do. Great numbers of sleek cattle were in the rich pastures, and vast flocks of geese marched along the tow-path under the command of urchins. The day, though windy, was sunny and warm, so the haymakers were busy on the banks, a jolly lot of fellows who addressed us cheerily in unknown tongues as we sailed by. We passed several small villages, each with its ferry-boat traversing the river on a chain, like the "grinds" at Cambridge. The scene was always lively and cheerful, and I soon came to the conclusion that the Eider is one of the pleasantest rivers in Europe for a yacht cruise.

"Hullo! look there, Sir. What's that great bird on the bank?" cried Wright suddenly. It was a stork standing on one leg and gazing at us with an expression of profound melancholy. Then it flashed upon me that we were in the land of storks, and as a student of Hans Andersen I should have remembered this before. We saw many more of these birds in the course of the day; they were always alone. The stork seems to be a very meditative bird and fond of solitude.

We passed a good many vessels, schooners and ketches of about ninety tons, clumsy-looking craft with lofty square sterns, but very handy; they turned to windward in the narrow reaches of the river as smartly as a Thames barge will. Those coming from the Baltic were generally laden with timber, those from Bremen and Hamburg with coffee, sugar, and other colonial produce.

The wind was abaft us most of the way, but in consequence of the windings of the river we were often reaching or tacking. We carried the flood with us for nine hours, and we sailed on, with no mishap save that we once missed stays and ran ashore on a hayfield, until nine in the evening, when we came to an anchor near a picturesque old farm. Having no chart or map of this river, I had no idea where we were, and did not much care, for there are no dangers on the Eider, and pilot directions are not wanted. It was a perfectly calm night, and it was pleasant to hear round us the lowing of cattle, the song of nightingales, and the chirping of crickets for a change, instead of the howling of wind and the dashing of waves.

I was awakened early the next morning by the cackling of hens and other noises of the farm-yard, and turning out I found that a cloudless sky was overhead and a light south-west wind was blowing. The haymakers were already at work in the fields, and the milk-maids were bustling about with their wooden pails. We got under weigh after breakfast and sailed to Rendsburg, which we reached early in the afternoon. This is a fortified town of about thirteen thousand inhabitants, quite as old-fashioned and quaint as Tonning, but far more lively and interesting. The remains of an old castle dominate the town, and a considerable Prussian garrison is now stationed here.

We made fast to the quay close to the sluice and remained here for the night. A crowd, as usual, gathered on the quay to stare at us; but the children did not annoy us at all. German boys are not so rough and troublesome as the Dutch, in fact I consider them to be the most staid youngsters in Europe. They are so hard-worked at school, and such massive learning is driven into their young heads, that they have little life and energy left for mischief. If boys had any voice in the matter, they would refuse to be born in Germany.

I reported myself to the Custom-house and paid the canal dues, which amounted to ninepence. A large ketch that had entered the Eider the same day as ourselves, came in shortly after us and brought up alongside. I chummed up with her skipper and we repaired to a public-house he knew of, whose host was one of those English-speaking ex-sea-captains, who seem to compose half of the population of these countries. He told me that many English yachts used to pass through the canal some twenty years ago, and that it was very rare to see one now. He said that a yacht flying the German flag, but in charge of an English skipper and crew, had been in Rendsburg the day before. She was drawing too much water for the canal, so it was found necessary to take all her ballast out. She had chartered a steamer to tow her to the Baltic while the ballast followed astern in the boats. I afterwards discovered that this was an English-built yacht, the *Carlotta*, which had been purchased by a German officer resident at Kiel, and that she was about to race at the Kiel regatta on the 24th. She is a fast boat, and I believe she carried off the first prize.

The skipper of the ketch told me that he had come from Bremen, where he had been weather-bound by the north-west wind for three weeks. Nearly all the profits of the voyage had been eaten up by this delay, for his freight was only five marks a ton, and out of this he had to pay a mate and three hands, and meet heavy dues.

The next morning, July the 14th, we were off at seven. This was another glorious day; and if I was charmed with the country we had traversed so far, I now became enthusiastic in my admiration. Few rivers can show such a succession of lovely scenes as the Eider above Rendsburg.

We passed through the sluice and then found that the river widens into a lake-like expanse at the back of the town, bordered with trees and presenting a very picturesque appearance. So fine a piece of water in the vicinity of an English town would be crowded with pleasure craft; here there were but a few skiffs and no sailing boats. There is no doubt about the English being far ahead of all other European peoples in what the Germans call the water-sport. Even in such maritime countries as Holland, Denmark, and North Germany the most glorious facilities for yachting are almost totally neglected.

After this the river narrowed, but to open out again shortly into a far more extensive lake of very clear water, surrounded by hills whose abrupt outlines made them appear far higher than they really were. It was a beautiful scene; the water, scarcely ruffled by the light breeze, lay blue under the cloudless sky; the hills, save in places where there were miniature precipices, were clothed either with woods or green pastures. At one corner of the lake was a pretty little village nestling among the trees. There were not many habitations elsewhere on the shores, and but few signs of man's presence, but of other life there was no lack. There were many well-fed cattle standing on the shingle beach by the water's edge; the air was full of birds; white swans were floating on the water; and the fish were jumping all round us. As I had no map of it, and had thought that the Eider would probably prove as uninteresting as a Dutch canal, it was very delightful to come thus unexpectedly on so beautiful a country.

I should recommend that village at the corner of the lake as a good place for a jaded man from the town to pass his holiday in. He is certain to find some cosy little inn there, and with a sailing-boat, a fishing-rod, and a few books, he might dream away a summer's month very pleasantly. Those sailing men, too, who wax so enthusiastic over the Norfolk Broads, should try this water. The cattle boat from London would carry a small centre-board boat on her deck to Tonning, and the voyage thence to Kiel will be found superior to anything that can be done on the narrow rivers and shallow pools of East Anglia. I may mention that between Rendsburg and the Baltic there is no perceptible current, and there are only three bridges to pass through.

We sailed on, now up the winding stream, now across other Brednings—the local name for Broad—lying under the smiling hills. Later on, the river became much narrower, but was no less beautiful. It flowed between steep high banks covered with timber. We were crossing what appeared to be a more thinly populated district, and there were few signs of cultivation, but it was a region of luxuriant wild vegetation. Honeysuckles, dog-roses, and other flowers in profusion were growing at the lower edge of the woods, scenting all the river. Tall bulrushes bordered the water, and we were often forcing our way through the white water-lilies that floated on the surface. The larks and other birds were singing merrily above us, and the bees were busy among the honeysuckles; and for almost the first time this year there was a genuine appearance of summer around us.

We had plenty of exercise on this journey, for when the wind headed us, as it often did, we took it in turns to tramp along the tow-path and tow the yacht—no light weight—and as the wind died away altogether in the afternoon this was our only means of progressing for nearly five hours; it was very hot work, and the gnats worried the man with the tow-line terribly. We passed through two more sluices, at both of which the guardian was, of course, an old sailor who could speak English, and at eight o'clock we went through the first bridge we had seen since leaving Rendsburg; it closed behind us, and then, hot, tired, and very ready for supper and bed, we made fast to the bank close to a schooner laden with bricks.

Soon a young man came down and talked to us a good deal in his own language. He pointed to our warps and went through an unintelligible pantomime, but we could make nothing of him till of a sudden

Wright called out, "Didn't he say 'pert' then, Sir? Why, that's something like the Dutch word for a horse!"

Of course! How stupid I was not to have recognised the word over which I had puzzled so long at Assen. No doubt "pert" was the Low German equivalent; so, calling to mind how our Dutch towing-man had conveyed his meaning to us, I brought out paper and pencil and made a rough sketch of a horse. I showed it to him. He knew at once what it was intended for. "Jah, jah! pert," he exclaimed in a delighted voice, nodding his head in the affirmative. Then, by pointing to the sky, by pantomime and by diagram, I endeavoured to explain to him that if the wind was not fair for us on the morrow we would be happy to engage his pert, otherwise we would dispense with his services. I believe he understood me; at any rate he went away seemingly contented.

We rose at six on July the 14th. It was another fine sunny day, and the wind was south-west, so we did not take the young man's pert, but got away under sail. At ten we reached the fourth sluice, and found that we had now attained the highest point on the canal; for at this lock we were lowered about ten feet. In another hour we passed through the fifth sluice, which is at a hamlet called Knoop. This was a lovely neighbourhood; magnificent beech-trees overshadowed the canal; and the manor-house, with its park and its gardens sloping to the water, called to mind some of the summer-palaces on the upper Thames. There is a pleasant beer-garden, too, under the trees at Knoop, for this sweet spot is a favourite resort of the citizens of Kiel.

At one o'clock we passed through the last sluice, and shortly afterwards we came to the village of Holtenau, where the canal opens into the sea. We sailed out into the salt water and were in the Baltic at last.

Before us lay the beautiful fiord of Kiel, surrounded by hills covered with beech woods, and about two miles up the fiord were visible the roofs and shipping of Germany's greatest naval station.

The fiord looked more like a lake than an inlet of the sea, and this we found to be the case with all the fiords on the coast; for the water of the Baltic is extremely clear, and it contains so much less salt than that of other seas that it nourishes a rank aquatic growth which rises to the surface of the shallows and much resembles the long weeds that choke some of our English rivers. Again the range of the tide is so small —a few inches in the Southern Baltic—that the trees and other vegetation grow to the very edge of the sea; and despite the rigorous climate there is a luxuriance in the plant life on the Eastern slopes of the Cimbrian peninsula that recalls tropical shores.

What a change was this after the North Sea! Here we would never have to trouble our heads about tides and currents; instead of coasting along dangerous shallows out of sight of land we could now sail for a thousand miles and always remain within a stone's throw of the shore, and in water so lucid that it would never be necessary to sound, a glance over the side would tell the depth; for here all the rocks and weeds at the bottom are clearly visible when many fathoms below a vessel's keel.

We tacked up the bay, and after passing many enviable country seats came to as pretty a suburb as any city in Europe can boast of. Here, embowered in fine trees, were the villas of great merchants, each with its lawn and well-tended flower-garden sloping to the tideless sea, and each with its little landing-stage at which a pleasure-boat was moored. The next thing that struck my attention was a nice-looking restaurant on the shore, with a large garden in front of it, in which an excellent band was playing to a crowd of well-dressed people, who were sitting over coffee or bocks of beer in the admirable German fashion.

This was just the sort of cheerful place I liked to anchor off, and as I saw that several small yachts were moored about here, and as the centre of the town could be little over a mile away, I thought it better to bring up where I was than to sail on to the commercial harbour. We let go our anchor some thirty yards from the shore, and I quickly put myself into shore-going apparel, for I was anxious to get my letters which had been waiting for me here more than a month. I hoisted the sail in the dinghy and tacked towards the restaurant. On the way I passed a yacht, which proved to be the *Carlotta*. Her English skipper had watched us coming in. "I did not expect to see a small boat flying the Royal Thames burgee out here," he shouted out as I went by him. I landed at the restaurant landing-stage, and while enjoying a bock of cool lager I was informed by the waiter that this was the Folker's Garten and that trams for Kiel passed the gate every few minutes.

I was driven to the town through an avenue of beautiful trees—Kiel is full of beautiful trees—and found my letters at the British Consul's. Then I set out to explore the streets. There is always something very fascinating in a first stroll through a strange city, but especially so when one has just landed from a little yacht in which one has been roughing it for some time. This sudden plunge into luxury and civilisation gives a charm to travelling that the railway-tourist can scarcely appreciate. The yachtsman too is in such rude health and high spirits that he is ready to enjoy everything keenly; and even the change from jersey and rough sea clothes to white shirt and decent apparel produces a sense of comfort and happy Jack-ashorishness that lends further zest to his amusements.

I found Kiel one of the pleasantest places I visited this year; but for what there is to do and see in it I refer my readers to the books of Baedeker. I stayed here three days, and I did not find the time hang heavy. When I wearied of the streets I sailed in the dinghy about the fiord and among the German men-of-war in the harbour. There were many fine vessels here at the time, but I could not quite fancy the German men-of-war's men, though they are no doubt excellent sailors. Militarism can perhaps go too far. One can put up with railway-porters, postmen, and other landsmen being uniformed and drilled to resemble soldiers; but to an Englishman's taste a sailor should be allowed to look like a sailor, and not be goose-stepped till he has the stiff bearing of a guardsman. The slouching ease of our own blue-jackets seems more appropriate for one whose profession it is to tumble about the seas. There was a Chinese man-of-war in Kiel. Her men did not look like either sailors or soldiers; after thinking it over some time I cannot say what they did look like.

On the morning after our arrival I was reading an English paper in the cabin, when I was startled by a sound that was very familiar, but the last I should have expected to hear in Kiel Fiord. Had I been dreaming, or was I still lying off the Doves at Hammersmith? It was a human voice screaming and cursing in the purest Thames tow-path dialect, reckless of aspirates, rich in horrible invective. It was a Cockney addressing men whom he called respectively Five, Four, Three and so on as if they were so many convicts. He was urging them in impassioned language not to feather under water, to keep their something eyes in the boat, not to sugar, and to do or to avoid doing several other things. How often had I been bullied in a similar fashion by a similar tyrant on the Cam! I leapt on deck and lo! there was a genuine racing four pulling by! There were several other fours and funnies on the bay, and it was evident that the "Wasser-sport" was much patronised at Kiel.

I afterwards learnt that the rowing regatta was soon

coming off, so all the rowing men were in training, and this particular crew of young Germans had imported a professional coach from the Thames to teach them how to row. They were very enthusiastic and plodding, but the coach with all his skill and blasphemy could not drive any real style into them. It seems strange that the North Germans, well set-up as they are physically, can never approach the English in any athletic sport.

"It's all that d—d lager they drink," said a professional oarsman, who had been to Hamburg, to me; "it swells them out till they're all wool and flabbiness."

The Kiel rowing men made a good deal of their tutor, admired him greatly, and bore his fearful language with patience. They wanted to learn rowing at any cost, and they had been led to understand that it was quite impossible to become a true English wassersportsman unless one has been well cursed through one's apprenticeship.

Our berth opposite the Folker's Garten was certainly the best we could have selected in Kiel Bay. The gate of the garden is open all night, so that I could leave my dinghy at the landing-stage and return on board at any hour. It is possible that I ran some risk in doing this, for several boats on hire are moored to this landing-stage, and the University students have a habit, after a heavy kneipe, of coming down here at three in the morning and going away with the first boat they find, to take a sail on the bay and cool their fevered brows.

The University of Kiel is famous for its school of medicine. Of an evening, when the band played, there were generally a good many of the students in the Folker's Garten. I had never before seen German students at home, and they struck me as being somewhat swaggering young gentlemen. Many of them, especially those who had no good looks to lose, proudly carried on their faces the ornamental scars of their duels.

At sunset the scene from our yacht's deck was always an animated one. The gardens were illuminated, and pleasure-boats glided round us, usually containing pretty and well-dressed girls, who amused themselves by burning coloured fires while their husbands or brothers or others took the oars.

The narrow locks of the Dutch canals had taken a good deal of the varnish off the *Falcon's* sides, and she was beginning to look very disreputable, so before proceeding on the voyage I took the yacht back to Holtenau and laid her alongside the canal bank for two days, while Wright and myself set to work scraping, cleaning, varnishing, and painting till she looked quite smart again.

And now, having reached the Baltic, I had to decide whither we were to journey next, not an easy task, for a great choice of delightful cruises lay before me. I studied the charts, and longed to explore all the deep-winding fiords of these seas. There was Liim Fiord, in the North of Jutland, the largest and most interesting of all. There was the Gota Canal, which would take me through lakes Wenern and Wettern to Stockholm. There was Lubeck and the coast of North Germany, Dantzig and the Vistula—how splendid it would be to sail up the Vistula to Warsaw! Then there were the lakes of Finland, St. Petersburg, and—but I was too ambitious, and I sighed as I remembered that the end of July was near, that my holiday was almost finished, and that I had no time to carry out even the least of the above projects.

I realised that it would be impossible for me to see much of the Baltic and sail back to England this year; so I gave up all idea of taking the boat home and made up my mind to cruise about these waters as long as I was able, and then to lay her up for the winter in some convenient place to which I would return the following summer and complete my voyage.

My intention was to sail to Copenhagen, not directly, but by a circuitous route through the Little Belt into the Kattegat, and so to the Sound. I should thus see some of the most beautiful coast scenery of Schleswig, Jutland, and Zealand.

CHAPTER X.

THE FIORDS OF SCHLESWIG.

WE set sail at six in the morning of June the 20th. It was not a pleasant day, the wind had got round to the north-west, it was cold and squally and the rain fell steadily. We found the climate of the Baltic to be even more changeable than that of the coast of Hanover. One day it is hot as at Marseilles in August, the next, a blustering north-wester brings with it the bitter weather of an English March at its worst. We soon discovered that whenever the wind means mischief in these seas it shifts to the north-west. We never encountered bad weather from any other quarter. Another discovery we soon made was that a dangerous sea can get up in the Baltic with extraordinary rapidity. This is without doubt not only due to the shallowness of the water but also to the small proportion of salt contained in it. A well-pickled ocean is always more sluggish than a fresh-water lake.

But the north-wester could not do us much harm

during the first portion of the journey before us; for we would be generally coasting northwards with the main-land to the east of us, so were not likely to encounter unpleasantly rough seas except at the entrances to the fiords.

We sailed down the long bay of Kiel and doubled Bulk Point, which forms the extremity of the promontory known as the Danish Wold. Here the land trends in a north-west direction to the mouth of Eckernford Fiord, and we had a dead beat to windward. As the wind was blowing at us across eight miles of open water the sea was very choppy; we ran our nose into the short waves, smothered the yacht with water, and made very little way. After tumbling about for several hours we came off Nienhof Point. I had hoped to reach Slimunde before night; but seeing that this was impossible with a head wind, I altered my plans and sailed up Eckernford Fiord. This inlet of the sea is eleven miles long and three broad; at the head of it is the little town of the same name and an excellent harbour protected from all winds.

We crossed to the north shore in order to get into smooth water; but our luck was bad this day; the wind now shifted to the west and blew straight down the fiord, so that we had to turn to windward all the way to our port.

We came to the conclusion that if all the Danish fiords resembled this one we should be very content. Here was a noble sheet of water surrounded by grassy or wooded hills, while the red roofs of scattered farm-houses relieved the sombre tints of the pine forests with touches of bright colour here and there. For us there was deep water up to either shore, and we never went about till we could clearly distinguish the white sands and rocks, the weeds and anemones at the bottom. Like all bays of the Baltic, this one swarmed with brilliantly-coloured jelly-fish.

We came to an anchor off Eckernforde at five o'clock. Seen from the sea this town has a somewhat dishevelled and repelling appearance. The reason is that, unlike most sea-side places, it turns its back to the water. The fronts of the houses on the beach look inland, and we were gazing at a waste of blank back-walls relieved only by clothes hanging out to dry in dingy yards, dust-heaps, and the other unlovely household gods which are usually put out of sight in the rear of a dwelling. The shore itself was untended and had no road along it, but was covered with stacks of timber, hundreds of fishing-nets stretched on stakes, and rubbish of every description. The back view of Eckernforde certainly does not give the approaching mariner a high idea of the cleanliness or tidiness of its citizens; there was, however, a charm in all this slovenliness to one who had been so long tortured by the Dutch craze in the opposite direction.

But one may go too far even in uncleanliness, as I very soon found out. A creek pierces the heart of this town and forms a commodious haven along whose quays lie many fishing-boats—clumsy open craft rigged with three masts and sprit-sails. After dinner I sailed up this haven in the dinghy, and soon became aware of a peculiar and horrible smell. I was puzzled to account for this at first, as the water beneath me was absolutely pellucid; but happening to look over the side I perceived that the bottom was of a glittering white as if it had been paved with a mixture of silver and chalk. A closer examination showed me that thousands of dead herrings and other fish were lying there, and had no doubt been cast overboard by the fishermen as useless. Later on when it was dark I saw that the water was brilliantly lit up with the phosphorescence thrown out by this decaying matter. As there is no perceptible current in the harbour this custom seemed, to put it mildly, a rather unhygienic one, and I began to understand how it was that outbreaks of cholera have proved so deadly on the shores of the tideless Baltic.

I walked through the town, but did not find it interesting. The streets are broad and some of the houses pretentious in appearance, but there were very few people to be seen abroad, and those not of the well-to-do classes. There was a dejected and shabby air about the place like that of a town that has seen better days.

The next morning a strong north-west wind was blowing, and the climate was more wintry than ever. On consulting the chart I found that we could sail under shelter of the shore as far as Slimunde, which was twenty miles distant; but that beyond that lay the broad mouth of Flensborg Fiord, across which a heavy sea would certainly be running. So we weighed anchor at 10 A.M., bound for the Slei. When we got outside Eckernforde Fiord the wind, as usual heading us, veered to the north of north-west, so that we could not lay up the coast close-hauled on the port tack, but had to take a short leg inshore occasionally, in order to keep close under the land and avoid the tumbling seas farther out.

We passed by a hilly and wooded coast till about mid-day, when we skirted a low marshy country, which extended as far as Slimunde. At two o'clock we saw our port in front of us. It did not look an imposing place, consisting as it did of two houses and a lighthouse. When we came opposite to it we found that the entrance to the Slei was between two piers so very near together that tacking in between them was an awkward task even for our small craft. We got safely inside, and then entered an extensive lagoon, where we let go our anchor.

The scene was a strange and desolate one. A large expanse of shallow water, noisy with the doleful cries of multitudes of sea-mews, lay before us. It was bordered by swamps and sands on two sides, and, on the side farthest inland, by a flat well-wooded country. Long dark-green or brown weeds floated everywhere on the surface of the lagoon, adding to the gloom of its appearance. In every direction rose poles and booms indicating the channels across the shallows, and also an extraordinary number of stakes running in parallel ranges, with withies interlaced between them, which

13 *

are used by the herring fishermen for their nets. The only houses we could see were those I have mentioned as standing by the pier, and the only other vessel here besides ourselves was a German revenue cutter. The only human beings visible were two men who had waved directions to me as I sailed in.

Of all the inlets of this coast the Slei is the most remarkable in its configuration. It is the longest of the Schleswig fiords; but, unlike the others, it does not open out into the sea by a broad gulf but by a channel only eighty yards in width, the original entrance having silted up. The length of the Slei from the mouth to Schleswig is thirty English miles; it forms a succession of narrows and lakes, the largest of which is the Store Bredning near Schleswig.

Having stowed the sails, I pulled off to the pier to call on the two inhabitants of this lonely place. I discovered that they both spoke English. Of the two houses I had seen, one was a hotel and the other the pilot station, and one of these men was landlord of the first, while the other was one of the pilots resident in the second. I was surprised to find the hotel quite a capacious and luxurious establishment; for several German families come each summer to this healthy spot, where they can live at a very moderate rate and enjoy excellent sea-bathing. About a mile farther up the coast there is a little row of lodging-houses for the accommodation of the visitors.

The only family now staying at the hotel was that of a merchant from Hamburg; but his progeny was numerous enough for several average families. He of course spoke English, and we quickly struck up an acquaintance over the usual bock of beer. He had hired a little fishing-boat, in which he went out every day fishing with his wife and children. He was a wise man, for he evidently did not miss his clubs and town society, but was enjoying his holiday in this quiet place as keenly as the boys themselves.

He told me that I ought to visit Mæsholm, a little island that was divided from us by two miles of shallow water overgrown with weeds. This island lies at the old entrance of the fiord, and is exclusively inhabited by fishermen, who form a race apart like the people of Urk and Marken. Here they still keep up the customs of their forefathers, and speak the Danish language. As these islanders will not intermarry with the inhabitants of the main-land they are all related to each other. There are only four or five surnames among them, and as the number of Christian names deemed by them orthodox are also limited in number, it comes that many people have the same names and so have to be distinguished by nicknames expressive of some personal or other quality. For instance, there are thirty Peter Mass's here; and I saw a letter addressed to one in which he was described as, "He that is the eldest of the two Peter Mass's that have red hair." The duties of the Mæsholm postman must be arduous and sometimes delicate.

I pulled off to this queer island in the dinghy, and landed among a crowd of fishermen who were mending their nets. They looked at me with evident astonishment, for they perceived that both the dinghy and myself were foreigners; and they had not seen the yacht, so were naturally puzzled to know where I had fallen from. I was not surprised to find that one of these men had served on British vessels and spoke English. He piloted me up to the village, where he introduced me and told my tale to a number of honest fishermen, who gave me a hearty welcome.

The island is well-wooded and the village is a tidy, pretty little place. I entered the one inn, and soon some of the notables came to interview me. Among others was the schoolmaster, who spoke a little English acquired from books and not by practice, and therefore not very easy to understand. But he was very pleased to have an opportunity of speaking to an Englishman. He was a nice young fellow and remarkably well-educated for the dominie of a fishing-village. He discoursed to me on science, literature—he was a student of Shakespeare and Dickens—and contemporary politics. He told me that the fishermen were no longer as prosperous as they used to be. Some years back fifty ocean-going vessels belonged to the people of Mæsholm, but now they only owned fourteen. However, there is still a large fleet of small open herring-boats here, and some of the wealthier inhabitants own schooners; in these they sail up the fiord and purchase cheeses and other agricultural produce from the farmers, which they carry to Copenhagen for sale.

The fisherman who spoke English told me that his

brother kept the "Jolly Sailor" at Gravesend, and he made me promise to look in there when I was next in that port; "for," said he, "I don't suppose my brother ever meets anyone in England who can talk to him about Mæsholm."

The sun had set, and as I knew that it would be difficult to find my way in the dark through the labyrinth of herring-stakes and shoals that lay between me and the yacht, I rose to go. I first went to the village store, where everything useful can be bought, from a marline-spike to an onion, and purchased a quantity of eggs and potatoes, which I carried down to the dinghy. A crowd of friends accompanied me to the shore to bid me farewell. It was with regret that I left this jolly little island with its simple sturdy race of fishermen.

I reached the yacht, and after dinner examined the charts of the coast over my pipe. The plan of Slei Fiord so fascinated me, with its indications of winding lakes, woods, and islands, that I could not resist its temptation; and I decided not to put to sea the next day, but to leave Wright in charge of the *Falcon* while I made an expedition to Schleswig in the dinghy. As the journey was a long one—nearly sixty miles there and back—it would be necessary to start at day-break, so I made my preparations over night by boiling hard half a dozen eggs.

At 3 A.M., June 22nd, I put the needful stores into the dinghy, the eggs, bread, cheese, a bottle of rum and water, pipes, matches, and plenty of tobacco, a sketch-book and compass, and I did not forget to take a blanket in case I was benighted and had to sleep out.

The wind no longer howled from the north-west, it had shifted to the south-east and was very light, so that I had to take to the oars. I pulled across the lagoon towards the first narrow, passing several of the Mæsholm fishermen in their sprit-sail boats, with whom I exchanged greetings. The sun was just rising above the horizon as I left the broad water and entered the channel that leads to the town of Cappel. The water was beautifully clear and full of gorgeously-coloured jelly-fish. On either side were sloping lawns and woods of fir and beech, while picturesque wooden farm-houses, with tall thatched roofs, peeped out here and there from the rich foliage. It turned out to be a magnificent sunny summer's day, so the country looked at its best.

It is impossible to describe the peculiar charm of the scenery of these fiords. There is not here the wild grandeur of the fiords of Norway, but a soft and peaceful loveliness of which one never wearies. Word-pictures of these sweet landscapes could not fail to be monotonous to the reader; for they are all composed of the same elements—clear water, grassy slopes, and woods of fir and beech. But there is no monotony in the reality; each reach in a fiord presents some fresh feature of its own; and there is a great variety in the tints of both vegetation and water, a variety intensified by the ever changeful northern sky. The sea-coast of the Cim-

VILLAGE OF SLIEBY.

orian peninsula is to be understood and enjoyed in a boat and not to be described in books.

I pulled away under the hot sun and soon found that a current of some strength was running against me; for, though there is no perceptible tide in the Baltic, a strong wind will bring a current with it and cause the water to rise several feet in the narrow gulfs and sounds. Fed as it is by many great rivers, the Baltic has a tendency to flow into the North Sea, and it has been calculated that the current sets outward for five-sevenths of the year. But when the northwest wind has been blowing for some days a contrary effect is produced, and the waters of the German Ocean are driven into the land-locked sea. This had been the case for several days past, and, now that a calm had set in, the water was pouring out again and so causing the adverse current which I experienced.

I rowed by Cappel, a picturesque old town where the Slei narrows considerably and is traversed by a bridge of boats; by Arnis, where the Prussian troops forced the passage of the fiord in 1864 and routed the Danish army; and then came to the Lange Bredning, a fine sheet of water, where, the wind freshening, I was able to lay down the oars, set the sail, and admire the scenery at leisure for a time. The village of Slieby looked so pretty and inviting that I landed there and repaired to the inn for some beer. Here I found a lot of merry men, who, as far as I could make out, had just returned from a yeoman's wedding. These

Schleswiger farmers were fine-looking fellows, stalwart, clean of complexion, very English in appearance, as indeed were most of the people I came across in the course of this summer's voyage; for were not these regions the cradle of our race, and had I not been sailing along the coasts of the Saxons, Danes, Jutes, Frisians, and Angles, those brave and ferocious old pirates once the scourge of Christendom, whose descendants on the continent have for some strange reason become the most peaceful and amiable of all Europeans?

The jovial farmers insisted on my joining in their carouse, and we attempted conversation, but could not manage it. I was always meeting people who understood English on this cruise, yet in no previous wandering had I ever realised the curse of Babel so intensely. I know something of the Latin languages, so can get on tolerably well in Southern Europe. I have travelled among savages and semi-savages on the other continents without understanding a word of their tongues; but this enforced silence did not trouble me much, except when I wanted something to eat and did not know how to ask for it; for it was probable that their discourse would not be very amusing or interesting if it was intelligible. But now it seemed to me to be horrible and unnatural not to be able to hold intercourse with these pleasant people so nearly allied to ourselves by blood, whose habits so closely resemble our own, and between whose dialect and ours there is so slight but insuperable a difference. We could not talk together, but we could drink beer together, and we did so—there again in the love of beer our kinship showed itself; then I dragged myself away from my jovial friends and rowed on again under the hot sun, for I was yet only half-way to Schleswig.

After travelling for some hours through a succession of delightful scenes I came to the Store Bredning, a lake three miles broad; thence a short strait brought me into the Lille Bredning, a beautiful sheet of water, and there before me at last stood the ancient city of Schleswig. Its situation is exceedingly picturesque; it may be said to consist of one street, upwards of three miles in length, which is carried round a deep bay at the extreme end of the fiord, having for a background the spires of churches and the not beautiful ducal castle of Gottorp.

I had refreshed myself with sundry snacks of bread and cheese on the way, but my long journey had given me an appetite; so, as it was now two o'clock, before landing in the town, I sailed to a little island, anchored under its shade, and did justice to my hard-boiled eggs. I was surprised to find that this island, notwithstanding its proximity to the city and its distance from the sea, was crowded with sea-gulls, who appeared to be almost as tame as those birds which dwell on desert islands and are never molested by man. I was afterwards told that the gulls on this island, which is called Movenburg, have been protected by law from time immemorial, and that a heavy fine is inflicted on anyone who lands here during the breeding season.

I had but little time to explore Schleswig, which is a delightful old town full of historical interest; and as it is a sleepy place, with no trade worth mentioning, it has not been modernised by progress, and preserves many of its mediæval characteristics. This is one of the oldest cities of the North, and was the capital of the Danes in the days of Charlemagne. The first Christian church in Denmark was erected here on the site of the present cathedral; and—but all this and much more is in Baedeker, to whom I am indebted for these facts.

I visited the old cathedral, with its many monuments of kings and dukes, and should liked to have driven to the ruined Danevirke, but I thought of my long pull home and refrained. The Danevirke was to the ancient Danes what the Great Wall was to China. The head waters of the Eider and the Slei are within a few miles of each other, and, as the swampy shores of the first and the broad deep lakes of the second form an almost insurmountable obstacle to an invading army, the Danish kings commenced, even in pre-historic times, to fortify the intervening space and so form a complete line of defence from the North Sea to the Baltic. Queen Thyra set the whole of her nation to work for three years in constructing a gigantic rampart nine miles in length, forty feet in height, and surmounted by oaken pallisades. From behind it the Danes defied their enemies for many centuries, but when the province of Holstein was added to the Danish crown in 1460, and the frontier was moved farther south, the Danevirke was considered of no further use and was allowed to fall to ruins. However, in the war of 1864, the Danes once more fortified the old rampart; all in vain, the luck of the Danevirke had departed, and the Prussians forded the Slei and turned the position. Many a good old-fashioned battle has been fought by here, but this is not the place to chronicle them; though I could not resist the temptation, despite my resolve to forswear description of lions, of having something to say concerning this grand blood-stained old Danevirke.

The south-east wind freshened in the afternoon, and, as the current was now with me, I accomplished the thirty miles that divided me from my yacht in much less time than the journey out had occupied. However, there was still some hard pulling to be done, and I did not stop anywhere till I reached Arnis, where a *café* on the beach tempted me to land for beer. Near here I noticed a cutter yacht of about ten tons, which was evidently of English build. Two men were engaged in rigging her; they told me that she was entered for the Kiel regatta, that her owner intended to sail to Kiel the next day, and that she was called the *Widgeon*, and had been purchased at Hamburg from an Englishman thirteen years before. This was somewhat of a coincidence, for I was familiar with the history of this boat, and the book in which her voyage is chronicled was on board the *Falcon*. If Mr. Robinson, the author of *The Cruise of the Widgeon*, reads these pages he will learn that his old vessel is in good hands, almost as sound as ever, and does not show her years.

I did not reach the outer lagoon until long after dark. I picked my way with difficulty among the herring-stakes, and lost myself several times in the labyrinths of hurdles, which led me into *culs de sac* amidst the weed-grown shallows—a queer and weird navigation; but at last, shortly after mid-night, I found the yacht, and turned in to sleep soundly after my lengthy expedition.

The next morning was hot and windless, but the barometer had fallen two-tenths in the night, so we surmised that one of those rapid changes which are so frequent on these coasts was not far off. We pulled the *Falcon* out of the harbour with the sweeps at ten o'clock, and then set the sails; there was not a breath to fill them, so they hung useless; but the current was still setting to the northward, and we drifted in a very leisurely manner up the coast, putting out an oar occasionally to obtain steerage-way. We had no idea what anchorage we should reach before night, and it was nearly always thus with us in the Baltic. In these regions of capricious weather there was a charming uncertainty about our movements, and yet, as a rule, an absence of anxiety on the matter, for a port to which we could run for shelter was never far off.

On both seas there is a preponderance of wind, but in no other respect do the Baltic and North Sea resemble each other. On a sultry day such as this was a haze would be hanging over the chilly waters of the German Ocean and obscure the low eastern shores; but here the atmosphere was marvellously clear, and we could discern plainly, far away across the Little Belt, the Danish islands of Langeland and Arroe. The water, too, seemed almost as pellucid as the air; we could distinguish every object at the bottom of the sea fathoms below our keel, even the individual grains of sand. A brightly coloured vegetation, almost tropical in its luxuriance, clothed the coast. This looked indeed like a summer sea, and the German Ocean can never put on so fair an aspect.

A light south-east wind sprang up, so we hoisted our square-sail and got along a little faster.

The glass had not fallen without good cause. At one o'clock, having finished my own lunch, I sent Wright below to get his, and took the helm. There was not a cloud in the sky or the slightest appearance of bad weather. About a mile ahead a topsail-schooner was sailing in the same direction as ourselves, and I was watching her to see whether we were gaining on her at all, when suddenly there was a commotion on her deck, her sails shook violently, down went her topsail, inboard came her sheets, and lo, she was now sailing close-hauled, her lee gunwale under water, on precisely the same course on which she had been running free the moment before! Then I saw a suspicious black line rapidly coming towards us across the smooth blue water.

" Up you come, Wright! In with the square-sail. We 'll be all taken aback in a second," I shouted as I left the tiller and hurried forward to cast off the main-boom guy.

We had just time to get all ready when down it came on us, a violent squall from the north-west driving the water up before it in a foaming yeast.

"Well, this beats everything yet!" exclaimed Wright, "I don't think the weather-prophets would be much good out here."

The Baltic is certainly the match of any tropical ocean for the suddenness of its squalls. We took down a couple of reefs in the mainsail and put the yacht on the port tack. Leaning well over till the water hissed through her lee scuppers, she took the bit in her teeth and tore away up the coast like a race-horse. But not for long; the sea quickly got up, and soon—when we rounded Abue Point and were off the mouth of Flensborg Fiord, where the land afforded us no shelter—the short tumbling waves that opposed her knocked all the speed out of the *Falcon*. We thrashed to windward across the fiord, making very little way, driving the yacht's bows into seas that looked like walls of water, and which, burying her bowsprit and jib and falling on her decks, would often stop her as completely as if she had struck a rock.

The sky and water had now assumed a uniform leaden hue, down poured the rain in torrents, and it was bitterly cold. No, there is no monotony about the weather here. Those to whom their medical advisers recommend a change of climate should try this country; a voyage from the Equator to Siberia will not present a more utter change than can be constantly experienced here in the course of ten minutes.

I had thought of sailing to Flensborg, but as it is situated at the very head of the fiord, and as I should have had a dead beat to windward most of the way there, I now altered my plans and tried to make Sonderborg in the Als Sound instead.

When we were half-way across the great arm of the sea which forms the opening of Flensborg Fiord the wind freshened and the sea became so confused that the yacht scarcely progressed at all, and was certainly making far more lee-way than head-way. Occasionally four or five steep breaking waves would charge down on her in rapid succession, when, as if stunned and dazed, she would stop altogether, and merely rise and fall to each billow in a heavy lifeless manner. It began to look as if we should be unable to reach the opposite coast, but be driven out into the open sea. Though we always waited for a "smooth" to go about, the *Falcon* several times refused to stay, so that we were obliged to wear her round. Hour after hour passed in this manner, but at last, in spite of wind and sea, we got across to Als Island. We made the land close to the lighthouse on the peniusula of Kekenaes some miles to leeward of Als Sound, and being now in smoother water we were not long in tacking up the south side of the island.

At seven in the evening we opened out the deep inlet of Horup Haff, which is about four miles from the Sound; and, coming to the conclusion that we had had enough tumbling about for the day, we gave up Sonderborg, slacked off the sheets, put the helm up, and after sailing with a beam wind for three miles up the perfectly smooth water of the bay let our anchor go off Horuphav, a pretty little fishing village on the north shore.

We thus put into a port which we had not the slightest idea of visiting, and whose very name was unknown to us when we had sailed in the morning; but I was not sorry that stress of weather had brought us here, for Horup Haff is a beautiful piece of water and Als Island one of the fairest in Denmark. This fiord is seven miles long and one mile broad; as it turns round upon itself the inner portion is completely landlocked, and, the water being deep throughout, affords a most safe and commodious harbour, which, though now frequented only by a few coasters, was of great importance to the Danes during the last war. Most of the fighting was done in this neighbourhood, and this was used as the chief port of embarkation for troops and stores.

As it was still raining hard I did not go on shore that evening, but informed Wright that the next day being Sunday we would make it a holiday and remain at Horup. We became strict Sabbatarians in the Baltic, but as long as we were in the North Sea we could not afford to lose any slant of fair weather on whatever day it might come.

When I awoke on the following morning I found that winter had departed and summer come back again. A hot sun was shining, and the wooded hills and downs that surrounded the fiord looked very fresh and lovely

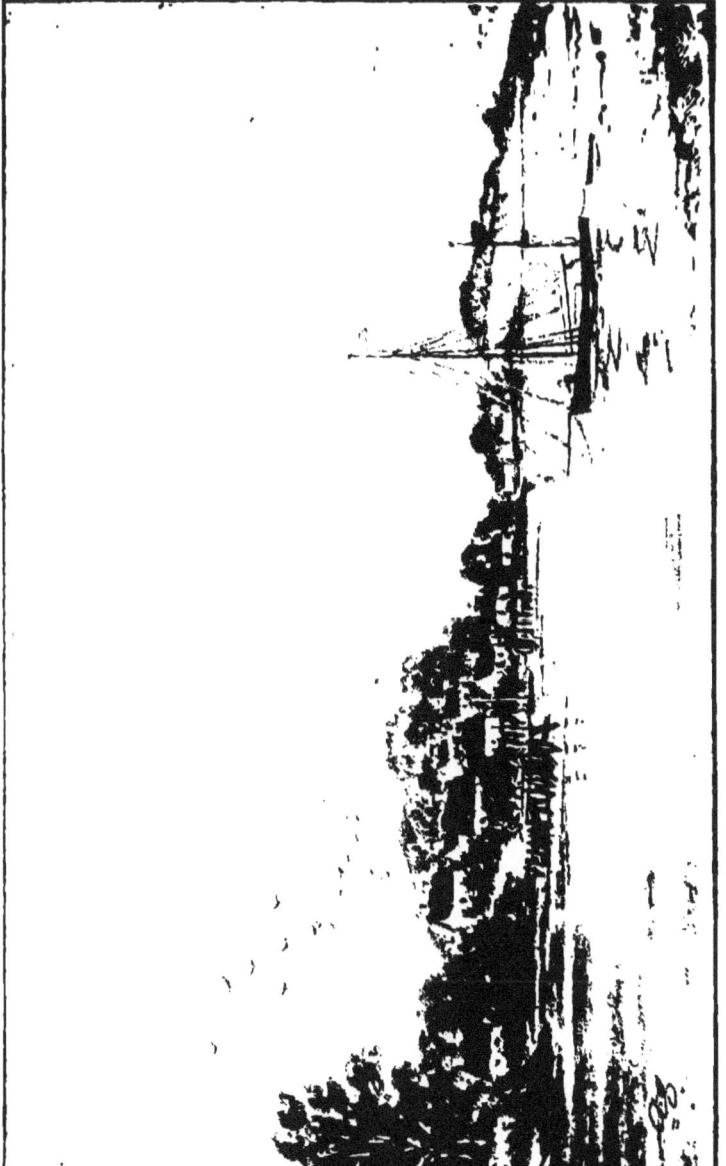

VILLAGE OF HORUP-HAV.

after the recent rain. The song of multitudes of birds filled the air—the extraordinary number of birds and the tremendous musical energy they display is another pleasant feature of these regions. As I gazed at the shore I came to the conclusion that the climate of Denmark is after all one of the best in Europe; better even than our own, which is saying a good deal. What though it is changeful, no sensible person would like every day to be monotonously fine; and when it is fine in this land of wind and rain Nature puts on a fresh and tender loveliness which is unknown in those so-called perfect climates which lie under the hard Southern skies. So I thought just then; but I have no doubt that the next time I was caught in a north-wester I set to reviling the Danish climate in no measured terms, even as I had done before.

Seen from our anchorage, Horuphav appeared a comfortable little place. It was half concealed by the green bushes that fringed the shore; there was no formal street, but the fishermen's cottages were scattered through a pleasant grove of beech and other trees; most of these cottages had deep thatched roofs, and all had glaring whitewashed chimneys, which produced a rather curious effect. A sloping forest formed a fine background to the scene.

"Now I wonder if we shall come across anyone in this out-of-the-way place who speaks English," I said to Wright as we pulled off to the rough timber jetty.

We landed, and, as we had exhausted our store of bread, I inquired the way to the baker's in English of the first man we met. He looked surprised for a moment, and then replied to me in my own tongue. He of course proved to be an old sea-captain. When I made some remark as to our good luck in thus having found at once someone who could understand us he denied that there was any luck in it. "For," said he, "this place is full of men who speak English better than I do; most of them have been gold-diggers in California in their day."

He told me that he had given up the sea and was now the landlord of the "Baltic Hotel," the only inn in this village. He led the way there, and I was astonished to find it a spacious and seemingly comfortable hostelry, commanding a splendid view over the fiord, and surrounded by a well-laid-out garden. A good many visitors from the neighbouring towns put up here in the summer months, for Horuphav, having the pure sea in front of it and the balmy pine-woods behind, is a very healthy place.

As it was Sunday the local gossips were sitting in the public room enjoying their pipes and beer after the sedate Northern fashion. I noticed that they were all speaking Danish and not German. The North Schleswigers still adhere to the tongue of their old country, and have not yet abandoned all hope of being some day freed from the foreign yoke—no heavy one, by the way, for the German Government is very indulgent to Schleswig-Holstein, and does all it can to reconcile the natives to the new rule. I was introduced to several of the old California diggers, none of whom seemed to have been very successful in their search for gold.

Had I yielded to the importunities of my new friends I might have passed the whole of the glorious day in consuming thin beer and listening to yarns long spun out, in this stuffy room; but I managed to slip away and took a long walk through the woods. I noticed, while going through the village, that every fisherman's cottage had its little carefully-tended garden, in which roses, stocks and other old-fashioned flowers were blossoming. Very pleasant-looking, too, were the good wives who sat knitting at the cottage porches.

When I returned on board, Wright told me that he, too, had been yarning with the gossips at the hotel, and that when he was leaving the landlord had come up to him, and said in a mysterious voice,

"Does your captain like fish?"

"He likes anything that's good," was the reply.

"Well, I want you to take him from me a little present. It's one of those big fish, I don't remember how you call it in English."

"Turbot," suggested Wright.

"No, not turbot. It's that fish which turns about and bites you if you catch hold of him, you know."

"Lobster?" ventured Wright again.

"Ah, yes, lobster, that's it! I've got a lot of them down in my cellar, but I can't leave the customers just now, so if you'll come back by-and-bye I'll fetch it for you."

So, in pleasurable anticipation of a rum and lobster

supper, I sent Wright back to the hotel in the dinghy. He returned, and, with a quiet chuckle, produced—a large dried eel. Our worthy host had unintentionally disappointed me; however, the eel, when stewed, proved to be excellent.

CHAPTER XI.

THE LITTLE BELT AND VEILE FIORD.

On the following morning, July 25th, the climate had again changed. Up till now we had experienced in the Baltic rapid alternations of hot cloudless summer and blustering wintry weather; but this day an entirely new climate visited us, which may be compared to that of Plymouth in autumn. The glass had fallen nearly half an inch in the night, and Wright, who had marvelled at its rapid movements since we had been on these seas, drily remarked that I should have brought two aneroids with me, as one was likely to wear out if it was left to do all this work by itself. The sky was overcast and threatened wind, and the rain fell steadily, but so far it was almost calm; a very light air creeping up occasionally from the south-west. Distant thunder could be heard rolling over the hills on the mainland.

As Sonderborg was but six miles distant I thought we could reach it before the storm broke; the anchor was accordingly weighed after breakfast. It was a most ominous-looking morning, but nothing much came of it. We tacked slowly out of Horup Haven, and had reached the mouth of Als Fiord, when the wind suddenly shifted to the north-east, and a violent squall of rain and wind as usual heralded the change. But we had not far to go, and a few more tacks brought us within the sheltered sound. We luffed alongside the quay of Sonderborg, lowered our drenched sails, and made fast. So very narrow is the Sound at this point that a large vessel cannot come to an anchor, having no room to swing, but the water is deep up to either shore. The current sets through this strait with such velocity that it has never been known to freeze. The chief street of Sonderborg borders the quay, and at one end of it rises the old Schloss of the Dukes of Augustenborg, a somewhat imposing edifice, but ugly, as are most of the ducal castles of Schleswig-Holstein.

A bridge of boats here crosses the river, and on the opposite shore rise the famous heights of Dybbol.

With the exception of the castle, few buildings in Sonderborg have an antique appearance, for the town was almost completely destroyed by the Prussians during the bombardment of Dybbol, and has for the most part been rebuilt quite recently. It now contains about 6,000 inhabitants, and if one may judge from the number of vessels that lie along its quays, a considerable trade must be carried on here. It has recently become one of the favourite watering-places in these parts, and large hotels for the accommodation of visitors have been built in the southern suburbs of the town.

Shortly after we had entered the harbour this interesting climate changed yet once more, this time to that of the traditional English April, by which I mean that perhaps mythical April described by the ancients as forming a portion of the spring, and not of the winter, as has been the case in recent years. The sun shone brightly, the birds sang merrily, and now and again a brief shower would pass overhead, leaving the dripping woods more beautiful than ever.

And now I had to make that pilgrimage which is obligatory on all who visit Sonderborg. I crossed the bridge of boats to the mainland, and after ascending a broad steep road for about half an hour reached the summit of the Dybbolbjerg, that memorable hill-side which the Danes defended so valiantly for two months in 1864, and whose battered entrenchments were at last stormed by the overwhelming forces of the Prussians.

It is not within my province to chronicle that plucky but hopeless defence, but of the Dybbolbjerg itself it may be said that it would be impossible to conceive a more majestic scene for a vital struggle between two nations. The Dybbolbjerg is a dome-shaped hill, one of the highest of the peninsula of Sundewitt; its summit commands a very extensive and magnificent view. From here the armies could overlook half the beautiful country for which they were fighting—a vast panorama of blue water and undulating green land, interlocked with each other, as it were, by many an irregular promontory and isthmus, and intricate winding gulf and sound. To the north and east are Als Sound, the long fiord of Augustenborg, and Als Island with its forest-clad hills; to the west and south stretches the great gulf of Flensborg, with its countless capes and bays; and to the north, across the fertile downs of Sundewitt, and to the south-east are obtained glimpses of the open Baltic.

On the top of this green hill, where the sea winds wave the long grass and the bright-hued northern flowers that are growing so rankly over the graves of warriors, rises a lonely monument, an admirable work of art, and singularly in harmony with its surroundings. This is a lofty obelisk in the Gothic style, not unlike the Albert Monument in appearance, which commemorates the Prussian victory. The bas-reliefs round the base illustrate incidents of the siege, and so careful have the conquerors been not to hurt the feelings of the vanquished that it would be difficult for anyone to discover from the carvings and inscriptions what had been the issue of the contest. Here the individual gallant deeds of Danes are pictured side by side with those of their German foemen. The monument is dedicated to the fallen, but to the fallen of both nations, and, unlike most erections of the kind, this is no monument of self-glorification, but of proud respect for the valour of both armies; it can arouse no sentiment of animosity in the breast of any spectator but a feeling that here fought two generous enemies well worthy of each other. Near it are the ruins of the Danish intrenchments and a cemetery where stand many simple gravestones bearing such inscriptions as, "Here lie one hundred brave Danes," "Here lie fifty brave Prussians," "Here lie many Prussian and Danish soldiers."

Such are the relics of the wars that have been, but here also are to be seen extensive preparations for possible wars to come. Defensive works of great strength have been raised on these heights and also round Sonderborg, which are supposed to have made this important position and the Als Sound unapproachable to the army or fleet of an enemy. Even in these days of peace there was a martial air about the old battle-field. I met here many more soldiers than civilians; the engineers were working on the new fortifications, and ever and anon I heard in one direction or another the sound of bugle call or military music.

I returned to Sonderborg, and visited the old castle which was built in the thirteenth century. It has been converted into a barrack, and now contains a considerable Prussian garrison. The chapel and the adjoining vault are alone open to the public; in the latter are piled up a large number of ancient and sumptuous coffins containing the remains of members of the Augustenborg family. A lugubrious old man who acted as cicerone insisted, despite my repeated asservations that I did not understand a word of German, on telling me who all these dead grandees were, when they had lived, and what their achievements had been.

In the evening a German gentleman, who spoke English well, called on me. He told me that he too was skipper and owner of a yacht, that he had sailed here from Lubeck, and intended to follow the coast as far as Assens. I went with him to inspect his vessel, which was lying above the pontoon bridge. She was a ten-tonner, and had a large open well in which was a small steam-engine. When he encountered a calm he got up steam, and could make about two knots an hour. His wife, two children, and two sailors, were on board with him, so it can be imagined that they were too much crowded up to enjoy much comfort. The steam-engine, too, must have got terribly in the way, and created plenty of dirt. He had a steel life-boat, which he had constructed himself, as a dinghy. This somewhat eccentric craft was the only native yacht I met cruising in the Baltic. These people do not deserve to own such a splendid cruising-ground.

There was no wind at all on the following morning until nine o'clock, when, a southerly breeze arising, we pushed off from the quay, passed through the pontoon bridge,—the toll for opening which to a vessel is one mark—and sailed up the Als Sound.

This strait, which divides the island of Alsen from the mainland, is twelve miles long, and its extreme breadth, in its northern part, is two miles. The scenery on either side of us was charming, as it always is on this coast. Verdant slopes came down to the edge of the clear blue water, contrasting with the darker colouring of abrupt pine-clad hills; and here and there stood a beautifully situated country seat, with noble park around it, or a snug little village with its rough wooden jetty and group of fishing-boats. The Sound broadened as we advanced; but about a league above Sonderborg there is a spot where the land, jutting out on either side, once more contracts the channel. Here, on the western shore, is an extensive beech wood, and on the eastern the village of Arukiel. It was at this point that the Prussians forced the passage of the Sound in 1864; and we perceived, standing by the sea-side, a Gothic monument, resembling that of Dybbol, which commemorates this event.

Shortly after passing this we opened out Augustenborg Fiord, which looked so beautiful that I was almost tempted to ascend it. After sailing another seven miles we came out of the Sound, and were once more in the open waters of the Little Belt, which here attains its greatest breadth of sixteen miles. Across it, on our right, we could see the blue hills of the distant island of Fyen, and before us lay the extensive bay into which opens the fiords of Apenrade and Gienner. As the weather still looked fine I decided not to put into any of the nearer ports, but to cross the bay to its northern point, Cape Halk, and thence, following the coast, reach the sheltered sound inside Aaro Island before night.

The gentle south-west wind carried us slowly before it till we were in the middle of the bay and off the wooded islet of Barso. Wright was on deck steering, while I was having a nap below.

"There are breakers ahead, Sir," I heard him cal. out.

I glanced at the chart. "Nonsense, Wright; there are fourteen fathoms about here, and there are no shoals to pick us up between this and the shore."

"There are breakers ahead, though, Sir; and if there is no shallow water it must be a squall coming down on us."

I hurried on deck and stood by the haulyards. A line of foam, dazzlingly white under the bright sunshine, and therefore giving us the impression of more commotion than really existed, was crossing the smooth water. It soon reached us, and we were relieved to find ourselves, not as we had expected in the midst of a violent north-west squall, which would have been an awkward customer to tackle in this open water, but of a fresh and steady east wind which enabled us to hold our course close-hauled on the starboard tack.

The Little Belt, separating as it does the territories of Germany and Denmark, is closely watched by the preventive services of either nation, and smuggling craft must find it difficult to avoid the cruisers. The captain of a Prussian revenue cutter, that was hove to to windward of us, evidently thought the *Falcon* a suspicious-looking vessel, for he let draw his foresail, bore down on us, and turned close round our stern. He perceived our blue ensign and appeared satisfied, for he waved his cap to us, wished us a good journey, and then sailed back to his post of observation. Half an hour afterwards a Danish revenue cutter went through exactly the same performance with us.

We passed Halk Head and saw before us the little island of Aaro, which is about two miles long, and is flat and desolate in appearance. At 6 P.M. we entered the narrow sound which divides the island from the mainland. There is a harbour at Aaro and one on the Schleswig shore; as the latter, which is called Aarosund, looked the most cheerful of the two, we stood in between its piers and lowered our sails.

This port can only be used by very small craft. The entrance is but thirty-seven feet wide, and as the piers take a sharp turn to the northward it is an exceedingly inconvenient place to get into. Once within, one is in a snug little harbour capable of accommodating half a dozen fishing-boats at the outside.

We secured the yacht to the wooden quay and then looked round us. On the shore three houses only were to be seen, and behind these was a grove of beech-trees. Of the houses, one was a small tavern, one a coastguard station, and the third an imposing-looking restaurant or refreshment-room, whose presence in such a lonely spot somewhat puzzled me. I afterwards discovered that the passenger steamer which plies between Haderslev and Assens calls here twice a day, and that the citizens of the former inland town are fond of making excursions to this little sea-side place to avail themselves of the excellent bathing it affords.

We had purchased some fish from a smack that was in the port, and were doing justice to them at dinner, when I heard a heavy body bump against our sides. I looked out, and found that this was the Lubeck yacht which had followed us from Sonderborg, and was now making fast alongside.

While lying in most of the Baltic ports vessels are not allowed to have fires or lights on board, the many wooden houses and stacks of timber making this precaution necessary. We had disregarded this troublesome prohibition on more than one occasion, but now we cooked our dinner and lit our lamps with an easy conscience, for our pilot-book informed us that there is no rule of the sort in Aarosund, and it would, indeed, have been superfluous in a town of three houses.

I only visited one of these houses, and that, naturally, was the tavern. We had run short of potatoes, and I went there in the hope of purchasing some. I was received by a nice-looking old woman who knew no English. I tried to recall the German word for potato but could not do so; all I remembered about it was that it sounded something like the name of the Evil One. I did not like, therefore, to experimentalise on the language, in case I might shock the old lady with unconscious profanity.

"Madam," I said in English, "I want potatoes, but I am English, and speak no German."

"Neither do we, Sir; we are Danes," a voice behind me said proudly, in the purest Anglo-Saxon.

I turned round and perceived the host, who had just come in, at the door; a tall handsome old man, but with dim eyes that were evidently almost blind.

"What is it that I can have the pleasure of doing for you, Sir?" he continued.

I told him my wants, and he sent his wife off for a sack of potatoes.

This was a very pleasant old chap; he was dignified and courteous, and to my surprise he spoke our language as an educated Englishman would. His accent and vocabulary were not such as foreign seamen pick up in British forecastles and Wapping lodging-houses. He seemed pleased to meet an Englishman, so I called for beer and had a long yarn with him as he sat with closed eyes in his chair and smoked his long pipe. His good wife—they were an affectionate couple, and always addressed each other as "fadder" and "mudder"—could not understand our conversation; but her honest face beamed with satisfaction when she perceived how this recalling of olden times was brightening up her old man. He told me that he was nearly ninety, and that he had not had occasion to speak English for nearly half a century. He had been a sea-captain, and had evidently passed much of his life in the tropical Atlantic, for he seemed very familiar with the Brazils and the West coast of Africa. I heard, afterwards, that there was some mystery about the old fellow, and that strange rumours were afloat concerning his past. He was possibly a retired buccaneer, slaver, or other sea-adventurer, of the sort.

I stayed two days in Aarosund—the first because the weather was stormy, and the second because I was lazy and bethought myself to take a trip on a steamer for a change.

On the night of our arrival the wind was howling again in a wintry fashion, and on the following morning it was blowing half a gale from the north-west; so the two yachts shirked the sea and stayed in port.

About a mile to the northward of Aarosund, Haderslev Fiord opens into the Little Belt. This fiord is about nine miles in length; it is narrow and winding, and at the head of it lies the town of the same name, which has a considerable shipping trade. The chart showed me that I could safely venture to Haderslev in the dinghy, as the wind was off shore and the sea would be quite smooth on this side of the Belt.

I therefore left Wright in charge of the yacht, set the balance lug in the boat, and sailed away. I entered the mouth of the fiord and was tacking up the first reach when the steamer from Assens overtook me, crowded with jovial excursionists and having a brass band on board that did its duty well, and never ceased playing throughout the voyage. The skipper hailed me, threw me a rope's end, and I was towed all the way to Haderslev, having nothing to do but to sit at luxurious ease in the dinghy's stern, smoking my pipe and admiring the scenery. The banks of the fiord were, of course, well-timbered and pleasing. In describing one of these fiords one describes all of them, though, as I have said before, there is no monotony in their loveliness, only in the attempt at reproducing them in words.

On reaching Haderslev the captain of the steamer, a jolly North German, volunteered to show me round. This is a very old town, with lofty and picturesque houses.

Extensive barracks are now being constructed for the accommodation of the Prussian garrison. The Germans evidently maintain a great number of troops in these two conquered provinces; not that the natives, who are a long-headed race, are likely to attempt such a hopeless piece of madness as a rebellion against their powerful masters, even should the outbreak of a war between Germany and some other great power appear to afford an opportunity. In Holstein there is, of course, little or no ill-feeling towards the Germans, as the bulk of the population is of German blood and was ever disaffected towards Denmark. In quite two-thirds of Schleswig, again, the people seem to have reconciled themselves to the new regime, and have come to the conclusion that they are better off as citizens of a great nation like Germany than of poor little Denmark, now so helpless, and of so small account in the affairs of Europe.

But here, in the extreme north of Schleswig, it is another matter. Here the people are Danes to the back-bone, detest the German, and still entertain some hope that Germany will, one day, be compelled to restore this country to Denmark. In a town like Haderslev, which is only a few miles from the frontier, and whose inhabitants have, therefore, much commerce with their neighbours in more fortunate Jutland, it is patent, even to a passing stranger, that no love is lost between the two races.

This was, indeed, soon brought before my notice. In the chief street there are two *cafés* opposite each other, which are frequented by the men of position in town. At one of these *cafés* the Captain and I lunched. On looking round at the other tables I saw several Prussian officers, burly merchants of the true North German type, refreshing themselves in the intervals of business, and at one table was a group of Protestant parsons, also smoking and drinking beer, and who, I was told, had been attending a synod which was being held in Haderslev. By the way, how is it that in most countries a haphazard group of clergymen is almost sure to contain a noticeable proportion of sour-looking, or foolish or physically weak, or otherwise disagreeable types, while, on the contrary, in Denmark or North Germany, the clergy seem to be above the average of their countrymen in robustness, intellectuality of features, and prepossessing appearance generally ? Now, I noticed that everyone present, were he soldier, parson, merchant, or waiter, was speaking High German, and that none but German papers were lying on the little marble tables.

"How is this?" I said to my friend, the Captain; "I thought the people spoke Danish in this part of the country."

He laughed, and replied, "So they do; but we happen to be sitting in the best German *café* of Haderslev. Just over the way you can see the best Danish *café*;

if you go in there you'll hear nothing but Danish spoken round you, and see none but Danish papers. I did not take you in there because I am a German, and they would scowl at me, and perhaps make themselves objectionable."

Not only is it thus with the *cafés*, but with the churches, and with the places of public amusement. The two races have their own, and keep entirely apart. The steamer that runs to Assens, of which my friend was skipper, belongs to a German company. Some Danish merchants have determined to start an opposition boat. Then there will be none but German passengers on one steamer, and none but Danes on the other. They do, indeed, cordially detest each other. The Germans I met in this part of Schleswig had all sorts of bad things to say about the Danish character; so, too, had the Danes on the contemptible features of the Teuton nature. I have no doubt that my friends spoke from conviction, but the charges they made against each other were often grotesquely false; and, as far as my limited experience goes, they were all gross slanderers, and jolly good fellows on either side.

The Captain towed me back to Aarosund, and, before going on to Assens, he persuaded me not to sail on the following morning, but to take a voyage with him.

Accordingly, when his boat came alongside the quay, at mid-day, July 28th, I got on board, and we steamed between the isles of Aaro and Baago, across the Little Belt to Assens, on the island of Fyen. There was again a large party of excursionists on board, mostly robust business men from Haderslev, with a capacity for food, beer, and tobacco that was refreshing to behold in this dyspeptic age. A lunch was served on the way, consisting of cold fried fish, Russian sardines, cold pork sausages, black bread and mutton sandwiches, kummel, and Danish aquavit. The dwellers by the Baltic have clearly not yet lost their gastric juices. The journey was uneventful, save that some Danish yeomen got drunk, sang songs which I could not understand, but which were evidently not complimentary to the Germans if they were not absolutely seditious, and at last had to be repressed.

We reached Assens, and, for the first time, I set foot on Danish soil. There was nothing here to indicate that we had crossed from one country to another, save the difference in the uniforms of the soldiers and custom-house officers, and the fact of the latter being somewhat more officious than the same class in Germany—not that they troubled me, for I had no luggage, but they thoroughly rummaged the boxes, baskets, and bags of my fellow travellers. There was little to see in this clean sea-port, save the cemetery on the hill-side, which commands a beautiful view, and where are monuments to the Danish troops who fell in 1864. In the evening the steamer took me back to Aarosund, and then, sitting in the *Falcon's* cabin, I proceeded to consult pilot-books, charts, and Baedekers as to whither I should sail on the morrow. But I found that in going up the Little Belt I should have on either side of me so many good ports and pleasant places that I decided to leave my next night's destination to chance, or rather to the pleasure of the inconstant Baltic breezes.

On the morning of July the 29th, the weather, as Wright remarked, could not have been better had it been made for us. A warm sun was shining, and a fresh south-east wind was curling the waters of the Little Belt. This was, I think, the pleasantest day's sail we had on this voyage. We got under weigh at 6 A.M., and, after travelling about fifty-two English miles, through ever-varying scenery, composed of extensive bays, narrow sounds, islands, and fiords, we reached Veile at three in the afternoon.

We sailed out of Aaro Sound, across the shoals that lie to the north of it, the feeding-ground of many birds, by the flat uninhabited island of Linderum, into the Little Belt, which is here nine miles broad, but is much contracted in places by the promontories that project from either shore. Then we came to the little island of Brandso, well-wooded, and having a fishing-haven on its southern side. On the main-land, opposite to this, we opened out the bay of Heilsminde, which forms the frontier between Jutland and Schleswig; so from here we had Danish land on either side of us, and were leaving astern the territories of the Kaiser.

Next we entered the rougher waters of the Bredning, where the Belt broadens to ten miles; and now, ahead of us rose ranges of steep wooded hills, loftier than any we had yet seen in the Baltic, through which no opening was visible, so that we appeared to be in a great land-locked bay. But, steering our course, we came to Stenderup Point, at the farther end of the Bredning, and before us there opened out a narrow strait like the entrance to a fiord, but through which all the waters of the Belt were pouring out. This is known as the Narrows of the Little Belt, a winding channel, more than ten miles in length, and, in places, not half a mile in width, formed by the convergence towards each other of Fyen and Jutland. Through these Narrows the current runs with great velocity to the northward, often causing dangerous races. My pilot-book told me that the current here is, indeed, stronger than any on the Danish seas, and that when the wind is north-east the sea is so high, short, and irregular, that even the well-protected anchorage off Fredericia is unsafe for vessels. The water is deep in the Narrows, attaining forty fathoms in one spot.

The southern entrance of the Narrows is divided into two branches by the island of Faeno. We went up the smaller channel on the Fyen side, which is called Oinaes Sound, and here we passed scenery more charming than any we saw on this voyage. On our left was Faeno Island, two miles long, high, and clothed with magnificent beech trees, save in places where the wood was cloven by smooth sloping lawns. A lovely island, indeed; the sort of place one would like to own in the Monte Christo fashion, and convert into a splendid summer yachting-box. On the Fyen side the land was steep and rugged, but also well wooded with beech and pine, while the strip of shore beneath was not a desert of pebbles, or of mud left bare and hideous at low water as on the coasts of our tidal seas, but a rich pasture crowded with cattle. At the end of the Sound, on a steep peninsula of Fyen, we saw a country seat, which drew from both of us exclamations of astonished admiration. A light fairy-like châlet, nestling among masses of brilliant flowers, stood on the heights, and the well-timbered slopes that descended from it to the water's edge had been converted into beautiful pleasure-grounds with open glades, gardens, drives, winding paths, and summer-houses. This, I learnt afterwards, was the manor house and park of Hindsgavl. Blind, or far too perfect for this world, must be the man who does not break the Tenth Commandment, when, on a fresh Danish summer's day such as this was, with the song of innumerable birds filling those pleasant groves, he gazes at this paradise. I came to the conclusion that I would have no objection to passing the rest of my days here, if anyone presented me with this manor and a suitable income.

I had intended to put into some port within the Narrows for the night, but I was unwilling to waste this fresh and favourable breeze, so pushed on. Faeno Island passed, we saw before us the broad mouth of Kolding Fiord opening into the Narrows. Leaving it to port, we doubled Gals Point, and entered the narrowest reach of the straits, which here runs in a south-easterly direction, so that we found the wind and current opposed, and had to tack through a confused sea, which did not curl in waves, but resembled the commotion at the bottom of a lock when the water is being let in. We had only three miles of this bubble, and the strong stream soon carried us past the picturesque and ancient town of Middlefart into the last reach of the Narrows, where the wind was fair again and the water smooth. Then we sailed close under the dismantled fortress and the decayed old city of Fredericia, and were out in broad water once more; the Belt widened out rapidly into the open Kattegat, and ahead of us, to the north-east, no land was visible.

We followed the coast of Jutland to Kasserodde Point. The wind freshened, and came down on us in stiffish squalls from the defiles above Baaring Bay, raising a somewhat choppy sea; but the wind was on our beam, and we reached along fast, at one o'clock rounding the beacon which marks the limit of the extensive shoals off Kasserodde, and opening out the broad entrance of Veile Fiord. This deep gulf is reputed to contain some of the fairest scenery in all Denmark. The distance from Kasserodde Point to the town of Veile, at the head of the fiord, is sixteen English miles; and the wind being now right aft, we accomplished this in two hours, getting alongside the quay at 3 P.M. The fiord presented a succession of lovely landscapes; the steep wooded hills were higher than they generally are in Denmark, and were cloven by deep valleys, while pine-clad promontories jutted out from either shore.

As is the case on most of the Danish fiords, a rank

vegetation here covers the bottom of the sea, and where the water is shallow the heads of the long weeds float on the surface, and smooth the troubled waters much more effectually than oil can. The bay opposite the town, which forms the termination of the fiord, a piece of water two miles long and one broad, is entirely overgrown by these weeds. As we approached it, running before the wind over a tumbling sea, we saw before us a line of breakers stretching right across the bay, exactly as if a shoal had been there, but which was caused by the waves dashing against the edge of the weed-choked water; and beyond the breakers was a dark green expanse, rising and falling sluggishly in smooth undulations. Through this strange marine growth a narrow channel, half a league in length, has been dredged, by which vessels, of not more than ten feet draught, can reach the town quays.

CHAPTER XII.

ACROSS THE GREAT BELT.

WE had at last brought the yacht into a Danish port, and we were not allowed to forget this fact for a moment, for hundreds of Danish flags were flying in the strong breeze from the masts in the harbour and the houses on shore; while at least two of the brass bands which were blaring in different portions of the town were performing the National Anthem of the Danes.

It was the cattle-show week, and Veile was *en fête*. The quay was crowded with holiday-making peasants in their best clothes, who gazed at the *Falcon* with open-mouthed surprise when they heard that the little ship had come from England. The harbour-master, a very aged mariner, who spoke English, stood by our vessel, and delivered lectures on us to all who would listen. He told them that we had sailed all the way from England to visit the fair city of Veile, and that the citizens ought to be very gratified to hear this; that we had timed ourselves to arrive while the *fête* was in progress; and that he trusted we should be able to commend the well-conditioned cattle at the show. He translated each sentence of his lecture to us as he went on. He was a foolish, garrulous old chap, but it was so pleasing to observe the simple joy and pride he took in acting as our showman that it was impossible to be bored.

Veile is a town of 7,000 inhabitants, and is the centre of a rich agricultural district. It does not appear to carry on much trade as a sea-port, so we did not here come across as many English-speaking people as usual, and the natives stood on the quay and stared at us with the same wondering curiosity we had experienced in the inland Dutch towns.

But the old harbour-master was not the only one we met who understood our tongue; a queer young fellow found us out, and afforded us considerable amusement. He was so typical of a certain class of his countrymen that it may be worth while to describe his peculiarities.

This individual, who appeared to be about twenty-four, met Wright in the street, and, seeing that he was an Englishman, accosted him thus, in an exaggerated Yankee accent—

"Stranger, you must be God-dam lonely, I guess, with no one to talk to, so come and have a glass of beer along with me."

Wright complied, but, it seems, soon wearied of the company of his new acquaintance; and, on his return to the yacht, warned me that a great bore had expressed an intention of calling on me. We had just finished our dinner when the "great bore" paid me his threatened visit; he was a remarkably free and easy, *sans cérémonie* young man, and at once made himself quite at home in our cabin. He informed me that he was a native of Veile, but that he had emigrated to the United States when he was sixteen; that he now ran an hotel in the U. S.; that he had a sweetheart in Veile, had come over to marry her, and to take her back with him to the U. S.; that the U. S. was the only country fit for a man to live in. He invariably spoke of his adopted home as the " U. S," and, to believe him, Paradise before the Fall must have been a shabby sort of place in comparison with the least desirable fragment of the Great Republic. " No man can know what's what," he said to me, " unless he's been in the States. Of course you've been to the U. S., Sir?" I was obliged to admit that I had not. " You don't mean that!" he exclaimed in great astonishment, " you seemed smart-like, and to know what's what, so I made sure you had been there."

After a pause he cackled on again.

" Ah, I am so glad I met you! I felt so lonely here; I had no one to talk to; you see they're all God-dam fools here. England or the U. S. for me! I could not live in this hole. My gel's nice enough, but she's a fool, poor thing; she can't help it, being a Dane; however, we'll smarten her up in the U. S."

" You'll be glad to leave Denmark again," I said to this unpatriotic person.

"I guess I will; I have been almighty dull here. I calculate I have been walking up and down this village for two weeks, and not a God-dam soul could I find to talk to until I met you two Britishers."

"But did not you say that you belonged here; have you no relations?" I inquired.

"Oh, I've a father and mother and sisters, and that sort of folk, you know, living up in the town there; but I can't get along with them; they ain't been away from home, like me, so they're God-dam fools, and I can't hold conversation with them no how."

"And what do they think of you, do they say that you've improved since you have been away?" put in Wright, with a sarcastic smile, which was quite lost on this young man; no shafts of ridicule could pierce his self-conceit.

"Well, they can't quite make me out," he naively replied; "they don't understand Yankee ways, poor souls. They are a slow lot in this old country. The young men here think they can play cards, but I tell them they are God-dam asses; what do they know about poker? These Danes, too, turn over a ten cent piece a dozen times before they'll part with it. Don't they stare to see this Yankee boy chuck the gold about!"

And so he went on reviling his country, his countrymen, and all their ways. The polite continental custom of taking off one's hat on entering a shop or *café* prevails in Denmark. "Such a nigger-slave trick it is," he exclaimed indignantly; "I tell them that it disgusts an independent free-born American. It makes me feel sick to see it, and I won't take my hat off to no one; so that poor old stay-at-home fool, my father —what can he know about things?—pitched into me the other day, and told me I was a bad-mannered pig."

Wright and myself burst out laughing at this; but this serene young man, far from taking offence, joined in, no doubt under the impression that his father's folly was the object of our merriment.

There was a monument on the quay, near the yacht, dedicated to the brave Danes who fell in the war of 1864.

"What is that?" I asked our friend.

"I guess I don't know," he replied; "I think it's something to do with a little fight—a war, these Danes call it—which once came off here. God-dam idiots! they don't know anything about wars, I reckon. I guess, now, that civil war in the U. S. was something like a war."

This youth, who, in his own estimation, was so almighty 'cute, had passed through England on his way home, and he told us a simple tale about his adventures in a train which caused the tears to run down our eyes in streams. I wish I could remember his exact words, and describe the innocence of his manner: "There were two men in the carriage with me," he said, "and one brought out a pack of cards, and taught the other a game I had never seen in America. It's done like this: A man turns down three cards, and the other bets which of them is the knave. I saw the man who was betting win a lot of money; then he nudged me, and, while the other wasn't looking, he made a scratch with his thumb-nail on the back of the knave, and winked at me. I had been smartened up in the States, and I saw his meaning at once. The cards were turned down again, and we both saw the marked knave, and we each put a sovereign on it, and of course we won. Then the other man went mad, and swore against his God-dam luck, and put his cards in his pocket, saying he wouldn't play any more as he had lost all his money.

"So you went away a pound to the good," I said.

"No, I did not; for, you see, the man who had won the money chaffed the other, and said he was afraid to play with such a cute Yankee as I was; and for a long time the man wouldn't play, but at last we bullied him so that he said, 'God-damme! to show that it ain't because I'm afraid, I will play once more. I've got no more money, but here is my gold watch and chain; it's worth a hundred guineas; now, if you'll stake fifty pounds against it, why, demme, here goes to try my luck; but, mind you, win or lose, this will be the last time. I suppose you would like me to lose my very trowsers to you.' So I put on all I had in my pocket, twenty pounds, and the other chap put on the rest."

"And you won the watch," said Wright, maliciously.

"No; and I can't understand how it was, nor could

the other chap. I could have staked my bottom dollar that we had backed the marked card; but we could not have done so, for, when the card was turned up, it was not the knave. We must have been darned careless not to have made quite sure of that marked card before we put the money on. And the other chap kept his word, and wouldn't play any more."

Wright and I could not now restrain our laughter, and this innocent young American citizen looked from one to the other of us with a puzzled expression, not being able to see where the joke came in. I could not resist the temptation of enlightening him on the subject, and when I told him that the three-card trick was a very ancient British trap to catch gulls with, and explained to him that the man who had marked the knave was the accomplice of the other, his cock-a-hoop manner suddenly vanished, his cheeks turned scarlet, and, terribly humiliated, he seized his hat, said in a mild voice, "I must now say good night to you; they will be waiting supper for me at home," and slunk off. He certainly had proved the reverse of a bore; with his beautifully unconscious humour, he was the most amusing person we came across on this voyage.

This youth was but an extreme example of a very large class. I have observed that many foreigners, especially Scandinavians, after having passed a few years in the States, altogether outyankee the most outrageous of Yanks, and render themselves as ridiculous in the eyes of the genuine Americans as they make themselves astonishing and disgusting to their own

people on their return home, by their foolish arrogance and ignorant contempt for all belonging to the fatherland. I should like to have heard what the poor old man and woman, who had brought this renegade Dane into the world, thought of him. What an extraordinary conception, too, they must have formed of the Anglo-Saxon from their son's report; what an ill-mannered lot of savages they must consider the British, and their transatlantic cousins! I have met some Englishmen, who, after a residence in America, put on a similar affectation, and revile what they are pleased to call the rotten old country; but, out of the vast number of British abroad, only a foolish few do this; whereas, of the Danes and other foreigners, a large proportion are inclined to this weakness.

On the afternoon of my arrival ¡I ascended a steep hill that overhung the town on the north side. From here the view over the winding fiord and its forest-clad capes was simply magnificent. The great sheet of water, clear as crystal, and so revealing what lay beneath, assumed various colours, from brown or darkest green where the bottom was overgrown with weeds, to emerald green or turqoise blue where it flowed over rocks and sands. But fairer even than the majestic fiord was the vast scene that stretched before me into a hazy distance when I looked over the town, inland. Veile lies at the end of a long valley, which is bordered by hills of bold outline, covered with forests; but the vale itself, which is broad and level, consists of a gigantic pasture, a beautiful prairie, whose vivid

16 *

green is in strong contrast to the dark colours of the woods that surround it. The port, and the picturesque scattered little town, with its avenue-bordered white high-roads radiating from it, formed a fore-ground to this extensive and delightful landscape.

I felt an irresistible desire to ascend and explore this great valley; for the farther one looked up it the less cultivated and more wild it appeared to be, till at last, far away on the horizon, I could see that low bare sand-hills took the place of the wooded heights and black moorland of the verdant prairie. This seemed to be the gate-way to some mysterious and inhospitable inner region, even as are those fair valleys I had seen on the African coast, which, at first giving promise of such rich country beyond, lead only to the black gorges of the Atlas, and the wastes of the Sahara. And so, too, will the traveller who follows one of these deep valleys, which, descending from the heart of Jutland, open into the fiords on the east coast, soon find himself in one of the most desolate tracts of Europe. He who has only seen the beech-clad hills and rich pastures of the Baltic coast is likely to form an exaggerated idea of the fertility of the Cimbrian peninsula; for there runs all down the middle of the peninsula, like a back-bone, a broad strip of barren country, a great plain, or rather steppe, of dark heath, almost treeless, with here and there morasses, sandy wastes, and drifting sand-hills; here a hard stratum, called the Ahl, a conglomeration of sand and iron, exists a little distance below the surface of the soil, causing great obstruction to the growth of vegetation. This district slopes towards the west, where it joins the equally inhospitable land that borders the North Sea; a sandy wilderness for the most part, swept constantly by the bitter and plant-killing north-westerly winds. Thus the smiling country, along which I had been coasting, where the rich vegetation overflows hill and dale to the water's edge, is but the delusive face of the true Jutland; a narrow strip of fertility bordering and concealing the inner desert.

The view from this hill-top excited my curiosity, and I wished to see something of that desolate country beyond; so, instead of sailing the next morning, I left the yacht in port, and started on a long walk up the broad valley of the Veileaa and across the hills that bounded it. It was a glorious, sunny, windy day; one of those that make the little there is of the Danish summer so agreeable. I followed the valley for some way, then turned off into the woods, and reached the village of Jellinge, where I saw two mighty barrows rising high above the houses, which my guide-book told me were the burial-places of two ancient pagans—King Gorm of Denmark, and his queen Thyra Danebod. In the church-yard, too, I was shown two well-preserved and beautifully carved Runic stones. The whole of this neighbourhood abounds in relics of the præ-Christian days, and is highly interesting to the archæologist.

After leaving Jellinge I still proceeded westward. The country gradually lost its fertile appearance, and at last I found myself on a lonely road crossing the bleak Jutland heath. It was almost impossible to face the strong wind that was howling and sweeping over this great treeless expanse. It certainly looked as desolate a region as any I have ever seen—sands, heather, and bog stretching to the horizon, and no sign of human life, save an occasional shepherd, clad in sheepskins, minding his wiry-looking flock.

I did not return to the yacht until late in the evening, having found my walk a most interesting one; it enabled me to form a good idea of the various features of this country from the bleak Ahl to the fertile shores of the fiords; from Runic stones to mediæval castles and modern country seats.

The next day being Sunday, the yacht remained in port. I put some provisions in the dinghy, and set out on a cruise down the fiord. First I sailed to the fishing village of Tirsbaek on the north shore, which lies at the foot of a little valley, and is surrounded by magnificent woods. Then I crossed the fiord to Munkebjerg, the favourite pleasure-ground of the citizens of Veile, and celebrated throughout all Denmark for its beautiful scenery. Here the steep hills, cloven into picturesque defiles, are densely clothed with the beech-trees that flourish so well on this sheltered eastern coast; and from the bathing-station on the shore a labyrinth of zig-zag paths leads to the summit of a dome-shaped hill, where a restaurant stands on a natural terrace, and overlooks a splendid scene. In the summer months a little steamer—called the *Falken*

VILLAGE BELOW TIRSBAEK AND ENTRANCE TO FIORD OF VEILE.

by the way, a namesake of our own—runs between Veile and Munkebjerg. On this fine Sunday she made several voyages, and landed a large number of excursionists on the wooden pier by the bathing-place. The whole of Veile seemed to be taking a holiday on the water. Many small open pleasure-boats were sailing on the fiord, some on hire, and others which were evidently private yachts; all were rigged in the same fashion—two sprit sails and a jib; and some had top sails above the sprits. They were clumsily-built craft, and sailed very badly; my little dinghy, with her small sail, could have beaten the largest of them, especially when it came to turning to windward.

Apropos of craft, the *Falcon* was moored by the starting-place of a quaint ferry-boat, which plied between Veile and some neighbouring village on the shore of the weed-grown bay I have described. This boat was of considerable size, and was capable of carrying a large number of passengers. She was very shallow, and was propelled by great paddle-wheels which two men turned with a crank, while the skipper, a very ancient and impatient person, steered. She seemed well adapted for her purpose; she skimmed over the surface of the shallows at a good speed, and was not impeded by the entanglement of weeds as any other boat would have been.

On my return to Veile in the evening I found that some other English-speaking people had found us out, and were standing on the quay talking to Wright. These proved to be an old sea-captain, his wife, and little girl. They had been settled for ten years in New Zealand, and had come home on a holiday to see the old people. The child, who had been born in the colony, spoke no Danish, but English only. I found that the captain, though he liked New Zealand well enough, and was making money there, loved his own country better, and intended, when he had acquired a competence, to pass the remainder of his life at Veile. He was thus of a different way of thinking from our young friend from the States. Is it that the Great Republic is so infinitely superior to a slower-going British colony? or, is it that the unpatriotic youth is an ass, and this sturdy sea-captain a wise man, who, "in spite of all temptation, &c.," remains what he was born, and insists on believing that his native land is far the best of any?

And now we had to leave the eastern shore of Jutland, which had so far protected us from the fury of the north-west wind, and to cross the open Kattegat to the coast of Sweden, a voyage which, unless our luck was to be much better than it had been hitherto, was likely to bring us some tumbling about and anxiety.

The weather had been magnificent during the two days we had passed at Veile, but, of course, when we turned out on the morning of Monday, August 1st, and prepared to start, things looked bad again. The glass was falling, the sky was stormy of appearance, and the wind was cold and blowing from the dreaded quarter again—north-west. However, we got under weigh at 7 A.M., as the chart showed me that for the first forty miles of the journey we should never be far from some port or sheltered anchorage under the lee of one of the islands.

The wind was nearly aft, so we soon left the red roofs of Veile behind us, and ran past the forests which were now swaying wildly, and groaning beneath the freshening breeze. Hard squalls rushed down upon us from the mouths of the ravines, throwing the yacht on her beam ends, and driving her through the hissing water at a merry rate. It was a splendid day for a sail on the sheltered fiord; but, as we approached the open sea, and saw the steep white-capped waves ahead of us, we felt some disinclination to scudding away to leeward from the protection of the mainland.

We reached the mouth of the fiord, and were abreast of Rosenvold Point; so I had now to decide whether to run on into the Kattegat, or adopt some more prudent course. I was still in doubt when the weather very opportunely settled the question by showing us clearly what were its intentions. Above the hills to windward there rose suddenly a dark mass of vapour, with a menace in its speed and wild shapes that was not to be disregarded. We took in the mizen, and scandalized the mainsail; no sooner had we done so, than the squall was on us, and a pretty stiff one it was, accompanied by cold rain. All having been made snug on board, I went below to consult the chart, and decided to make for the small bay of Sandbierg, which lies to the north of Veile Fiord, and where there is a sheltered anchorage with the wind from north-west. This was not much out of our course, and would bring us twenty miles nearer our destination.

From Rosenvold Point we sailed up the coast with the wind abeam, our lee gunwale under water, at as fast a rate as I have ever seen the little yacht attain, for ten miles, when we came to Biornsknude Point. We rounded this rocky wedge-shaped cape, giving it a wide berth; for a dangerous shoal extends from it some way out to sea, and then we opened out the rougher waters of Sandbierg Bay. We tacked into it, making very little progress, as usual, against the choppy sea; the *Falcon* is a very good sea boat, but I should certainly not like to have to claw off a leeshore with her in a gale of wind, and I had always to take this failing of hers into account when cruising on these coasts. Sandbierg Bay did not look particularly inviting on this stormy rainy day; its shores were flat and desolate, and only a few houses could be seen standing among some trees at its farther end. The mouth of the bay is encumbered by extensive shoals, the limits of which are not indicated by beacons; but we found no difficulty in knowing when it was time to go about, for, rough as the water was, it was still perfectly clear, and we could always see the rocks and sands beneath us, and so estimate the depth with sufficient accuracy.

At twelve o'clock we came to an anchor close under the shore, opposite a little wooden jetty. Before us was a treeless expanse of country; about a hundred yards from the water's edge stood what appeared to be a railway-station, in front of which was brought up an engine with a train of cattle-trucks. This sign of civilization surprised me, for, according to my charts and maps, there was no railway or village anywhere in the neighbourhood. There was only one other house in sight, a large red brick building, which was ugly enough and deserted enough to be a railway company's hotel. But not a single human being was to be seen on the shore, and not a craft of any description, save our own, was in the bay. We had, in all conscience, found a quiet anchorage this time, and here we were not likely to be disturbed at day-break, as we had been while lying in the harbour at Veile; for there, each morning, the paddle ferry-boat used to bring across the weedy bay successive cargoes of cackling market women, and disembark them on the quay just above our heads, where they would stand and discuss us shrilly until it was time for them to commence their business.

I pulled off in the dinghy, and landed on this desolate shore in the hope of coming across some of the natives, but no one could I find; the railway-station was deserted, and the railway-hotel was as yet a delusive shell. I tried the door, and found it locked, and, peering through the window, I discovered that the building was unfurnished and unoccupied. So, balked of my anticipated conversation with the fair barmaid of this lonely terminus, I took a walk along the sea shore, which would have looked pretty had the sun been shining and the rain been absent. There was but a narrow margin of pebbly beach, and up to this came a lovely carpet of soft grass and many flowers—thyme, harebells, yellow snapdragons, and others. After a while I reached some sand-hills, where I saw several rabbits dodging about among the tough sea grass. These I stalked, and attempted to kill with stones, a healthy sport, but one which is so monotonously unsuccessful that I soon wearied of it, and returned to the jetty where I had left the dinghy. As I approached I, to my delight, at last perceived a human being; this was but a small specimen of the natives, a boy, who was standing on the pier, gazing down at my dinghy with so profound an interest that he was not aware of my approach till I was close upon him; then, suddenly seeing me, a look of horror came to his face, and, with a shriek, he fled precipitantly from the terrible foreigner. My experiences on the shores of Sandbierg Bay having thus proved somewhat dispiriting, I returned on board, and indulged in a short swim round the vessel; short, firstly, because the water was cold after the rain, and secondly, because it swarmed with huge jelly-fish of brilliant hues, which had to be carefully dodged, for some of the medusæ of the Baltic inflict very painful stings, and will occasionally produce serious illness.

I had despaired of holding any intercourse with the natives, but, just as we had finished dinner, I perceived a man pulling off to us in a boat from the further end of the bay. He came alongside, and, without ceremony, threw up his painter, and stepped on deck.

He was a pale and anxious-looking youth. After glancing quickly from Wright to myself he came to the conclusion that I was the skipper, and, drawing from his breast a coloured official envelope, crumpled and worn as if with much handling, he presented it to me with a bow.

We could not speak, or understand each other's tongues, but we got along somehow, and the conversation that took place was more or less as follows.

"What is this?" I asked in English.

"I am the telegraph clerk, and I have brought you this telegram, Captain," he replied in Danish.

"Oh, that is not possible; I expect no telegram here."

"It is for you, Captain," he said positively. "Yours is the only vessel in port; read the inscription."

I tried to decipher the address, and it appeared to be, "To the captain of the vessel which will come to Sandbierg Bay." I shook my head again. Then he became very voluble, almost angry, and I understood him to say that the evidence of the telegram being intended for me was conclusive, as, not only was mine the only vessel now in the bay, but that there had been no other in the memory of man, and that the message had been awaiting me here for a great number of years. Patiently I endeavoured to explain to him that when I had sailed that morning I had no intention of visiting Sandbierg, that I had not even then heard of the existence of such a place, and that, consequently, it was impossible that anyone could have telegraphed to me here. He seemed, at last, to grasp the force of this reasoning, for he thrust the telegram back in his breast, sighed deeply, and looked wistfully round the horizon as if in search of the mysterious vessel that had been so long expected, and never came. This telegram seemed to be a terrible weight on this poor young fellow's mind; the whole object of his life was evidently to rid himself of it; he was like a second Vanderdecken. I gave him some refreshment to keep the cold out, and said a few hopeful words to him in English, on which he seemed somewhat happier, and, getting into his dinghy, he pulled off to the shore, where he is still, no doubt, lying in wait to carry that undelivered document on board any rare vessel that may visit this weird and deserted bay.

All that afternoon the wind had howled, and the scud driven across the Kattegat; but in the evening it became finer, no doubt in consequence of our refusing to accept Vanderdecken's fatal telegram; had we taken it of him a hurricane would surely have overtaken us. The wind fell altogether, and after a wintry day followed a calm, cloudless, and warm summer's night. Far away seawards we could see the flashing lights on the different islands, and so clear was the atmosphere that, when the moon rose, we could distinguish the shores of Endelawe and Aebelo Islands, which had been invisible all day.

We got under weigh at six o'clock the next morning. Just as we were off the engine attached to the train of cattle-trucks whistled loudly. It sounded like a mocking farewell to the foreign yacht. But we were amazed to see that there were still no signs of life on the shore—no passengers, no officials at the station, not a human being was in sight. I looked through my binoculars, but could not distinguish driver or stoker on that demon engine. Sandbierg Bay was clearly uncanny, and the sooner we were out of its haunted waters the better.

It was a sunny morning with a moderate west-south-west wind. We set all sail, and steered out to sea, towards the island of Endelave, which was about ten miles distant. We reached it in two hours, and sailed close along its southern shore, which was low, and seemed very fertile. From here we made for the larger island of Samso, and doubled Vestborg Point, a rocky headland on its south-west extremity, at twelve o'clock.

And now dark clouds rose suddenly behind us, and the wind shifted to west-north-west, a bad sign. Prudence now suggested that we should bring up under the lee of Samso, and wait there till we saw what the weather was going to do. There was all the more reason for doing this, as, for the next fifty miles of our journey, we should be quite exposed to a north-west wind sweeping across the broad Kattegat, and would have no port to run for; the harbourless bays and rocky reefs of the north of Siaelland presenting only the most dangerous of lee shores.

I hesitated, but referred the matter to our faithful aneroid, which was high and steady, and said, "go on."

We accordingly ran before the wind from the safe shelter of Samso, across the mouth of the Great Belt towards the north of the island of Seiero, twenty miles away. When we had sailed half the distance, the weather began to look very menacing; a mass of pitch-black cloud, like a solid wall, was rising along the whole western horizon. I had, by this time, learnt some of the tricks of this eccentric Baltic climate, and knew that the sky had a habit of threatening considerably more than it performed; and that, though violent squalls are very frequent, they last but a short time. Ominous signs that would keep one in port in England must be disregarded on these waters, else one would not get far on one's cruise; and, on the other hand, the finest looking sky is the most treacherous here, and cannot be relied on.

My barometer had not deceived me, there was no gale of wind about; but a violent thunder-storm overtook us, accompanied by such torrents of rain that the sea, which had been slightly choppy, was completely beaten down. This downpour continued all the afternoon, hiding the land, so that nothing but universal moisture was visible round us.

At five o'clock the sky cleared a little, and we saw a few miles ahead a lonely light-house, which I knew must be the one on Seiero Island. The wind now fell light, and we did not reach the north point of the island until after six. As we would find no port if we sailed on, I decided to stay here for the night. We doubled the point, and anchored off its east shore. I

SEIERO ISLAND AND LIGHTHOUSE.

knew that this would be a very exposed position should it come on to blow from the north-west, but there was no help for it; there was no secure anchorage between this and Ise Fiord, forty miles away.

Seiero Island is five miles long, but it is very narrow, and its two extremities are like sharp wedges; it runs north-west and south-east, and, therefore, though it affords shelter from all other winds, both sides of it are exposed to the most frequent and most dangerous wind of all. Not only this island, but the long lean promontories that jut out from the north of Siaelland —that of Siaellands Odde for example—also tend in a north-west direction; so that a vessel that is caught by a north-west storm on this coast has no pleasant time of it.

However, the wind was now westerly again, and as long as it held in that quarter we had nothing to fear. We were anchored at some distance from the shore, as rocks and shoals surround the north of the island. In front of us was the stone light-house standing on a bare hill. There were no other houses in sight, and no human beings, merely steep downs and rocks that were covered with multitudes of noisy sea-birds, while the heads of seals were to be occasionally seen peering above the water. It was even more lonely an anchorage than that of the previous night, but very far from being so safe an one.

This, after all, proved to be rather an anxious night for us, or,rather, it would have been so had we not gone to sleep and forgotten all about it; for, after

17

dinner, the wind, which had been blowing right off shore, began to gradually edge round to the northward, and when I turned in it was only a little west of northwest, so that the island barely sheltered us. We tumbled about a bit in the lop, which the freshening breeze was rapidly raising, and we could hear the melancholy booming of the seas on the other side of the island. However, the glass was still steady, and we both slept soundly, knowing that if bad weather came on it would very soon wake us, and that it was, therefore, not necessary to set an anchor watch.

CHAPTER XIII.

THE KATTEGAT AND ISE FIORD.

At three o'clock the next morning I was awakened by that deafening jumble of noises which is produced when a small vessel is tumbling about at anchor in a seaway—the groaning of timber, the rattling of the contents of lockers, the clashing together of the various articles hanging from the forecastle roof, the creaking of the main-boom, the straining of the chain, and manifold other scrapings and gruntings and thumpings which perplex the listener to account for. I got on deck, and found that it was still dark, but that the first signs of day-break were appearing in the east It was not the sort of morning to cheer up a man who had just turned out of his comfortable bunk. The wind was gusty and bitterly cold, the sky was stormy-looking, and the bleak expanse of dark rough sea before me had an uninviting aspect; so I felt that I should have been better pleased had I wakened up and found myself in some snug harbour instead of at this exposed anchorage.

The wind had not only veered to the north-west in the night, but had even gone a point or so to the northward of that, so that we were now on a lee-shore. Under these circumstances it would not do to remain where we were any longer. I roused the peacefully sleeping Wright, and we got under weigh at once. We had a long day before us, and I thought we should be able to reach Elsinore, which was sixty-five miles away, before night.

We had first to sail in a north-easterly direction so as to weather the extremity of the promontory of Siaellands Odde, after doubling which we would have a fair wind all the way to the Sound. Siaellands Odde is one of the worst dangers to navigation on this coast. It is a remarkably shaped neck of land, twelve miles long, and generally under two miles in breadth, and from its point there extends for another sixteen miles out to sea a narrow strip of rocky reefs, dry in patches, but for the most part covered with water, on which many an unfortunate vessel has been lost. There are several navigable passages across this reef; one, with five feet of water in it, is close under the cape; but the pilot-book told me that there were no leading marks for it, and that "the only directions that can be given will apply also to the other channels, viz., that the agitation of the water is less in them than on the reefs." Seeing that the weather was thick, that a nasty sea was running, and that I had no good chart of this portion of the coast, I prudently decided to avoid these somewhat dangerous short cuts, and sail through the broad ship-channel between the Yder Reef and the Hastens Ground.

We were thirteen miles from the entrance to this channel, and could just fetch it, close hauled on the port tack. We were a long while getting there, and at times it seemed as if we should not be able to weather the Yder Reef; for a high steep sea was running, and the *Falcon*, as usual, when turning to windward under such circumstances, jumped about a good deal, but made very little head-way, and sagged to leeward in a disheartening fashion. At last we approached the reef, which certainly presented a terrible appearance; the seas were breaking on it with a great roar, and the shallow water beyond was whirling and foaming like the surface of a boiling cauldron. The rocks seemed to be all covered, except in one place where a small black patch was occasionally visible in the midst of the raging waters. On this dry patch stood a large beacon, or, rather, a refuge, called the Ronnen, a squat tower, painted with red and white horizontal bands, in which, the pilot-book informed me, provisions are stored, so that if a vessel be wrecked on the reef, and the crew succeed in reaching this refuge, they can support life until succour can be sent to them from the mainland.

Two miles outside the Ronnen is the beacon which marks the extremity of the Yder Reef. This we doubled at seven o'clock, then, slacking off our sheets, we ran before the wind, with far easier motion and much greater speed than before, across the broad bay which extends from Sieallands Odde to the entrance of the Sound.

The north-west wind was kind to us this day; it blew freshly, and was anything but warm, but it was not the blustering bully we had hitherto known. This was well for us, as the sea soon becomes dangerously rough on the open Kattegat, and even now that only a steady breeze was blowing, high wall-like masses of water rolled down upon us in so threatening a manner that we had to acknowledge that we would have preferred less to more wind.

At mid-day the sky suddenly cleared, and the wind fell. At one o'clock it was almost calm, and our mainsail began to flap about, despite Wright's persistent whistling for a breeze, so, as Elsinore was still many leagues away, and there seemed to be but a small chance of reaching it before nightfall, I altered my plans. We were now in the middle of the bay, and about five miles from the nearest land—the high capes that border the entrance to Ise Fiord. To the north of us, far away on the sea-horizon, rose a tower, the light-house on the little island of Hesselo, a remote spot, which, I understand, is inhabited by one man and multitudes of seals and rabbits. I decided to make for Ise Fiord, which abounds with harbours and safe anchorages; so, bearing away, we steered towards Spotsbierg Point. We did not reach it for three hours, so light was the wind, and we should not have got there then had not a squall opportunely come down on us while we were yet a mile away.

This inlet, which is the most extensive fiord in Sicalland, is well worthy of a visit. At its entrance it is only two miles wide; but within it expands into a great sheet of water, upwards of ten miles in breadth, having several long winding tributary fiords connected with it, amongst others, Roeskilde Fiord, a beautiful gulf, twenty miles in length, at whose further end stands the very ancient royal city of the same name. A whole summer's holiday might be well spent in cruising among the islands and inlets of Ise Fiord. It ought, indeed, to be the paradise of small boat sailors, yet I did not see a single pleasure craft upon its waters. It is a great pity that this inland sea, with its clear water, wooded shores, and all, cannot be transported bodily to the mouth of the Thames. The Cockneys would appreciate it, and know how to use it, and possibly to misuse it too.

As I entered the fiord I perceived a group of red-roofed cottages on the east shore of the Narrows, and a small artificial harbour of rough stones, inside which two or three fishing boats were lying. My chart ignored the existence of village or harbour, but, as this looked a snug little place, I sailed in and made fast to the quay. The harbour was a queerly constructed one. From the shore a rough jetty of timbers, filled in with great stones, extended across the shallows for about thirty yards, and then divided into two branches, which enclosed the tiny port, leaving a very narrow passage to the sea. A Y with its two arms bent round until their ends nearly met would serve as a plan of this primitive harbour. The village consisted of one store and about two score of fishermen's huts, not forming a street, but scattered over the shore, as if they had been thrown there haphazard. On the beach a number of fishing-boats were drawn up, and behind all rose breezy downs, on which cattle and sheep were grazing.

I went up to the store, and there found several fishermen and pilots, whom I saluted in English. They looked at me with some surprise, for, not having seen the yacht, they naturally wondered from whence I had turned up; but I very soon satisfied their curiosity, as not only the store-keeper but several of the other men spoke English well. An Englishman can never find any difficulty in making himself understood in the very smallest of Baltic fishing-harbours. As usual, all these honest hardy fellows were my friends at once, anxious to offer information, and be of any possible service. The store-keeper was—again as usual—a retired sea-captain, who now supplied the fishermen with everything they could possibly require, from aqua-vit to fishing nets; at his place they could purchase their simple provisions—stock-fish, salt pork, onions, and coffee—their clothes and furniture, even their coffins; he was the universal provider of the the place, the local Whiteley.

He offered to accompany me for a walk, and show me all that was to be seen in Hundested, as this out-of-the-way little settlement is called. First we crossed the downs—wondrously green and bright, with a pro-

THE KATTEGAT AND ISE FIORD. 265

fusion of thyme and harebells, as are all the downs in this fresh moist climate of Denmark—to the lighthouse on Spotsbierg Head. Here I was surrounded by a vast panorama, which included all the various features of Danish scenery. The waves were dashing on the base of the cliff on which we stood, and to the north stretched the boundless sea, with nothing to break its 'sameness but the small island of Hesselo. To the west the rugged bays and capes of the coast of Siaelland were visible as far as the entrance to the Great Belt. To the south lay the smooth blue waters of Ise Fiord, with its many islets and beech-crowned hills. And to the east the eye roamed over an immense tract of undulating country, having pastures and scattered villages, but consisting, for the most part, of wild and sombre forest-land, with here and there the gleaming waters of a lake or tarn; beyond the hills that formed the limit of this region the entrance to the Sound was faintly visible, and the lofty black promontory of Kullen, on the Swedish coast, rose from the sea like an island.

My friend, the store-keeper, was a very well-informed man, and was well up in the history of the neighbourhood. I noticed the remains of old earthworks on the downs near the light-house; these, he told me, had been thrown up by the Danes when they were at war with the English, in 1801. He was the chief man at Hundested, and, in addition to keeping the store, was a timber-merchant and owner of many fishing-boats. He had the interests of his native village very much at heart, and expressed great dissatisfaction at the way in which the little settlement had been treated by the Government. It seems that the following system prevails on the Danish coasts. If a sufficiently large community of fishermen represent to the Government that an harbour is necessary for their boats, an inspector is sent down to examine the proposed locality, and, if his report is satisfactory, the Government advances the necessary funds for the construction of the work; the fishermen give their labour, and afterwards repay the loan with interest by the levy of a harbour due—the *Falcon* was taxed sixpence for the use of this harbour. Now the energetic store-keeper, who was harbour-master as well as everything else in the place, had himself initiated the idea of Hundested Haven, and had drawn up a plan, which he showed me, representing what he considered his pet project should be like.

But the Government sent down its own harbour constructor, an unpractical official who had theories of his own, and who, despite the protestations of the fishermen, set them at work to carry out his plans, which resulted in the eccentric Y-shaped haven I have described. As was foretold by the sailors themselves, this has proved to be almost useless, and is gradually becoming entirely so. Its mouth faces the sea instead of opening out on the southern side towards the fiord, as it should do; hence it becomes impossible to get out when a strong wind is blowing from the Kattegat, as the waves would dash a vessel on the rocks before she could clear the entrance. Now, as it is only in rough weather that the fishermen can successfully carry on their occupation, they are liable to be detained in this unscientifically-devised harbour at the very time when they ought to be at sea. And, more than this, a gale has, on more than one occasion, completely filled the harbour with sand and weeds, so that the whole of the population, including the women and children, have had to turn out, and dig for days with great labour to free the imprisoned boats on which their daily bread depends. Again, even at its best, the harbour will not admit craft of more than four feet draught. Thus, in consequence of a government official's obstinacy, the unfortunate fishermen have saddled themselves with a heavy debt which they can never pay off; for now most of the skippers prefer remaining at anchor outside to entering such a rat-trap of a port, and consequently but few dues are collected.

I had noticed on entering the haven that the water, instead of being beautifully clear, as it is elsewhere in the Baltic, was of a thick white colour, as if quantities of chalk had been stirred up with it. The squall that was then blowing had, for the time, removed another unpleasant peculiarity of the haven, which, now that the wind had dropped, began to assert itself very strongly. This was a horrible stench, the like of which I have never experienced elsewhere, though I have been in many mal-odorous ports.

"Yes, we shall have cholera or the plague here some day, I expect," said the store-keeper when I remarked on it, "but it is nothing to-day: you should be here in really hot weather; then the stink is intolerable, and can be distinguished for a mile all round the harbour. Before that stupid harbour was built we had none of this. Then Hundested was becoming quite a little watering-place; Copenhagen people used to come here on account of the good bathing and the pure air. Few come here now; but to-day there is not much smell."

Hearing this, I tried to form an idea of what it would be like when there was "much smell," but gave up the attempt in disgust. Exceedingly disagreeable as this odour is I doubt whether it is prejudicial to health. It is put down to the masses of sea-weed that accumulate between the jetties. The Baltic water, probably in consequence of the small percentage of salt contained in it—one-seventh that of the ocean—seems to promote a vegetable decomposition differing from that which occurs in other seas, and it is certainly more offensive to the senses. The exhalation of this white water produced a remarkable effect; in the course of a few hours it turned all the grey paint inside our bulwarks and the white paint in our cabin dark brown. We found it not at all easy to wash off this stain, and, judging from its smell and colour, I think that the rotten weeds of Hundested throw off fumes of some sulphurous gas. It is quite possible that these stinking white waters, far from being unhealthy, possess valuable remedial properties, and that the much-reviled Government harbour designer has unconsciously proved a benefactor to the people of this hamlet, who should forthwith sell their fishing-boats, roof over their haven, advertise well, and all make their fortunes as the proprietors of the all-curing Hundested Medicinal Baths. Here, too, is a chance for some of our own company promoters. The inhabitants themselves do not belie the advantages of the scheme by their appearance; they are as robust, healthy-looking, clean-skinned a race as can be found in Europe.

Not only was my friend displeased with the Government on account of the unsatisfactory haven, but he sorely complained that Hundested, unlike other settlements of its size, did not possess a public school, and that very few of the fishermen could read or write—a rare exception to the rule among this well-educated people. He said that in consequence of this ignorance the poor mariners when they entered a Swedish port to to sell their fish were unable to reckon up their accounts, and were, therefore, woefully cheated by the Swedes. The Swedes, by the way, are not much liked by the lower classes in Denmark; they are accused of being cunning and dishonest. On the other hand, the Danes get along very well with the Norwegians, who speak their own language.

The store-keeper, who was evidently very anxious to forward the prosperity of unhappy Hundested, told me that he intended to go to Copenhagen himself in the autumn, interview the Minister of Home Affairs, and lay before him the grievances of the little community.

Hundested is one of the most important stations of the herring fishery on this coast. I was told that two weeks later hundreds of boats would be lying off here, and that a busy market would be held in the village attended by many wholesale fish-dealers from Copenhagen. Many of these fishing-boats were drawn up on the shingle beach above the haven, and were now being fitted out for the coming season. Each boat carries three hands, who, as a rule, own her between them. Three brothers, who owned one of the largest of the fleet, a craft of whose good qualities they were very proud, took me over her, and explained to me all the details of the fishing as it is carried on in these seas. Like most of the other boats, she had been built in Sweden, where labour and timber are much cheaper than in Denmark. She was not much bigger than the *Falcon*, was strongly built of oak, sloop rigged, sharp-sterned, like a whale-boat, with great sheer, a deep false keel, and stern and bow raking so much that her length on deck was nearly double that of the keel. She had no bulwarks, but there was a small cockpit aft for the man steering, and another forward for the hand working the net or lines—not a luxurious berth, this last, on a wild winter's night when the craft is running her nose into the icy waves. The rest of the vessel was occupied by the fish-well.

" And have you no cabin to sleep in? " I asked.

" We have not," was the reply of one of these hardy Norsemen; "you see we are young men yet, and can put up with the wet and cold; we can't afford to hamper up the boat with cabins."

A few years since none of these boats were provided with cabins, but most of the new ones have very confined sleeping quarters, mere lockers, opening into the cockpit. When it is remembered that these fishermen remain at sea for many days, even sailing as far as the island of Anholt in mid-winter, it will be understood that the islanders of Siaelland are by no means a degenerate race.

These craft, small as they are, can put up with a great deal of rough weather, though they are occasionally turned over by the dangerous breaking seas of the Kattegat. They can be readily beached; and, indeed, it often happens that when a fleet of them is overtaken by a sudden gale on an unprotected part of the coast they are run ashore, and the ballast—big stones from the beach—is thrown overboard, while the crews help each other to drag boat after boat out of the reach of the waves.

The solder having melted, the framework of our riding-light had tumbled to pieces; so I inquired of the store-keeper if there was a blacksmith in the place who could put it to rights for me. He said that there was no blacksmith, but that he knew of a man who might be able to do what I required. He then introduced me to a strange being who was a veritable Jack-of-all-trades, and, poor fellow, certainly master of none. This was the one pauper of Hundested, the village idiot, a harmless, hideously deformed, and crippled imbecile, arrayed in the filthiest of rags. His whole possession in the world besides his rags, and it is doubtful whether he could show a title to that, was a rough stone hut, open to all the winds of heaven, and destitute of furniture of any sort. He lived on charity, but would work when it pleased him. If one supplied him with tools and materials he would sometimes condescend to mend a pair of boots, undertake a bit of carpentering, repair fishing-nets, and, in short, do any odd job after a somewhat clumsy fashion. With some difficulty I persuaded him to try his hand at soldering, and purchased for him at the store the articles he asked for— a few lumps of coal, some wood, and a pennyworth of petroleum; he said he would beg or steal the other requisites. When he had completed his work he came into the store, and, to the amusement of the assembled sailors, held tightly to the lamp with both hands, and refused to even lay it down on the counter until he had received the stipulated payment. The poor idiot evidently entertained a profound mistrust of foreigners, which he did not attempt to conceal. When I handed him the money he seemed greatly surprised, and skipped about the floor with gestures and inarticulate cries of exceeding joy.

"What's the matter with you?" asked the storekeeper.

"The matter?" exclaimed the poor fellow, with an air of dignified pride, "I know now that you foolish people are all wrong in calling me an idiot. Because this man is a stranger I have charged him three times too much, and he paid it! The Englishman is more idiot than I am, being taken in so easily. Me an idiot, indeed! Why, even our clever host here only charged him the right price for the beer he is drinking. Oh, you idiots, you idiots!" and, shrieking with delight, he danced out of the store. I believe that one could find a moral somewhere in this story.

I think that our dinners must have been somewhat indigestible, for both Wright and I dreamt terrible dreams this night. I awakened several times with a start, under the impression that I had fallen asleep at the tiller, and had allowed the yacht to drive among the breakers on a shoal. The sounds around us were well calculated to suggest such a nightmare; for a fresh wind was blowing from the sea, and only the narrow jetty was between us and the waves, which dashed on the stones with a great roar, and occasionally washed right over and dropped a few buckets-full of water on our decks. Wright dreamt that he was in a house on fire, or in the infernal regions, or in some other burning place; and, no doubt, this train of ideas could be put down to the heavy sulphurous fumes that had crept into our cabin from the water outside.

On the next morning, August the 4th, a light wind was blowing from the east, and a pilot, who had just come in, told us that a strong northerly current was running out of the Sound, so that it was very doubtful whether we would be able to reach Elsinore that day. I was not at all loth to postpone my voyage, so as to have a day's exploration of the fiord in the dinghy; but there was something else to be considered. I had received no letters from home since I had left Kiel, and I knew that important correspondence was awaiting me at Copenhagen, which I was anxious to get without delay. Then I examined the chart, and found that the town of Frederikssund on Roeskilde Fiord was connected with Copenhagen by a railway twenty miles in length. This decided me ; I would combine business with pleasure, sail to Frederikssund in the dinghy, and thence take train to the capital and fetch my letters.

I had a voyage of sixteen miles before me. I started at seven o'clock, pulled up the coast, passed the little fishing-haven of Lyeness lying at the foot of a steep cliff, and then, leaving the Great Bredning, entered the narrower waters of Roeskilde Fiord. This fiord was much like the others I had visited, now narrowing, now broadening, and always bordered by charmingly green hills ; but this was the loneliest inlet I had yet seen on the coast; very few habitations were visible on the shore, and I perceived no signs of agriculture. The water was, as a rule, very shallow—so that I had to follow the channel even with the dinghy—and was overgrown with an extraordinary quantity of weed, which, in places, was beginning to assume rich autumnal tints. The whole of one small bay was of a deep crimson colour from this cause, and the vivid green pasture behind it and the bright blue sky above formed a treble band of such dazzling hues as are only seen in the brief northern summer.

After I had rowed eight miles in the hot sun, a northerly wind began to blow right down the fiord, and I was able to ship the oars and sail the rest of the way. At last I came to a point where the convergence of two promontories leaves but a very narrow passage for the waters of the fiord, and here there is a bridge of boats from one shore to the other. I passed under the bridge, and there before me, on the left bank of the fiord, which had again suddenly expanded into a broad lake, stood the little town of Frederikssund.

And now I had to discover where I could leave the dinghy while I went to Copenhagen, for even Danish boys cannot be trusted not to meddle with an unguarded boat. Danish boys, by the way, are infinitely less naughty than Dutch; but, being somewhat less overworked at school, are more mischievous than German lads. As I approached the bank I saw half a dozen urchins eyeing me with an interest that betokened danger. Then, to my great relief, I perceived that there was a vessel in the harbour—a good sized schooner that lay along the quay, discharging coal. In her I recognized my natural protector; the skipper of a collier would be certain to speak English; I would enter into a defensive alliance with him, and all would be well. So I made fast to the quay, and called on the captain, who did speak English and had just arrived from Charleston in the Firth of Forth, having been eleven days on the voyage. He gladly consented to take charge of the dinghy during my absence; so I brought her round, and secured her to the other side of his vessel, where the boys could not get at her without swimming, and he promised me that if they tried this his crew would pelt them with the British coals he had on board.

18 *

My mind being thus set at ease I walked up the chief street, rather a smart one for a town of only 1,300 inhabitants, and lunched at a comfortable hostelry called the "Ise Fiord Hotel." There is something very homely and pleasant about the Danish inns. They are like what tradition tells us the English inns were in the good old days, when there was plenty of solid comfort; when the guests were jovial beings who supped heartily and feared not dyspepsia; and the host was a host indeed, and became one's friend before one had been half an hour under his roof; but the Danish inns have the further advantage of being scrupulously clean, which I rather doubt anything was in the England of those same good old days. The host here could not speak English, but his father-in-law was—even yet another of them—an old sea-captain who spoke our language well. He was a jolly old gentleman who had been in the China trade; he seemed very interested in our cruise, so much so that he sent his little grandson to fetch the editor of the local paper, who forthwith came with note-book and pencil, and proceeded to cross-examine me at length—the captain acting as interpreter—while he jotted down my history, which, he told me, would appear as an article in the next day's edition.

As there was no train to Copenhagen for some hours I crossed the pontoon bridge, and visited Jaegerspriis, an old royal palace and park which belonged to the Crown of Denmark nearly six hundred years ago, and where many interesting statues and other curiosities are to be seen; but what pleased me most was the wood to the north of the park, which I had noticed while sailing down the fiord, whose waters it borders for some distance. The glades in this wood are singularly beautiful; there are spots where one could imagine oneself to be in one of those primeval forests, long since destroyed, which once covered all these northern lands. The oaks here are the largest in the country, and the King's oak—I quote from Murray—is the largest in all Denmark; it is now reduced to a hollow trunk with green branches issuing from the inside as well as from the outside. Its circumference is forty-two feet.

I then returned to the railway-station of Frederikssund, and took my place in a third class compartment with a family of handsome peasants, who, to judge from their anxiety and utter helplessness, had never travelled by train before. They all began to address me together in eager voices; they were, no doubt, asking me whether they were in the right carriage, when they would reach their destination, and the many other questions with which the inexperienced are wont to worry their travelling companions; and when I informed them in English that I was a foreigner, and did not understand what they were talking about, they became suddenly silent, and sat eyeing me with open-mouthed consternation, as if I had been some strange and dangerous beast; and the little children, who, displeased with their unfamiliar surroundings, had been ready to weep on the slightest provocation, now broke out into a chorus of vigorous bo-hoo-ing, and would not be comforted. The whole party looked upon me with profound suspicion; and when one of the stalwart sons had filled his pipe, and could find no match to light it with, he would not ask me for one, and when I handed him a box he hesitated to take it until his little wife, relenting towards me, nudged him, and whispered to him to remember his manners. This made matters worse, for the young man now seemed to wax jealous, and frowned and glared savagely at me with his big blue eyes for the rest of the journey.

It would be difficult to find anywhere in Europe a jollier lot of people to travel among than the seafaring population of Denmark—the honest, open-hearted, hospitable and intelligent herring-fishers of the coast villages. But from what I saw and heard of them I doubt whether the peasant proprietors are quite so agreeable a race. In character they much resemble the same class in some parts of Normandy; they have all the solid and unornamental virtues; they are thrifty, very shrewd at a bargain, suspicious of foreigners. These small freeholders form the strongest party in the country, and hold exceedingly democratic and radical opinions—an anomaly for a class which represents the landed interests—whereas the townspeople and fishing population are, for the most part, what we should call Conservatives. The farmers are all for the doing away with army, navy, and even the Crown, so that the taxation may be lightened. There may be reason in some of their complaints against the present system of things, but their policy seems to be "Cut down the taxation which affects us at whatever cost to the rest of the community." They are apparently blind to all other considerations but the saving of a penny here or a penny there, and I understand that but too many of these selfish and short-sighted boors would welcome Anarchy or Socialism if they could be thereby relieved of some petty rate. But it is not only in Denmark that men grudge the penn'orth of tar necessary to keep the ship of State sweet and taut.

At last I was landed in Copenhagen, and on leaving the station found myself among broad bright boulevards, so that I could have imagined myself in Paris were it not for a glimpse of the port with its forest of masts. But Copenhagen, notwithstanding its animated aspect, imposing squares and fine streets, is, as I very soon discovered, not a small Paris by any means, very happily for itself, no doubt. For its size, it is, I imagine, the soberest, quietest, most early-to-go-to-bed, in short, the most respectable city in Europe. The casual stranger would call it distinctly dull.

I found that the Consulate was closed, so I could not get my letters until the next morning, and I had to find a lodging for the night. I avoided the swell hotels, among other reasons because I had no luggage with me, and wandered about in search of a more modest establishment. I soon came upon what I required in the "Amalia Gade," close to the Custom House, a little inn frequented by skippers, and kept by—I need scarcely say it—one of the great legion of English-speaking ex-sea-captains.

I took a stroll in the evening, and retired early to bed, my mind filled with a profound astonishment that a city of 240,000 inhabitants should be so entirely free from any signs of dissipation. As a rule, the first impressions of a lonely traveller who finds himself in a strange town at night depend very much on *café-chantants* and such-like places of frivolous amusement, which, perhaps, he does not visit once in a twelvemonth when at home. And yet, I believe, there are some travellers who, having finished their dinner at the hotel, do not, like ordinary mortals, say to the waiter, "What's going on here to night? Which is the best music-hall?" but pass the evening reading up their guide-books, and reserve all their energies for the visiting of museums, picture-galleries, churches, and other sights of an improving description; unfortunately I had not been educated up to this. Later on, when I saw more of Copenhagen, I somewhat modified my views; for has not this city its Tivoli and its Opera-House, famous for its beautiful ballets? Still the amusements of Tivoli are rather childish, and it cannot be denied that this capital seems very dull to the trivial tourist.

But when one really knows Copenhagen, has friends in it, and mingles in its charmingly unaffected and bright society, it soon becomes to him one of the pleasantest of European cities. I saw something of this real and inner life—and hope to see more of it—

with the result that, if I were told that I must leave London and take up my residence in some other large town, I am not sure that I should not select the fair capital of Denmark.

CHAPTER XIV.

GILLELIE AND THE SOUND.

The next morning I went to the Consul's and my letters were delivered to me. One of them, I found to my dismay, necessitated my speedy return to England. " Still, I shall have time," I said to myself, " to see something of the Sound and its ports on both the Swedish and Danish coasts before I lay up the yacht at Copenhagen, and take steamer home?" So I planned, reckoning without my host. "Host," as I learnt at school, is derived from a Latin word signifying "enemy," which at last, in consequence of the unfriendly disposition of most landlords, came to acquire its present meaning; I am using the word in its original sense, for the host I allude to is our old foe, the north-west wind.

I took train to Frederikssund, and thence, tide and wind being against me, and a choppy sea running on the fiord, I had a hard pull back to Hundested, which I did not reach till after dark. I found that the fumes of the haven had still further deepened the brown stain on our paint, which Wright had been vigorously scrubbing with hot water and soda, but all in vain ; he now abandoned the attempt in despair, for nothing but a scraper could take the stuff off. Should the Medicinal Bath scheme not come up to the expectations of its promoters, there might be a fortune in the Hundested Patent Indelible Brown Stain.

The next day, August the 6th, was too fine. Not a cloud was in the sky, and a very light breeze from the north-east scarcely ruffled the water ; this would be a head wind for us as far as Gilbierg Head, the most northerly point of Siaelland, twelve miles away. We tacked up the coast, progressing very slowly, by barren sand-hills, pine-forests, and bleak heaths, a land that appeared to be but sparsely inhabited. We passed one little red-roofed fishing-village with a row of brown fishing-boats drawn up on the sandy beach in front of it, and with sombre pine-woods rising immediately behind, the whole forming a very picturesque scene. A Swedish square-topsail ketch had come out of Ise Fiord with us ; for many hours we could not shake her off; with every tack either we passed close under her stern or she under ours, and her skipper became wild with annoyance that he could not show a clean pair of heels to so small and clumsy-looking a craft as ours. We heard him using dreadful language to each of his men in turn, reviling them for their careless steering, and at last he took the wheel himself to show them how the thing was to be done. Then, no doubt to his great astonishment and disgust, we crossed his bows on our next tack quite one hundred yards ahead, and rapidly left him astern.

Later on, the wind fell away altogether, so we tried a mode of progression which certainly seemed a strange one to adopt on this open and usually stormy sea, with no land to the northward between us and the far-off coast of Norway. We got close under the shore in four feet or so of water, and punted the yacht along the coast with the quant. The bottom was well adapted for punting, being of hard sand, with rocks here and there. The sun was shining full into the clear water, so that it assumed a beautiful pale emerald tint, and we could see the submarine gardens beneath us, the swaying sea-weeds growing to the rocks, the delicate-hued anemones, and the dark sea-mosses; while the grotesque crabs crawled amongst the stones, and the transparent rose and violet-coloured medusæ floated lazily half-way down. The fish did not like the look of us, and we could see them darting away as we approached.

We picked our way through crowds of rocks, shoving off from one to the other with the boat-hook, and sometimes our keel grated on the bottom. It was a queer sort of navigation, but interesting for a change, and we got along at a good rate.

In the afternoon a south-east wind sprang up, and, forsaking the shallows, we set sail again. But there was not enough wind to do us much good, and at nine o'clock it had all fallen away once more; so we brought up under the shore for the night in four fathoms of water, being still about five miles from Gilbierg Head. And now I saw that the glass was falling rapidly, and the moon rose over the land with a lurid and watery appearance like a bonfire seen through a haze. Bad weather was evidently coming on. But had we not had three fine days in succession? More than this cannot be reasonably expected on the fickle Baltic.

We enjoyed a quiet night, for the breeze was off shore; but the next morning brought dirty weather —a fresh and squally wind from the south-east, and heavy rain. The glass had fallen half an inch in the night, and was still going down. It did not look much like getting to Elsinore, for the south-east wind was a head one for us, blowing as it does right down the Sound, and the northerly current the pilot at Hundested had spoken of would, most probably, be still setting out. Between us and Elsinore no port existed, to my knowledge, and my charts indicated no harbour under the rugged cliffs on the opposite coast of Sweden. The prospect before us was not a pleasant one. It seemed very doubtful whether we should get anywhere if we proceeded on our voyage; but we felt so disinclined to give it up and run back to Hundested that we decided to push on and trust to luck; the wind might change at any moment, and make it all right for us.

We tacked towards Gilbierg Head in the smooth water under the shore, but I knew that after we had rounded this point we should encounter a wind right in our teeth, and, most probably, a nasty sea as well.

As we approached the headland we saw a good-sized village lying at the foot of it, lavishly decorated with Danish flags as if some festival was in progress. Wright took up the glasses, and scanned the place.

"Hullo, why, what's this?" he suddenly cried in tones of amazement; "do you know that there's a fine harbour there, Sir, and fishing-boats in it?"

I could scarcely credit such good news; but, looking through the glasses, I saw that it was even as he had said; a well-sheltered haven was before us, situated at the very spot where it would be of the highest service to us; for round the point, a mile farther on, the sea was already in violent commotion, and we should have been unable to make any way to windward.

This harbour was altogether ignored by my chart, and the pilot-book did not allude to it, so its existence was a pleasant surprise. Seeing good-sized herringers within, I knew that there was water enough for us; we therefore tacked up to it, and passed between the jetties. On the beach, in front of us, was the fishing-village with the usual large wooden building in which the herrings are salted. The haven was constructed on a more scientific principle than that of Hundested. Two rough jetties, formed of great stones rounded by the sea, and kept together by balks of timber, had been carried out from the shore at a distance of sixty yards apart, and from the end of the northern jetty another stout breakwater turned off at right angles towards the southern jetty, so that the entrance of the haven was on the southern side, and protected from the prevailing storm-wind. Here there is no tendency to silt up, and a depth of five feet is always maintained. The harbour was crowded with smacks, all gay with bunting, and many others were drawn up on the beach between the piers. The whole of the population were promenading in their Sunday best, seemingly in a very merry mood, and not one, but even three or four of the inevitable English-speaking sailors were alongside of us in a moment as we touched the quay.

"What's going on here to-day?" I asked one of these as he lent me a hand to make the yacht fast.

"It is the annual regatta for our fishing-boats," he replied; "you've just come in time to see it; they will start in an hour."

My informant, whose name was Andersen, was himself a fisherman, but his boat was on the beach undergoing repairs, so he could not compete. He took me under his charge during our stay, and showed me round. The boats were of a larger size than those of Hundested, and the race would have been interesting were it not that each vessel started when it pleased, so that, unless one carefully timed and remembered the exact moment when each passed the buoy that served as starting-point, it was impossible to say which was winning. And again, the vessels were so much alike that even the spectators on shore, who had taken the time, at last got very puzzled, and were unable to recognise the craft of their own relations. But I ought to mention that the people of this place have a very confused idea as to their relationships; they are all connected with each other in some way, for the fishing families will not intermarry with strangers. Every fisherman we met was introduced to me by Andersen as his cousin, and he said that the old lady who kept the grocer's shop at which we bought our provisions, was his step-grandmother-in-law. Such a relationship requires some thinking over, but it seemed clear enough to him, and, no doubt, was a comparatively uncomplicated one for this much connected community. But to return to the regatta. The boats carried plenty of spare canvas—huge squaresails and balloon jibs— and seemed to be well handled, and to be travelling fast. Each boat was crowded with the relatives of the crew—only some of the nearest ones, of course— women, children, and even babies, and dozens of bottled beer were placed in each hold for the thirsty mariners. The wind was fresh, and one vessel lost her mast, and another her bowsprit in a strong squall. At last one smack was declared the winner, and the regatta was over. But the best part of the festivity was still to come.

I learnt from Andersen that the village was called Gillelie, and that the haven, like that of Hundested, had been constructed by the fishermen, but that here the harbour had proved a success, so that the Government loan was being rapidly paid off by the dues. Our share was tenpence.

This, he said, was the greatest holiday of the year for the fishermen; by-and-bye there would be great fun on the hill above the village, as a *fête* had been organized, the proceeds of which were to be devoted to buying an organ for the church. The fishermen intended to amuse themselves, for this was the last day of their idle season, and all the herringers were ready for sea, and were about to sail to the fishing-grounds round the island of Anholt on the following morning.

"I suppose you will be starting at the same time," he added.

"I don't think that any of us will sail to-morrow," I said.

"How's that?" he asked; "the herringers must sail."

"It will be blowing a gale from the north-west," I replied.

"Ah, you are wrong, Captain; you don't know this coast like I do; it looks wild now, but it will be fine to-morrow."

"I don't know anything about the coast; but come below, and look at our glass."

It had fallen another quarter of an inch, and was now much lower than on any occasion since we had left England. I was sure that a strong, if a short, blow was coming. I was willing to stake my reputation as a weather-prophet on it, and, if I was wrong, I would never trust in a barometer again. As a man must be who cruises on strange coasts in small boats, I was always a close observer of the glass, and understood its ways and warnings pretty well; one's life depends upon such a knowledge. But my friend scouted the idea of an approaching gale, said he did not believe in glasses, and, what was more to the point, did not understand them.

"The wind's south-west," he urged; "we never get bad weather from that quarter."

"Then it will shift to the north-west by-and-bye," I replied; "I am sure that I, at any rate, will not sail to-morrow."

He told some of the other fishermen standing by what I had said, and I noticed that the older men shook their heads as they looked round the sky, and were evidently inclined to be of my way of thinking.

It was a day of revelry in Gillelie, and the men were making the best of it, for were they not to be off at dawn to spend the wild northern autumn on the fishing-grounds? and those who do not know the fisherman's life cannot picture to themselves what this means. A pine-clad hill rises above the village, commanding a fine view of the Sound and the opposite Swedish coast. On this tents had been pitched, and all the fun of a rustic fair was going on. There were refreshment-booths, shooting-galleries, merry-go-rounds, swings, and the other usual attractions, and in the evening there was to be a grand ball, a display of fireworks, and a theatrical entertainment.

I have been at a good many gatherings of this description in many parts of the world, but never at one which impressed me with such a high opinion of a people. True, there was a little drunkenness—for northern races will drink on occasion—but very little of it, and not one of these fishermen became objectionable in the slightest degree in his cups. It was very pleasant to watch the hearty enjoyment of these sturdy men, their well-dressed and comely wives and sweethearts, and pretty children—the Danish children are true children, and are just the jolly innocent little beings that one would imagine Hans Andersen must have lived amongst and been inspired by when he wrote his delightful tales.

Another noticeable feature of the *fête* was that a good many people of the higher classes were present—the "quality" of the neighbourhood—and also several ladies and their children from Copenhagen, who had come to Gillelie for the bathing, and were lodging for a few weeks in the fishermen's cottages. In Denmark all classes mingle together quite naturally in places of public entertainment in a way that is altogether unknown even in the most democratic lands, and it says a great deal for all that this is possible. This is the case not only in the country but in Copenhagen itself; for there is a charming simplicity in Danish life, which, it is to be hoped, what is called progress will not do away with. The peasant proprietors and their belongings were also present; and these farmers, ultra-radicals as they are, did not consider it necessary to prove their sturdy independence by an aggressive rudeness, but were as well-bred as the rest; there were some jolly clergymen also who put on no clerical airs, but enjoyed themselves as much as any. I was introduced to the leading fishermen and their families, and was soon very much at home;

and I do not think I have ever been at a more delightful ball than the one which took place in the big tent among the pine-trees, and at which, by the way, the ladies from Copenhagen were dancing with their friends in the same country dances as the buxom fish-wives and peasant girls. In Denmark the different classes evidently respect each other; but where else are the working people so refined and courteous in their manners, and, I may add, so neatly dressed, so cleanly in their habits?

After the ball the wood was illuminated with Chinese lanterns, and the firework display took place, unfortunately in the middle of a violent squall, which somewhat spoiled the effect. The wind had now shifted to the north-west, and was sweeping over the hill, howling through the bending pines, while the Sound beneath, which was only visible occasionally, when the moon gleamed out between the swift-driving clouds, was white with foam.

"What do you say to the weather now?" I asked Andersen.

"I think you may be right, Captain; it looks bad; but wait till to-morrow; it may fine down," replied that oracle.

At about midnight all the revellers returned to the village, and I went on board, crawling carefully along the narrow slippery jetty so as to avoid being blown into the sea by the fierce gusts. It was now blowing a heavy gale; the waves were washing over the weather-jetty, and showers of spray were being driven across the harbour. Before turning in Wright and I shifted the yacht; for, being on the lee side of the harbour, we were banging about against the jetty and the fishing-boats alongside of us. We took an anchor to the middle of the harbour, and, slacking out our stern-line, hauled out clear of everything.

On waking shortly after daybreak on August the 8th I found that the glass had fallen still lower, and that a regular hurricane was blowing from the west-north-west. The fishermen, far from putting to sea, were all busy securing their vessels, for there was some danger of these being dashed to pieces even in this sheltered harbour. It was as wild a morning as I have ever seen. The sky presented an extraordinary appearance, being of a cold green colour, while high up masses of cirrus clouds traversed it in parallel white threads, following the direction of the wind. The lower strata of clouds seemed to have been blown right out of the heavens. We were battened down all this day, for not only spray but solid lumps of water were hurled right across the haven, and fell upon our decks. We were wetter than we had ever been at sea.

After breakfast I clambered along the jetty, being, of course, soaked through long before I reached the shore, and walked up to Andersen's house.

"I shall believe in barometers for the future," were the first words he said; "as soon as I can afford it I will get one for my boat."

I had made an enthusiastic convert of him, and he

was anxious to learn all I could teach him on the use of the aneroid.

"It is a very fortunate thing for us fishermen," he said, "that yesterday's *fête* kept us all in port. Had it taken place two Sundays ago, as was originally intended, we should now have been off Anholt, where there is no harbour, and I think that many vessels and lives would have been lost. A few years ago a gale came on suddenly like this one, and twenty boats were capsized by the seas on the Anholt shoals, and all hands drowned."

He told me that none here remembered a summer in which the weather had been so unsettled, and in which strong north-west winds had been so frequent. All the fine weather had left this part of Europe for the English Jubilee. This was, at any rate, encouraging for me; I could look forward to getting along a little faster when I resumed my cruise on the following summer, instead of being weather-bound half my holiday, as had been the case this year.

In the afternoon, the storm being now at its height, I walked along the hills bordering the coast to the light-house on Nakke Head, and thence overlooked a seascape not easily to be forgotten. Nakke Head is a steep bluff surrounded by drifting sand-hills and heaths, with here and there clumps of dwarfed firs and black thorns, a desolate wind-swept tract on which only the hardiest plants can support existence. The scene landwards was of vast extent, and had a dreary grandeur that was very impressive; but on such a day

LIGHTHOUSE ON NAKKE HEAD.

as this it was the turbulent sea beneath that riveted all one's attention. Before me was the mouth of the Sound, and on the Swedish coast, twelve miles away, rose the promontory of Kullen—a huge isolated mass of granite, 900 feet high, standing out dark and gloomy in contrast to the verdant hills that elsewhere bordered these straits.

The Sound, that narrow gateway of the Baltic through which all the vessels that sail between the Ocean and the inland sea must pass, is at all times crowded with a remarkable quantity of shipping; but on this day the aspect of this great highway was exceptionally wonderful. Many hundreds of craft of all sizes and nationalities—transatlantic steamers, full-rigged ships, barques, schooners, and fishing-smacks were running into the Sound from the open sea, making for the shelter of the roads of Elsinore. Not a single vessel was heading the other way, all were scudding in before the tempest; many of them, no doubt, had put to sea several days before, bound round the Skaw into the German Ocean, but had been compelled to turn back by the violence of the hurricane. They were all staggering along under the smallest possible amount of canvas, pitching heavily into the frightfully high seas; here a full-rigged ship under close-reefed topsails; here a schooner under fore and main trysails; here a brig under bare poles; here a pilot-cutter under spit-fire jib, and the balance-reef down in her mainsail. Several vessels had lost spars or portions of their bulwarks; one Norwegian barque was evidently water-logged, and in a sinking condition, and was floundering slowly into smoother water, but just in time; and outside the Sound, on the raging Kattegat, were hundreds of other vessels, some hull down on the horizon, making for the same refuge, their fate still uncertain among those gigantic rollers, and, no doubt, with many an anxious heart on board of them.

I had brought the glasses with me, and, crouching under the lee of a thorn-bush, I watched vessel after vessel coming into the Narrows. There was a terrible fascination in the scene, and it was impossible to turn away from it. It seemed like a battle-field between the elements and vast fleets, the latter routed, and in full retreat, crippled and disheartened. There was one old brig that must have been caught by the gale on some bay on the Swedish coast, and was now endeavouring to weather the dark crags of Kullen. She was close-hauled under reefed topsails, and seemed to be doing little else but plunge into the furious seas that washed over her decks, while she slowly but surely sagged towards the iron-bound coast to leeward. But at last she got an offing, and, just before sunset, wallowed into the Sound, and was safe.

The storm lasted for three days, and detained us in Gillelie till August the 11th. This upset my calculations, and instead of visiting some of the towns on the Sound on my way I had to sail straight for Copenhagen. But the four days during which I was weatherbound in the little fishing-port passed pleasantly enough. The Danish fishing folk are exceedingly kind to the stranger who visits their shores in a small yacht, so that he leaves each hamlet with regret, as if it were his home, and he were saying good-bye to old friends.

There was one old fisherman—I suppose he was old because he had been upwards of thirty years at sea in big vessels before adopting the profession of fisherman, but he looked like a young man, and behaved like a boy—who became my particular chum during my stay. He was the most popular man in the place, especially with the children, a world-wide wanderer with the heart of a child. He had been a terrible rascal all his life, all out of boyish thoughtlessness and love of mischief, for none could look into his frank blue eyes and believe him capable of a mean or ill-natured action. This old boy, whom I will call Frederiksen, lived with his sister in a little hut among the fragrant pine-woods by the beach. There I dined twice with him during my stay, and his sister put on the table in honour of the guest the beef-steak and onions of Old England by the side of the rye-bread and aqua-vit of Scandinavia.

Frederiksen had quite a little library of books, among which there was one, he said, which was very interesting, as it was all about Kronborg Castle and Elsinore and the old kings who used to drink and fight there; he wished that I understood Danish, and could have read it. He showed me this volume, and I found that its title was—Hamlet. It was Shakespeare's play paraphrased and set out in the form of a prose narrative. When I told him that a dramatic version of this novel had been produced in England, and had met with considerable success, his national pride seemed to be highly gratified, and he said he was glad to hear that Danish literature was appreciated in England. In his version of the story all ends well: Hamlet and Ophelia marry and live happily ever afterwards.

In the evenings, while the storm was shrieking outside, and the *Falcon* was tumbling about in the haven as if she had been in a sea-way, Frederiksen used to smoke his pipe with me in our cabin, and spin strange but true yarns in an inimitable manner. His career had been varied and adventurous enough to fill a dozen boys' story-books; but he had never saved a penny till he gave up wandering, and settled down as a fisherman in his native village. He told me that he was now a rich man, having put by a thousand kroners —fifty-five pounds—and on the strength of this he was about to build himself a new and larger house. Unlike most sailors he had seen as much of the land as of the sea; for it seems that he was always shipping on vessels with something wrong about them, and then deserting them. He had dug for gold in California, and diamonds in the Cape. He had served with the Confederate army in the American Civil war, and had on two occasions narrowly escaped hanging as a "bounty jumper." He was before the mast on a British man-of-war during the Crimean war. He had fought for the Chinese rebels. He had cruised on the Pacific and Indian Oceans in a Yankee schooner which carried on a trade scarcely legitimate, indeed, almost piratical. Some of his tales of those experiences were exquisitely funny, and his Yankee skipper was a character who would make the fortune of a nautical novelist. Among other things he had been a policeman in Calcutta, and a jailor in a West India prison. After one of his many desertions he had walked from Trieste to Hamburg without a penny in his pocket; he said that all the people he met on the road were very kind to him, and fed him well because he looked jolly, and had not the hang-dog aspect of the ordinary tramp. He would sing Danish and English sea songs to the German and Austrian peasants at night, and, like Goldsmith, earned many a supper by his musical talents.

One night Frederiksen came to me and said, " My mother has got a little sing-song in her house this evening; you must come up there with me. I 'm the black sheep, the ne'er-do-well of my family, but they 're always glad to see me and my friends."

I, of course, gladly accepted the invitation, and accompanied him to one of the larger houses of the village. We entered a room comfortably, and even in a way luxuriously furnished—for though the Danish fishermen endure great hardships at sea, at home, thanks to their womankind, who are the best of housewives, their life is an easy one—and there found a very pleasant-looking, handsome old lady, and about twenty people of both sexes—sturdy young fishermen in blue jerseys, and some very bonny lasses. I was introduced to everyone. I had been prepared to find that they were all relatives; for, as I have explained, anyone in Gillelie is at least a cousin to anyone else, but now I learnt that everyone in the room was a descendant or a descendant-in-law of our hostess.

"There," said Frederiksen, "are my mother, brothers, sisters, nephews, and nieces, or, at least, some of them. Now make yourself at home."

It was indeed a jolly evening. The girls played the piano, and sang the simple and beautiful ballads of Denmark; many of the men, too, had good voices, notably Frederiksen, who rolled out the sea songs of England to perfection; one young fellow played admirably on the violin, and several glees were sung to the accompaniment of both instruments. I was ashamed to find that I alone was unable to contribute to the evening's amusement, till I remembered that I had once acquired some renown as an amateur conjuror, and succeeded in extemporizing an entertainment that seemed to amuse and astonish my audience.

There were some well-executed water-colour drawings on the walls representing views of the neighbourhood. These, I was told, were the works of some of the young people present. All that I saw and heard showed me that this was a family of cultivated tastes, and yet it was but typical of many another family among these noble Danish fishing-folk. I marvelled

GILLELIE AND THE SOUND. 301

to find poor men who live such rough and arduous lives having such gentle manners and such refined homes. The natural and well-bred courtesy of these kindly people made this reunion contrast very favourably with the average evening party of the London society of to-day. After a supper of home-made cakes, coffee, and aqua-vit, the glee-singers sang the Danish national hymn and "God save the Queen," and, bidding each other good night, we returned to our several homes.

The following information, which I picked up in Gillelie, may be of use to any of my readers who projects a yachting cruise in the Baltic. A strong oak boat, like those used by these fishermen, can be built at Malmo or in any of the Swedish ports on the Sound at a very moderate cost. For instance, a four-ton oak boat fastened with galvanized iron bolts, twenty-eight feet in length, with nine or ten feet beam, and three and a half feet draught, with all spars, ropes, sails, anchor, chain, four sweeps, and two boat-hooks, will cost forty pounds. The builder could be instructed to put in a commodious cabin in place of a fish-well, and then the yachtsman would have a craft in which he could cruise comfortably from one end of the Baltic to the other.

CHAPTER XV.

COPENHAGEN AND HOME.

On August the 11th the glass had not yet commenced to rise, and the sky looked as wild as ever, but there was a lull in the storm; the north-wester had subsided for a time into a moderate breeze with stiff squalls only now and then. So I decided to be off, and after bidding good-bye to all my friends shoved out of the haven at 9 A.M., and was soon scudding fast before the wind over the heaving seas which, though still high, were no longer steep and dangerous.

After following the coast for twelve miles we came to the narrow entrance to the Sound, where the shores of Denmark and Sweden are little more than two miles apart. Here the spectacle before us was most impressive. On our right, at the foot of a well-wooded promontory, the massive castle of Kronborg with its four graceful towers rose high above the town of Elsinore; on our left was the Swedish port of Helsingborg surrounded by green hills; and the whole of the Sound

KRONBERG CASTLE, ELSINORE.

between the two countries was crowded with vessels lying at anchor, the same that I had seen from Nakke Head running in for shelter from the Kattegat. None of these had yet been able to put to sea again; for the north-west wind and the strong current that sets into the Sound after a gale from that quarter rendered it impossible for anything but a steamer to get out. This vast weather-bound fleet, which was being ever increased by fresh arrivals, now stretched from land to land; so dense a forest of masts that from a distance it seemed as if even a little craft like the *Falcon* would not find room to work her way between.

As the proud rights of Denmark over the Sound have been abolished, and vessels have no longer to strike their topsails off Elsinore and pay toll to the king, we sailed on, still keeping close to the Danish shore, for twenty-two miles farther, passing delightful scenery of the usual Danish character—a succession of beech-woods, lawns, and fishing-villages, and, as we approached Copenhagen of bright-looking watering places and pretty villas. We sailed by Hveen, Tycho, Brahe's island, by—but the Sound deserves a volume to itself, and, no doubt, many solid tomes have been devoted to it, so I will say nothing more concerning it; and at last we let go our anchor, at 5 P.M., off the Lange Linie.

This is the Bois de Boulogne, the Hyde Park of Copenhagen, a very pleasant promenade, having the sea on one side, lakes, gardens, and groves of fine trees on the other.

It was the fashionable hour for "doing" the Lange Linie when we arrived, and, as the weather was now quite fine, and the sun shining, the view from the yacht was an animated one. The walks were crowded with a well-dressed crowd, in which the bright colours of the ladies' dresses and the officers' uniforms predominated over the sober black of the male civilians. Among the trees a military band was "discoursing most excellent music"—quotations from Hamlet are *de rigeur* from all British tourists when writing of these classic shores, so I suppose I must not be an exception.

It seemed strange to burst thus suddenly from stormy seas and little fishing-hamlets upon what looked like Hyde Park in the middle of the season, and Wright, after gazing shoreward with amazement for some time, said very justly, " Well, Sir, we've got to somethiug like a town this time."

Our cruise had now come to an end, and all that remained was to find a suitable place in which to lay up the *Falcon*. This I soon discovered in a boat-builder's yard, about a mile from the city.

But we had one last sail in the old boat, and a very pleasant one it was. I took some Danish friends out for a day's picnic. We landed at the village of Tirsback, and strolled through the fashionable watering place of Klampenborg to the royal deer-park, and as far as the King's shooting-box, known as the Hermitage. The environs of Copenhagen are all beautiful, but no other excursion can come up to a walk through this splendid forest with its great beeches, lovely glades, and great herds of stags, affording, too, as it does, frequent magnificent views over the Sound.

Then Wright and myself set to work for two days, and completely dismantled the yacht, taking everything, including masts and ballast, up to a shed that had been placed at our disposal. This done, the *Falcon* was hauled up on to dry land, and with a rough sloping wooden roof built over her deck, to prevent the snow from accumulating, she will remain there for the winter.

The laying up of the boat, the hospitality of my friends, and one thing and the other, detained me in Copenhagen for a week. In that time I saw most of the sights of the Capital, even religiously "doing" all the museums—Thorvaldsen's being, of course, anything but a penance. Tivoli, that huge but respectable Cremorne, which attracts great crowds every night with its open-air theatres, fireworks, dancing, and all manner of amusements, was my favourite resort after dinner. Copenhagen is proud of its Tivoli; and here, even as at the fishermen's *fête* at Gilleleie, all classes rub shoulders. Even Royalty, and English royalty on occasion, patronises these gardens without risk of being insulted or mobbed by roughs, swell or otherwise. I also visited a wonderful collection of horrors—a gallery of war pictures, painted by the Russian artist Wereschagin, clever, but full of anachronisms and other inaccuracies; for instance, the British soldiers blowing Sepoy mutineers from guns are attired in the helmets and uniforms of 1887. I was told that this collection was to be taken to London in the winter, and I have no doubt it will astonish some of the critics.

The police of Copenhagen, I understood, were very anxious during our stay, not on our account, but on that of the Czar of Russia, who was expected to arrive shortly. It was supposed that several determined Nihilists had preceded him, and the city was full of detectives, both Danish and Russian, who were closely shadowing all strangers. A very intelligent Russian who passed himself off as a commercial traveller came down to the boat-yard while we were laying up the yacht, and took a keen interest in our cruise. He conversed with me in a pleasant manner, but quietly, without appearing inquisitive, contrived to pump me very thoroughly as to my movements and antecedents. I was afterwards told that this was supposed to be one of the Russian secret police. I think he left me quite satisfied that I was only one of the ordinary English lunatics who like to travel in strange and uncomfortable ways, and not a dangerous villain cruising about with a cargo of dynamite and infernal machines.

On Thursday the 18th we embarked on the Danish steam-ship *Tala*, and, after a remarkably smooth voyage round the Skaw and down the North Sea, arrived in Millwall docks on the morning of the 21st. My travelling companions were some young Danish naval officers, who, with a crew of blue-jackets, were bound for Hammersmith, whence they were to take two of Thornicroft's torpedo boats back to Copenhagen for the Danish Government.

So the old *Falcon* lies buried under the northern snow for the winter, but I hope to return to her next summer, and resume my exploration of the Baltic, of which I have as yet had only enough experience to whet my appetite for much more. It is pleasant sometimes on a winter's evening to look over the charts, and plan the coming campaign. So far, I have not decided between the many routes that are open to me. I might sail home by the south of Siaelland, Lubeck, and the Eider canal; but for the greater portion of this journey I should be revisiting familiar coasts, and working my way along tedious Dutch canals. To see much of the Baltic, and return to England with a small boat in one short summer's holiday is no easy task; so the scheme that commends itself most to me is the following: to put aside all idea of returning home in the yacht, and to sail away from Copenhagen for a couple of months or so to the less-known portions of the Inland Sea, and when I have reached my farthest point to take everything of any value out of the yacht, then sell her for what she will fetch, and take passage home with my belongings in a sailing vessel. Old lifeboats are to be picked up cheap enough in the London docks, and it is not worth while to spoil a really good cruise for the sake of bringing such a craft home.

If I made up my mind to do this I could cruise among the Danish and Swedish islands, and ascend the Vistula to Warsaw. The river journey through Poland must be very interesting; but there seems to be a good chance of war breaking out shortly in these regions, and, if such be the case, the Russians will not look with favour on English yachtsmen. I have, in my time, been taken for a Russian spy, and I nearly lost my head in consequence; I do not wish to renew such unpleasant experiences. If there is a war I shall certainly have to avoid the Russian shores; but I might undertake a long cruise up the Gulf of Bothnia to Lapland and the verge of the Arctic regions; or, if that be too ambitious a scheme, I might sail to Gotenborg, thence, by the Gota canal, lakes Wener and Wetter, to Stockholm, and back to Copenhagen by the south Swedish coast, visiting the islands of Gothland, Ocland, and Bornholm on the way. In all probability this last will be the route I shall adopt. Wright, who is now before the mast on the Indian Ocean or South Atlantic, or some other distant sea, will be back in England ready to start with me on the first of June. A friend of mine, who is an artist, is also coming; so the *Falcon* will be well manned this year, and I am looking forward to making a very jolly cruise of it.

NOTE.

I returned to Copenhagen last June, and fitted out the *Falcon*. Her crew consisted of myself, Wright, and my friend, Mr. J. Leighton. After cruising for some weeks among the Danish islands, and on the coast of Sweden, we passed through the Kiel canal, and coasted from Tonning to Ostend, calling, among other places, at Cuxhaven, Hamburg, Harlingen, Utrecht, Dordrecht, Willemstad, and Terneuzen. The summer, as everyone knows, has been a villainous one, and especially so on the bleak eastern shores of the German Ocean. Our old enemy, the north-west wind, blowing right on to the land, perpetually persecuted us; so that stormy weather and heavy seas gave us plenty of anxiety.

At Harlingen we converted the *Falcon* into a regular Dutchman by having oaken lee-boards put on her. With these she can now turn to windward quite respectably, and they have even improved her appearance.

After having been much delayed by bad weather, we at last brought the *Falcon* safely up the Thames to Kingston on September 15th.

THE AUTHOR.

October 2nd, 1888.

www.ingramcontent.com/pod-product-compliance
Lightning Source LLC
Chambersburg PA
CBHW021209230426
43667CB00006B/618